In Dogs We Trust

In Dogs We Trust

An Anthology of
American Dog Literature

EDITED BY

Jacob F. Rivers III *and*
Jeffrey Makala

THE UNIVERSITY OF
SOUTH CAROLINA PRESS

© 2019 University of South Carolina

Published by the University of South Carolina Press
Columbia, South Carolina 29208

www.sc.edu/uscpress

Manufactured in the United States of America

28 27 26 25 24 23 22 21 20 19
10 9 8 7 6 5 4 3 2 1

Library of Congress Cataloging-in-Publication Data
can be found at http://catalog.loc.gov/.

ISBN 978-1-61117-966-8 (cloth)
ISBN 978-1-61117-967-5 (ebook)

This book was printed on recycled paper with
30 percent postconsumer waste content.

To Murray and Maggie, the best terriers in the world

As for love, a dog's love is more honest and unsullied, more faithful and true, than any other in this weary old world. A man may sink into the gutter and kill the affections of all who are nearest him, but his dog will cling to him through all.

Alexander Hunter, *The Huntsman in the South,* 1908

CONTENTS

ILLUSTRATIONS

ACKNOWLEDGMENTS

We would like to thank Patrick Scott, who first helped Jacob to formulate a definite idea for a project of this scope. Sharon Verba in Thomas Cooper Library at the University of South Carolina provided invaluable research assistance in identifying and locating long out-of-print paper-based sources and reference material. The Research and Professional Growth Committee of the faculty of Furman University provided research support at the time when it was most needed. Mark Perry at Furman helped us over one summer to identify sources. Elaina Griffith and the interlibrary loan staff of the Furman University Library were invaluable in their dogged (sorry!) work in tracking down obscure source material and delivering them to us. Jeffrey's colleagues at Furman have been models of support and encouragement, especially as he talked endlessly about dog stories with them. Thomas Hendrickson assisted with the translation of the epigraph to Governor William Livingston's "Thoughts on Dogs." The faculty and staff of the Special Collections Research Center at the College of William and Mary, home of the outstanding Chapin-Horowitz Collection of Cynogetica, provided important assistance.

Melissa Edmundson Makala, is, as always, a paragon of patience, support, and encouragement and a keen copy editor. And finally Roxie, Dixie, Peaches, Queen, Red, Torri, Buck, Joe, and all the other good dogs out there we have known and loved deserve our continual gratitude for their companionship, insight, assistance, and the necessary sense of perspective they have added to most aspects of our lives.

INTRODUCTION

Celebrating the American Dog

And also they [the Aztec] caused him to carry a little dog, a yellow one; they fixed about its neck a loose cotton cord. It was said that [the dog] bore [the dead one] across the place of the nine rivers in the place of the dead. . . .

And this, it was said, came to Mictlan tecutli. And when the four years had ended, thereupon [the dead one] went to the nine lands of the dead, [where] lay a broad river.

There the dogs carried one across. It was said that whosoever came walking [to the bank] looked over to the dogs. And when one recognized his master, thereupon he came to throw himself into the water in order to carry his master across. Hence the natives took pains to keep the dogs.

> Fray Bernardino de Sahagún, *General History of the Things of New Spain,* ca. 1575–77

Humans have spent millennia domesticating, selectively breeding, and using dogs for work, defense, hunting, and other forms of useful labor. European dogs made their way to the North American colonies of Spain, France, and Great Britain from their very first settlements. These dogs were workers, performing the same jobs they did in the Old World in rural and urban settings. Indigenous North American dogs, the domesticated companions and partners of Native Americans for millennia, feature prominently in their cosmography, religion, and mythology. In one of John White's watercolors (the first images made by Europeans in the New World), a dog is featured among the villagers in a view of the Indian village of Pomeiooc, near the Roanoke Colony. European settlers in the New World often erroneously equated Native Americans' companion dogs as little more than wolves, mostly wild animals loosely connected to (mostly) wild people. But different tribes used their companion dogs as sled pullers, hunting companions, and vermin killers, the same functions dogs performed for humans in other parts of the world.*

*Virginia DeJohn Anderson, *Creatures of Empire: How Domestic Animals Transformed Early America* (New York: Oxford University Press, 2004), 34–36.

In the nineteenth-century United States, several factors altered humans' relations with their household dogs and other animal companions: changing notions of domesticity; the rise of a relatively affluent middle class; and greater migration from rural to urban areas, all of which helped to influence and create new social relationships between humans and dogs. Later in the nineteenth century, the separate category of "pet" emerged and became widespread: a pet was a household animal whose purpose was solely to provide companionship and amusement for its owners instead of purposeful labor, most often within a domestic environment.*

At the same time, a significant interest in dog breeding, breed standards, and competitions in the form of dog shows became extremely popular in America. The emphasis on celebrating the purity of breeds and bloodlines among breeders and bench show competitors echoes nativist anxiety about an increasingly multiethnic society comprising significant numbers of recent immigrants to the United States from around the world. In the late nineteenth century, with the flourishing of unparalleled wealth, greed, and self-interest in a rapidly industrializing society—wealth often created at the expense of workers—serious questioning of human nature took place, with one result that people often turned with greater interest toward the positive qualities of their animal companions after becoming disillusioned with human nature. The literature of dogdom reflects all these phenomena.

More recently human bonds with our dogs seem to be closer than ever. Dogs not only share our homes and hearths but in some households have been elevated to the status of surrogate children: sleeping in our beds; being dressed up for Halloween; owning Twitter and Instagram accounts; and becoming the driving force of a huge consumer products industry. Dogs are also now trained to work with and for us in new ways, as service animals, therapy dogs, and emotional support companions. The highly developed olfactory skills of trained medical alert dogs have been shown to detect oncoming seizures in epileptic patients and may also help to provide early detection of some diseases such as cancer. Dogs are now literally closer to us than ever.

Contemporary dog literature is a vast universe, stretching far beyond the wide array of training and breed manuals that have long been its staple. Popular trade books about dogs have found a solid audience in America as we continue to attempt to better understand our canine companions. Alexandra Horowitz and

---

*See Jennifer Mason, *Civilized Creatures: Urban Animals, Sentimental Culture, and American Literature, 1850–1900* (Baltimore: Johns Hopkins University Press), 2005.

Cat Warren have recently written excellent books on dog behavior and psychology to describe what makes dogs tick and how they see the world.* The dog in America has also been the subject of recent works of social and contemporary history.†

Many of these historical changes are reflected in a large body of mostly forgotten American dog literature, some of which can be found here in this anthology. Dogs appear as subjects, and not just as minor characters, across the fictional and poetic landscape of early and modern America. Many authors wrote extensively about dogs in the vast periodical literature of nineteenth-century America, and their exploits regularly appeared in newspaper articles, which also excerpted and reprinted popular stories, accounts, and poems about them. They were also featured in specialized sporting journals that celebrated the persistence and sagacity of different breeds in the field. In countless manuscript letters and diaries, authors reveal the great value they placed on their dogs' companionship and fidelity. This volume explores a selection of some of the best and most memorable writings from the vast canon of American dog literature, mostly from the late eighteenth through the early twentieth centuries.

On Literary Dogs

Why are our dogs so compelling to us, and why are we compelled to write about them as much as we do? All fictional or poetic dogs exist, in some way, in relation to a human, because it is the human who writes about them, describes their exploits, loves them, and lives with them. Modern dogs still have some elements of wildness, despite their domestication. Dogs now live in mixed human-and-canine "packs;" at times their inherent wildness takes over when they become immoral opportunists, breaking their often extensive training when tempted with food, wild game, or even the neighborhood cat. Often they "train" their human companions to behave in certain ways to benefit them, and without our knowing it, at least at first. As the Spanish philosopher Jose Ortega y Gasset has

---

*Alexandra Horowitz, *Inside of a Dog: What Dogs See, Smell, and Know* (New York: Scribner, 2009). Cat Warren, *What the Dog Knows: Scent, Science, and the Amazing Ways Dogs Perceive the World* (New York: Touchstone Books, 2015). Both works were *New York Times* nonfiction best sellers.

†See Mark Derr, *A Dog's History of America: How Our Best Friend Explored, Conquered, and Settled a Continent* (New York: North Point, 2004). Ace Collins, *Man's Best Hero: True Stories of Great American Dogs* (New York: Abingdon, 2014). Elizabeth Thurston, *The Lost History of the Canine Race: Our 15,000-Year Love Affair with Dogs* (Kansas City, Mo.: Andrews and McMeel, 1996).

pointed out, "Man is at one and the same time a creature of today and of 10,000 years ago."* The same can be said of our canine companions. As such our dogs help to link us to the natural world, to its elemental wildness, and they create an important bridge between the wild and the civilized elements of our existence.

Even the most hearth-friendly family dog still retains this fundamental wildness deep inside its psyche. Because of this, and because of the fundamental virtues of loyalty and the instinct for protecting their human pack leaders at all costs, dogs become correctives to the dehumanizing effects of technology and a direct link to the ancient unity between humans and the nonhuman environment in which we live. Helping to recreate this primitive unity of nature and man encourages feelings of responsibility, not only to the natural world but also to one's human peers and subordinates. Dogs help link us to our own primitive past. Although these connections may be liminal, barely perceptive to the casual observer, they nevertheless serve to introduce us back into the natural world, guiding us there and protecting us from the ills of modern civilization. Dogs serve as guides who, through their dual natures, reintroduce us to our own more primal ancestral past. As they adapt to the civilized world of the town and the home, they help us to render the complexities of modern life into a more fundamental series of questions: Fight? Flight? Eat? Sleep? Play!

As many writers in this anthology have revealed through their stories and poems, the dog also functions as a restorative force for us. Observing dogs as they face their daily challenges and hardships helps to teach us independence, self-respect, and productive ways in which to live and function in a communal society. Proud dogs who stand up for themselves and their human families provide fine examples of the responsibility and courage necessary for productive human life. Despite their infrequent lapses into instinctive behaviors that may at times frustrate their owners, the dog has a decidedly moral center, a moral compass that always points true North.

In the nineteenth century, in writings of authors such as William Elliott and Johnson Jones Hooper, and in the immensely popular sporting journals such as William Trotter Porter's *Spirit of the Times,* the dog as companion and aid to the hunt enjoyed a tremendous popularity, providing the upper-class sporting fraternity an involvement with printed versions of the chase that succeeded in drawing them more fully into their authors' sporting adventures. On a different level, Ernest Thompson Seton frequently used dogs in his prolific literary career as stand-ins for their human counterparts, not only as representatives of

---

*Jose Ortega y Gasset, *Meditations on Hunting,* Howard B. Westcott, trans. (New York: Scribner, 1972), 136.

social and environmental change, but also to demonstrate correct behavior for young people and provide examples of loyalty, trust, and the importance of selfless generosity. Humorous stories were also an important part of American dog literature, from Mark Twain's loving, funny obituary of a beloved San Francisco Newfoundland, "Exit Bummer" (first published in the *Californian* in 1865) to O. Henry's "Memoirs of a Yellow Dog" (1906), included in this volume.

"Memoirs of a Yellow Dog" directly confronts masculine anxiety over the encroaching nature of domesticity and middle-class fears of emasculation at the turn of the century. Written from a dog's point of view, it humorously shows how one domesticated lap dog is rescued from his female owner's "civilizing" hands. The canine protagonist of this dog's version of *Huckleberry Finn* is in turn liberated by a master who takes him away from the confining spaces of domesticity as they decide to "strike out for the territories" together.

As a corollary it is no accident that the evolution of many dogs to the status of companions and nonworking pets in the late nineteenth and early twentieth centuries paralleled a great rise in sport hunting, with its own attendant corpus of literature. Both developments responded to American desires to recapture the spirit of intrepidity and independence of the hardy frontiersmen with whom they identified. Through their relationships with their dogs, whose courage and independence they admired, many American sporting writers were able to regain feelings of kinship with iconic wilderness hunters of previous generations such as Meriwether Lewis and Daniel Boone.

In a different vein, a surprising historical incident included in this volume is the account of James Smith, which first appeared in the antislavery newspaper *Voice of the Fugitive* in 1852. Smith fled slavery in Virginia in the 1830s and successfully made his way to freedom in Canada thanks to the constant companionship and aid provided by his hunting dog. Despite being told to go back, Smith's dog would not leave his side during his flight and saved his life several times. The two companions then settled into free life together in Ohio.

The prolific American writings about dogs in the late nineteenth and early twentieth centuries are an integral part of literary realism and naturalism. Since the great emphasis in these movements was on realistic descriptions of life and the inescapably atavistic nature of human existence, what better way to express those thoughts than to reference the dog, who shares both the civilized and the savage, the dual nature of humankind? In such canonical works as Stephen Crane's *Maggie, a Girl of the Streets* (1893), Theodore Dreiser's *Sister Carrie* (1900), and Frank Norris's *The Pit* (1903), we find competition and struggle in a rapidly industrializing society, one where the humanity of the characters is compromised severely and a reversion to savage instincts is necessary for survival. Likewise the canine heroes of Jack London's well-known novels *The Call of the Wild* (1903) and *White Fang* (1906) directly reflect the naturalist author's concerns about human helplessness in the face of natural forces beyond our control.

Marjorie Garber has noted that most dog literature that involves bonding between humans and canines involves boys or men and their dogs. With the two exceptions of Little Orphan Annie and Sandy, and Dorothy and Toto, girls and their dogs seem to receive scant literary attention.* This may be in part due to traditionally masculine pursuits such as hunting and camping that were extensively written about in boys' books and periodicals during the "golden age" of children's literature in the late nineteenth and early twentieth centuries. Nevertheless several selections included here clearly show deeply affective relationships between women and girls and their companion dogs. See especially Harriet Beecher Stowe's memoirs of canine domestic life in "Our Dogs," Anna Lea Merritt's story "My Dog (A Hamlet in Old Hampshire)," and the wonderful sporting elegy by Louis Imogen Guiney, "To a Dog's Memory."

There are many interesting, well-written, and occasionally provocative dog stories and novels that we wish we had space to include. Marshall Saunders's *Beautiful Joe* (1893), a touching novel from a dog's point of view, was written in the wake of the popularity of *Black Beauty* and was meant to raise awareness of animal cruelty. Excerpts from Jack London's better-known works have instead been replaced with his humorous short story "That Spot." The mysterious disappearing dog Tiger in Edgar Allan Poe's strange novel *The Narrative of Arthur Gordon Pym* remains one of nineteenth-century American literature's great enigmas. Mark Twain wrote a wrenching short story, "A Dog's Tale" (1903), about the unnecessary cruelty inflicted on dogs by the vivisection movement. Elizabeth Stuart Phelps's *Trixy* (1904) is an excellent novel also focused on antivivisection. Jennie E. Van's *Wise Old Deacon* (1903), written from a dog's point of view, is a witty and entertaining dog autobiography. And we could go on.

In the pages to follow, one will not necessarily find an anthology of sentimental stories about dogs. It is also not made up of many works written expressly for children or young people. The pieces included here do not tend to focus on the death of a favorite dog and their owner's bereavement, nor dogs who fight other dogs, for sport or survival, many examples of which can also be found in the vast corpus of American dog literature.

Many pieces of fiction from the nineteenth and early twentieth centuries betray much of the cultural biases of their times. Men kick dogs and pull on their ears, making *us* wince and cry out more than the dogs. The large and

---

*Marjorie Garber, *Dog Love* (New York: Simon and Schuster, 1996), 59–60.

traditionally celebrated corpus of dog stories and memoirs written by Albert Payson Terhune in the early twentieth century mostly ring hollow today. Terhune's descriptions of happy Anglo-Saxon homes and kennels in New Jersey and Long Island are constantly threatened by dark-skinned foreign immigrant hordes who are driven off by his purebred collie heroes. Like parts of the dog show genre, these tales become vehicles for writing about WASP-ish anxiety in the face of immigration and perceived ethnographic threats, elements that Terhune (like another contemporary of his, H. P. Lovecraft) unfortunately wrote about a bit too much. Only when sticking to dogs as dogs did he truly excel. Included here are a World War I story of Terhune's featuring the collie Bruce, which forms one chapter from Bruce's eponymous novel, and a boy's story, "One Minute Longer." The latter is admittedly a bit sentimental and more than a bit melodramatic, but it shows Terhune's talent for creating drama and getting into the mindset of the loyal dogs he justly celebrated.

This anthology includes a diverse selection of fiction, poetry, memoirs, and the occasional piece of journalism or creative nonfiction that celebrates the best qualities of American dogs in their own time and place: in the home, at work, and in the field; performing interesting and remarkable tasks and actions; and being written about from a variety of perspectives, some admittedly more "literary" than others. By including popular or vernacular pieces taken from almanacs and broadsides, cheap tracts, and folk or vernacular poems, we hope to show the range of emotion and feeling being expressed by owners for their dogs and not just the "finest" examples of literary complexity or merit. And so, the work of Emily Dickinson here appears equally alongside the anonymous provincial author of "Tumbler's Epitaph," a broadside from the 1840s, with both seeking solace as they remember and celebrate their favorite dogs.

All the texts included here appear with minimal editorial intervention, and in most cases as they first appeared to their audiences in magazine or book form. Thus, some spelling, uses of punctuation, and stylistic conventions in certain pieces lean toward the old fashioned or outright archaic. Complete bibliographical information appears at the end of each piece.

It is our hope that the selections included here represent not only a wide variety of literary forms and ways of expressing the unique bond between dogs and their humans, but can also be considered as literary works that (mostly) rise to the level of art. They are, if anything, among the most interesting, and as worthy of consideration for their literary and cultural merit as they are for the treatment of their subjects of interest. The pieces included here form a necessary part of understanding how Americans have thought about and expressed the presence of dogs in their own lives, over several centuries. American dog literature reflects every aspect of American life and culture, from the sixteenth century to the present. In other words, by taking dogs seriously, and by looking at American literature through a doggish lens, we can ultimately learn more about our animal companions, ourselves, and our national literature as well. Dog literature *is* American literature; it helps to explore and explain who we are, and who we wish to be.

DOGS.

Wood engraving showing several representative dog breeds.
John George Wood. *New Illustrated Natural History.* Chicago: Donohue,
Henneberry, 1880. Image courtesy of Special Collections and Archives,
James B. Duke Library, Furman University.

PART I

Working Dogs

"And every cur of them [Sioux dogs], who is large enough, and not too cunning to be enslaved, is encumbered with a car or sled (or whatever it may be better called), on which he patiently drags his load—a part of the household goods and furniture of the lodge to which he belongs. Two poles, about fifteen feet long, are placed on the dog's shoulder, in the same manner as the lodge poles are attached to the horses, leaving the larger ends to drag upon the ground behind him; on which is placed a bundle or wallet which is allotted to him to carry, and which he trots off amid the throng of dogs and squaws; faithfully and cheerfully dragging his load 'til night, and by the way loitering and occasionally

"Catching at little bits of fun and glee
That's played on dogs enslaved by dog that's free."

George Catlin, *Letters and Notes on the Manners,*
Customs, and Condition of the North American Indians, 1841

Little doubt remains in the minds of those who have studied the evolution of human and canine relationships that the first useful function of the dog for our prehistoric ancestors was as an aid to the hunt. Early humans were quick to recognize that the less aggressive and more gregarious of the wolves that had begun to visit their campsites were already superb hunters in their own right, aided of course by their marvelous sense of smell. The nose, and not the eyes or the ears, remains the touchstone of our canine companions, and even the most casual observer can watch their own dogs as they explore the world with their keen sense of smell. Dependent as they were on the meat they needed to survive, the prehistoric hunter discovered in the dog a valuable and willing working companion.

However valuable these early dogs were as locators of game, they simultaneously evolved a second trait that was no less valuable to their early masters. While access to good hunting grounds remains a privileged right, in the Pleistocene era it was a right that was frequently contested with the physical violence that characterized this early period of human life. Even before they were accepted into the family circle as valuable members of the tribe, early dogs lurking on the outskirts of the campsite would bark and howl at marauding intruders who tried to maneuver themselves into position for an attack on their rival hunting bands. This particular type of early warning system may originally have been more of a spontaneous outpouring of alarm than an effort to protect the group to which the dogs had attached themselves, but it was nonetheless valuable. It remains a valuable trait today and has been cultivated and elevated into a wealth of remarkable early-warning protective behaviors. In several of the selections that follow, most notably in "The Shepherd's Dog" and "The Cow-Boys and the Dogs," this canine willingness to alert their owners to the presence of outsiders continues to save their masters from surprise encroachments into what dogs consider their private spheres of life.

One reason for this kind of behavior is that dogs are pack animals who have inherited from their wolf ancestors the canine willingness to accept leadership and to respond to threats from outsiders on the group he depends on for survival. For this reason, and because humans have selectively bred different breeds for certain characteristics, dogs can be trained to perform a wide range of useful duties far beyond their abilities as hunters. As guides and battlefield messengers for our armed forces in "When Eyes Were No Use," as lifeguards in "Gunner, the Children's Rescuer," and as independent and spontaneous protectors of its owner's livestock in "The Sagacity of a Dog," this canine attachment to the lives and fortunes of the master and pack reveals something of the remarkable fidelity and faithfulness for which dogs are known.

As humans have progressed and developed, so have our canine friends. Their absolute attachment to their owners, their innate willingness to subserve themselves to leadership, and their ingenuity and intelligence have resulted in a symbiotic relationship that readily adapts itself to the technology and environment of the times. In the stories and accounts that follow, we should remember that the spectacular performances of its canine heroes represent but a small fraction of accounts and potential in the truly remarkable canine race.

Heroes of Fire and Water

I.—*"Sport," the Newark Fire Dog (1881)*

Among those who regularly call for their *Daily Advertiser* every afternoon at the counting-room of this office is an intelligent dog that rejoices in the name of Sport, and is the property of Hook and Ladder Company No. 1. At around 4 P.M. daily, as regularly as the hour comes around, Sport sets out for the *Daily* office, making a bee-line from the truck-house to the *Advertiser* counting-room. On arriving at the office he does not push or crowd, but, like the well-behaved dog that he is, waits until he can reach the counter. Those in charge know him well. A paper is folded and handed him, and he takes it in his mouth and starts on a bee-line for the truck-house. If he does not get the *Daily* immediately on reaching the counter, he rises on his hind-legs, places his forepaws on the counter and looks at the clerk as much as to say: "Don't forget me, please!" When the paper is handed him he wags his tail in thanks, and is off in a jiffy. Of late he has been muzzled, in accordance with the Mayor's proclamation, and the paper is put in the muzzle over his nose. On Sundays he never goes to the *Daily* office as he appears to know the office is closed.

Sport is a coach dog, and is between six and seven years old. He took up his residence in the truck-house in February, 1875, and soon began to run to fires with the company. As soon as the gong strikes in the house he is on the alert, and no sooner are the doors thrown open than out he bounds, rushing ahead of the horses, then darting back again, jumping up at the horses and dancing around them, and then rushing ahead again, barking furiously all the time. He will dart after vehicles that are ahead of the truck, bark at them and rush at the horses until they get out of the way. As soon as the company arrives at a fire, Sport goes on guard, watching the truck and the men's coats, and woe betide the person who should meddle with either. Sport has been injured several times. On one occasion he was run over by the truck and one of his legs was broken. He was carried to the truck house, where his leg was set, and he was kindly cared for by the members of the company. The leg got well, but is now a little stiff.

On the 22d of February, 1876, after a terrible storm, the members of the company found a little puppy in the Old Burying Ground. It was nearly dead with cold, but they took it to the house and were trying to warm it back to life, when

Sport appeared, took the little stranger in his mouth, bore it to his own bunk and tended it as carefully as a human father. It lived and thrived, the members of the company bringing it up on the bottle. The two dogs grew very fond of each other, and Sport would not suffer any but the members of the company to touch the little stranger, whom the firemen had christened Dash, or even to approach too near him. As Dash grew older he too ran to fires, and the two dogs were inseparable. One occasion a large dog of the cur species attacked Dash and beat him. The latter went to the trunk house where Sport was lying asleep on the floor, waked him up, nosed him, and evidently in some way made him comprehend what had happened. The dogs started off together, and members of the company followed at a distance to see what would happen, when they saw Dash and Sport set upon the unfortunate cur and give him a terrible thrashing. Dash was killed by being run over by the truck on its way to a fire and Sport mourned him sincerely.

Newark (N.J.) Advertiser.

"Heroes of Fire and Water I—'Sport,' the Newark Fire Dog." *Forest and Stream: A Journal of Outdoor Life, Travel, Nature Study, Shooting, Fishing, Yachting* 17, no. 2 (August 11, 1881): 34.

Heroes of Fire and Water

II.—*"Gunner," the Children's Rescuer (1881)*

Gunner is dead. Perhaps the average reader was not acquainted with Gunner, but every person who had been at Monmouth Beach within the past twenty years knew Gunner, and knew him well, the children especially. They had no better friend, companion or protector.

The story goes that one day twenty years ago there was a dreadful storm at sea. Many vessels were lost, and the damage to property on land was great. That night some fishermen walking the shore discovered a small water spaniel lying on the sand. Upon closer inspection they perceived that a child was tied to his back. The dog had struggled nobly with the waves, for he was helpless and nigh exhausted. He rolled his eyes appealingly toward his discoverers, and whined when they approached. But the exposure and heavy billows had been too much for the child, for it was cold and stark. The dog was picked up and carefully attended to, and the child was buried at Long Branch. It never was learned who and what the child was, or where it came from, but it was generally believed that the child came from a vessel that was wrecked with all on board, and that its parents, convinced there was no chance for them, entrusted it to the dog.

Gunner grew up the pride of Monmouth Beach. His romantic history attracted him to all, and his faithfulness to children drew him toward mothers who had never permitted their offsprings with animals of any kind.

Gunner's chief delight, however, was in the summer, when the place was filled and the sea alive with bathers. For hours and hours he sat by the breaking billows, running in as some favorite child came along, and for whole afternoons at a time he swam in and about the bathers, watching his chance to drag some venturesome or unskilled person from a watery grave. The number of lives he has saved is very large. Many, many children owe their preservation of life to Gunner's fidelity, watchfulness, and promptness. He was a large, shaggy beast, gentle as a kitten, with a high order of intelligence, and belligerent toward other dogs that ventured into the surf, believing no doubt that he had the proper right and that the interlopers were usurping his prerogative.

Yesterday afternoon his master ordered him to bring his cows home. Gunner started off with a joyous bark, and made for the supposed peaceful kine. But when he approached, one of them, a brown, vicious brute, turned and buried her horns deep into his body. In consequence of his death all the flags at the Club House have been placed at half-mast.

Commercial Advertiser, July 31.

"Heroes of Fire and Water II—'Gunner,' the Children's Rescuer." *Forest and Stream: A Journal of Outdoor Life, Travel, Nature Study, Shooting, Fishing, Yachting* 17, no. 2 (August 11, 1881): 34.

The Cow-Boys and the Dogs, in the War of the Revolution (1865)

In the time of our revolutionary war there was a class of marauders greatly detested by our suffering ancestors. They were called cow-boys, and were refugees from the British side, who kept up a kind of guerilla warfare by stealing the cattle of the Americans, driving them to New York, and selling them to the British.

You have read of, some of you may have seen, Washington Irving's beautiful residence upon the Hudson, called Sunnyside. The original building, or Wolfert's Roost, as history tells us, was erected by Jacob Van Tassel. He was a sworn enemy to these detestable cow-boys. His garrison consisted of himself, his wife, her sister

Nochie Van Wurmer, Dinah, a big negress, and Laney Van Tassel, his beautiful daughter. He owned one gun, of long range, called a goose gun. Our five mile Columbiads might laugh at the goose gun in these days, but it did its duty well, and that is all that little guns or little folks are asked to do, and happy are they if they succeed.

One day an armed vessel sailed up to the garrison. The men on board were aware, perhaps, that Jacob and his trusty gun were away, but the women resisted *manfully* until overpowered by superior numbers. Pretty Laney was seized, and the pillagers were hurrying her to their boat, when her father unexpectedly came to her rescue, and the cowardly invaders ran away as fast as their cowardly legs could carry them.

And now that you understand what the cow-boys were, we will relate a story which we learned from a gentleman who is very fond of dogs, because he has been for many years a thoughtful observer of their sagacity and faithfulness.

During the revolutionary war his grandmother—we will call her Mrs. Watson—was left in charge of a hotel, or tavern, as they called it then. She was like most women in those perilous times, a courageous woman, and she had two valiant defenders—two dogs named Bull and Tiger.

The cow-boys were, or would have been, frequent visitors at Mrs. Watson's if they had been allowed to come, but they never made very free with her fat cattle or nice cows, for Bull defended the house, while Tiger looked after affairs at the barn.

When a traveler approached the house in the day time, one of the dogs would go out to meet him, and decide whether he was friend or enemy. Woe to the cow-boy in disguise that hoped to deceive one of these brave dogs. A fearless spirit in a good cause made them look too dangerous to be meddled with. When they were satisfied that the new-comer was a true patriot without a taint of Toryism, why, then Tiger became a lamb, and trotted meekly along by the stranger's side until he had introduced him to his mistress, who entertained him hospitably, and Mrs. Watson never doubted any man that her dogs pronounced all right.

If, during the dog's examination of the new-comer, a cow-boy chanced to come along, the dog would eye them both keenly. If he saw a sign of recognition between the two he at once told them both by a menacing growl that they must not enter the door yard. If, on the other hand, the stranger did not appear to be acquainted with the cow-boy, he had permission to come in, while the cow-boy was escorted on his way in a hurry.

How could they know the difference?

Ah! how can we explain how a dog decides at first sight whether a man is a rascal or not, and tells with unerring instinct which man out of a crowd to attach himself to, and cling to and defend with generous forgetfulness of his own life? Of all God's gifts to man the faithful dog is truly the most remarkable.

At night Tiger took his post at the barn, while Bull lay down just inside the house door. The moment a cow-boy or any other enemy came stealing in on noiseless foot, Tiger went to the house door and told his fellow watchman of the fact, and Bull walked directly to his mistress' bedside and awoke her, and by the time the brave old lady and her servants were astir, the cow-boys would run off, cursing the dogs who had cheated them out of their expected booty.

One cow-boy, more adroit or bolder than the rest, broke in one night through a window, which closed upon him and held him fast until Mrs. Watson had beaten him soundly over the head with her fire shovel.

The gentleman alluded also to a little dog named Napoleon, that attached itself closely to a child of two years, and followed it all day with tender care, and when the baby went to its little bed upon the floor, lay down by his side, and rose every time the restless little fellow threw off the clothes during the night, and pulled them all about him with its teeth, and tucked them down as anxiously as any mother would have done. It was a pity to part them, but a sea captain saw and fancied the dog and took him to sea with him.

Another pet dog was fond of going to church. He behaved with the utmost propriety. When they sung a hymn he always wished to look over the hymn book with one of the family, and would put his paw on the corner of a leaf and look down the page with a ludicrous expression of wisdom on his little puppy face that we fear did not help the devotions of the bright young eyes in his vicinity much.

"The Cow-Boys and the Dogs, in the War of the Revolution." *Youth's Companion* 38, no. 12 (April 20, 1865): 61–62.

The Faithful American Dog (1798)

An officer in the late American army, on his station at the westward, went out in the morning, with his dog and gun, in quest of game.—Venturing too far from his garrison, he was fired upon by an Indian, who was lurking in the bushes, and instantly fell to the ground. The Indian, running to him, struck him on the head with his tomahawk in order to dispatch him: but the button of his hat fortunately warding off the edge, he was only stunned by the blow. With savage brutality he applied the scalping knife, and hastened away with his trophy of his horrid cruelty, leaving the officer for dead, and none to relieve or console him but his faithful dog.

The afflicted creature gave every expression of attachment, fidelity, and affection. He licked the wounds with inexpressible tenderness, and mourned the fate of his beloved master. Having performed every office with sympathy dictated, and sagacity could invent, without being able to remove his master from the fatal spot, or procure from him any signs of life, or his wonted expressions of affection to him, he ran off in quest of help. Bending his course towards the river where two men were fishing, he urged them by all the powers of native rhetoric to accompany him to the woods.

The men were suspicious of decoy to an ambuscade, and dared not to venture to follow the dog, who finding all his caresses fail, returned to the care of his master, and licked his wounds a second time, renewing all his tendernesses, but with no better success than before. Again he returned to the men!—In this attempt he was more successful than in the other—The men, seeing his solicitude, began to think the dog might have discovered some valuable game, and determined to hazard the consequences of following him. Transported with his success, the affectionate creature hurried them along by every expression of ardor. Presently they arrive at the spot, where—behold an officer wounded, scalped, weltering in his own gore, and faint with the loss of blood.—Suffice to say, he was yet alive.—They carried him to the fort, where the first dressings were performed. A suppuration immediately took place, and he was soon conveyed to the hospital at Albany, where, in a few weeks, he entirely recovered, and was able to return to his duty.

This worthy officer owed his life, probably, to the fidelity of his sagacious dog. His tongue, which the gentleman afterwards declared, gave him the most exquisite pleasure, clarified the wound in the most effectual manner, & his perseverance brought that assistance without which he must soon have perished.

> "My dog, the trustiest of his kind,
> With gratitude inflamed my mind;
> I mark, his true, his faithful way,
> And in my service copy Tray."

"The Faithful American Dog." *Key*, February 17, 1798: 1, 6.

Sagacity of a Dog (1831)

It is stated, in the *Poughkeepsie Intelligencer,* that during a great snow storm, last winter, a number of fowls, belonging to a farmer in that neighborhood, were missing at the hour when they usually retired to their roost. While sitting around the kitchen fire, talking of the subject, the attention of the family was roused by the entrance of the house dog, having in his mouth a hen, apparently dead. Forcing his way to the fire, the cautious animal laid his charge down upon the warm hearth, and immediately set off. He soon entered with another, which he deposited in the same place, and so continued till the whole of them were rescued. The fowls, benumbed by the extreme cold, had crowded together in the yard, when the dog, observing them, effected their deliverance.

"Sagacity of a Dog." *American Turf Register and Sporting Magazine* 2, no. 10 (June 1831): 2, 10.

A Canine Anecdote (1861)

C. J. ATKINSON

A gentleman connected with a Newfoundland fishery was once possessed of a dog of singular fidelity and sagacity. On one occasion a boat and crew in his employ were in circumstances of considerable peril, just outside a line of breakers, which—owing to some change in wind or weather—had, since the departure of the boat, rendered the return passage through them most hazardous. The spectators on shore were quite unable to render any assistance to their friends afloat. Much time had been spent, and the danger seemed to increase rather than to diminish. Our friend, the dog, looked on for a length of time, evidently aware of there being great cause for anxiety in those around. Presently, however, he took to the water, and made his way through to the boat. The crew supposed he wished to join them, and made attempts to induce him come aboard; but no! he would not go within their reach, but continued swimming about a short distance from them. After a while, and several comments on the peculiar conduct of the dog, one of the hands suddenly divined his apparent meaning. "Give him the end of the rope," he said, "that is what he wants." The rope was thrown, the dog seized the end in an instant, turned round, and made straight for the shore; where a few minutes afterwards boat and crew—thanks to the intelligence of their four-footed friend—were placed safe and undamaged. Was there reasoning here? No acting with a view to an end or for a given motive? Or was it nothing but ordinary instinct?

Rev. C. J. Atkinson, "A Canine Anecdote." *Flag of Our Union* (November 23, 1861): 8.

Pershing Honors Dog Mascot of A.E.F. (1921)

Pins Gold Medal on Stubby, Boston Bull, Who Was in 17 Engagements.

Wounded at Seicheprey

Many Decorations and is Life Member of Y.M.C.A., Red Cross and American Legion.

Stubby, a brindle Boston bull terrier, which served overseas as mascot of the American Expeditionary Forces, was today decorated as a wounded hero of the World War by General John J. Pershing, Commander-in-Chief of the American forces in Europe during that war.

The medal that General Pershing pinned on him was of gold, and bore on its face the single name "Stubby." It was not an army medal, despite the fact that Stubby wears the insignia of a private of United States infantry and participated with honor in seventeen engagements with the Twenty-Sixth Division, including the battle of Seicheprey, in which he received a shrapnel wound in the breast. It was a beautiful medal, however, of solid gold and nicely engraved, the gift of the Human Education Society, which has among its sponsors Mrs. Harding as well as General Pershing and many notables.

In presenting the medal the General made a little impromptu speech, but Stubby made no reply. He merely licked his chops and wagged his diminutive tail.

Stubby has been designated the official mascot of the A.E.F. He is said to be the only dog that made the trip to France and return with the same organization, the 102d Infantry, which when a puppy, he joined of his own volition and attached himself to former Corporal J. Robert Conroy of New Haven, Conn., and Washington, D.C., whose property he is.

While Stubby is now a trifle gun shy, and showed some symptoms of nervous excitement today when the camera men shot off a flashlight during the decoration ceremonies, there was a time when the big guns didn't frighten him. That was before he got his wound at Seicheprey, which necessitated his going to the hospital for six weeks. He returned to his regiment after his wound healed, but he never evinced his old time zest for battle. When the big guns started Stubby went A.W.O.L., though he always showed up, sober and ready for duty, when the tumult died down.

Stubby on parade is a gorgeous spectacle. He wears a leather blanket, beautifully embroidered with the flags of the Allies in natural colors, the work of nearly a hundred French demoiselles whom Stubby met in his travels. He wears also a Victory medal, with crossbars indicating the major engagements at which he assisted. His blanket is literally covered with badges and medals which have been thrust upon him by his admirers, and on the left side of his elaborate leather harness, also a gift, he wears three real gold service chevrons, while on the right side he has another gold chevron to indicate his honorable wounds. He is a life member of the Y.M.C.A. and has a membership card which proclaims him entitled to "three bones a day and a place to sleep" for the rest of his life. He is also a member of the American Red Cross and the American Legion, at the Minneapolis convention of which he was present as an honorary delegate.

But perhaps the greatest honor that has ever been bestowed upon Stubby was that given him at the Boston dog show, when the gold "hero dog" medal was awarded to him by unanimous consent of the judges.

"Pershing Honors Dog Mascot of A.E.F." *New York Times*, July 7, 1921, 4.

"Miss Louise Johnson & Stubby in Animal Parade."
Washington, D.C.: Harris and Ewing, 1921. Image courtesy of the
Library of Congress, Prints and Photographs Division,
Harris and Ewing Collection.

Another Dog (1895)

F. HOPKINSON SMITH

Do not tell me dogs cannot talk. I know better. I saw it all myself. It was at Sterzing,—that most picturesque of all the Tyrolean villages on the Italian slope of the Brenner,—with its long, single street, zigzagged like a straggling path in the snow,—perhaps it was laid out that way,—and its little, open square, with shrine and rude stone fountain, surrounded by women in short skirts and hobnailed shoes, dipping in their buckets. On both sides run queer arcades, sheltering shops, their doorways piled up with cheap stuffs, fruit, farm implements, and the like, and at the far end,—almost the last house in the town,—stands the inn, where you breakfast. An old, old inn, with swinging sign framed by fantastic iron work, and decorated with overflows of foaming ale in green mugs, crossed clay pipes, and little round dabs of yellow-brown, suggestive, no doubt, of cakes,— the whole typical of good cheer within. And with a great archway, too, wide and high, with enormous, barn-like doors fronting on the straggling, zig-zag street. Under this a cobble-stone pavement leads to the door of the coffee-room and out to the stable beyond. These great doors kept out the driving snows and the whirls of sleet and rain, and are slammed-to behind horse, sleigh, and all, if not in the face, certainly in the very teeth of the gale, while you disentangle your half-frozen legs at your leisure, almost within sight of the blazing fire of the coffee-room within.

Under this great archway then, against one of these big doors, his big paws just inside the shadow line,—for it was not winter, but a brilliant summer morning, —the grass all dusted with powdered diamonds, the sky a turquoise, and the air a joy,—under this archway, I say, sat a big St. Bernard dog, squat on his haunches, his head well up, like a grenadier on guard,—his eyes commanding the approaches down the road, up the road, and across the street; taking in the passing peddler with the tinware, and the girl with a basket strapped to her back, her fingers knitting for dear life,—not to mention so unimportant an object as myself swinging down the road, my iron-shod alpenstock hammering the cobbles.

He made no objection to my entering, neither did he receive me with any show of welcome. There was no bounding forward, no wagging of the tail, no aimless walk around for a moment, only to settle down in another spot; nor was there any sudden growl or forbidding look in the eye. None of these things entered his thoughts, for none of these things were part of his duty. The landlord would do the welcoming, and the blue-shirted porter take my knapsack and show me the way to the coffee-room. His business was to sit still and guard that archway. Paying guests, and those known to the family,—yes! But stray mountain goats, chickens, inquisitive, pushing peddlers, pigs, and wandering dogs,—well, he would take care of these.

While the cutlets and coffee were being fried and boiled, I dragged a chair across the road and tilted it back out of the sun against the wall of a house. I, too, commanded a view down past the blacksmith shop, where they were heating a great iron tire to clap on the hind wheel of a "diligence," and up the street as far as the little square where the women were still clattering about on the cobbles, their buckets on their shoulders. Thus it was that I fell to watching the dog.

The more I looked at him, the more his personality took possession of me. The exceeding gravity of his demeanor; his dignified attitude. The quiet, silent reserve about him. The way he looked at you from under his eyebrows,—not eagerly, or furtively, but with a self-possessed, competent air, quite like a captain of a Cunarder scanning a horizon from the bridge, or a French gendarme, watching the shifting crowds from one of the little stone circles anchored out in the rush of the boulevards, was a look of authority backed by unlimited power. Then, his hairy chops had a certain dignified cut to them as they drooped over his teeth beneath his black, stubby nose. His ears, too, rose and fell easily, and without undue haste or excitement when the sound of horses' hoofs put him on his guard, or a goat wandered too near. And with all this, one could see that he was not a meddlesome dog, nor a snarler,—no running out and giving tongue at each passing object,—not that kind of a dog at all. Just a plain, substantial, well-mannered, dignified, self-respecting St. Bernard dog, who knew his place and kept it, who knew his duty and did it, and who would no more chase a cat than he would bite your legs in the dark. Put a cap with a gold band on his head and he would really have made an ideal concierge. Even without the band, he concentrated in his face all the superiority, repose, and exasperating reticence of that necessary concomitant of Continental hotel life.

Suddenly I noticed a more eager expression on the face of my dog-concierge opposite. One ear was unfurled, like a flag, and almost run to the masthead; the head was turned quickly down the road. Then I heard the sound of wheels below the shop. Then his dogship straightened up and stood on four legs, his tail wagging slowly.

Another dog was coming.

A great Danish hound, with white eyes and black-and-tan ears, a tail as long and smooth as a policeman's night-club,—one of those sleek and shining dogs with powerful chest and knotted legs, a little bowed in front, with black lips, and dazzling, fang-like teeth. He was spattered, too, with brown spots, and sported a single white foot. Altogether, he was a dog of quality,—of ancestry,—of a certain position in his own land,—who followed his master's mountain wagon as much for love of adventure as anything else. A dog of parts, too, who could, perhaps, hunt the wild boar, or give chase to the agile deer. Moreover, he was not an inn dog. He was rather a palace dog, or a chateau, or a shooting-box dog, who, in his off moments, trotted behind dogcarts filled with guns, sportsmen in knee-breeches or in front of landaus when my lady went an-airing.

And with all this,—and quite naturally,—he was a dog of breeding, who, while he insisted on his own rights, respected those of others. I saw all this before he had spoken ten words to the concierge,—the St. Bernard dog, I mean. For he did talk to him, and the conversation was just as plain to me, tilted back against the wall, out of the sun, waiting for my cutlets and coffee, as if I had been a dog myself, and understood each word of it.

First, he walked up sideways, his tail wagging and straight out, like a patent towel-rack. Then he walked round the concierge, who followed his movements with becoming interest, wagging his own tail, straightening his forelegs, and sidling around him kindly, as befitted the stranger's rank and quality, but with a certain dog-independence of manner, passing the time of day, and intimating, by certain twists of his tail, that he felt quite sure his excellency would like the air and scenery the further he got up the pass,—all strange dogs did.

During this interchange of canine civilities, the landlord who was helping out the two men,—the companions of the dog, one round and pudgy, the other lank and scrawny, but both in knickerbockers, with green hats decorated with cock feathers and edelweiss,—assisted by the blue-shirted porter, who carried in the bags and alpenstocks, closing the coffee-room door behind them.

Suddenly the strange dog—who had been beguiled by the courteous manner of the concierge—realized that his master had disappeared. The man was hungry, no doubt, and half blinded by the glare of the sun, and, after the manner of his kind, had dived into this shelter without a word to the dumb beast who had tramped behind his wheels, swallowing the dust his horse kicked up.

When the strange dog realized this,—I saw the instant the idea entered his mind, as I caught the sudden loss of the head,—he gave a quick glance around with that uneasy, furtive, anxious look that comes into a dog's face when he discovers that he is adrift in a strange place without his master. What face is so utterly miserable, and what eyes so pleading—the tears just under the lids—as the lost dog's?

Then it was beautiful to see the concierge. With a sudden arching of the neck he reassured the strange dog—telling him, as plainly as could be, not to worry—they were only inside, and would be out after breakfast. There was no mistaking what he said to him. It was all done with a peculiar curving of the neck, a reassuring wag of the tail, and quick glance toward the coffee-room, and a few frolicsome, kittenish jumps, plainly indicating that as for himself the occasion was one of great hilarity, with absolutely no cause for anxiety. Then, if you could have seen that anxious look fade away, and the responsive, reciprocal wag of the night-club of a tail, and the sudden peace that came into his eyes, as he followed the concierge to the doorway, dropping his ears, and throwing himself beside him, looking up into his face, his tongue out, panting, after the habit of his race,—the white saliva dropping upon his paws.

Then followed a long talk, conducted in side glances, and punctuated with the quiet laughs of more slapping of tails on the cobbles, as the concierge listened to the adventures of the stranger, or matched it with funny experiences of his own.

Here a whistle from the coffee-room window startled him. Even so rude a being as a man is sometimes mindful of his dog. In an instant both were on their feet, the concierge ready for whatever would turn up, the stranger trying to locate the sound and his master. Another whistle, and he was off, bounding down the road, looking wistfully at the windows, and rushing back bewildered. Suddenly the thought popped into his head that the short cut to his master lay through the archway. Then it was that the concierge's manner altered. It was not gruff, nor savage, nor severe,—it was only firm and decided. With his tail still wagging, showing his kindness and willingness to oblige, but with spine rigid and hair bristling, he explained clearly and succinctly to that strange dog how absolutely impossible it would be for him to permit his crossing the archway. Up went the spine of the stranger, and out went his tail like a bar of steel, the feet braced, and the whole body taut as standing rigging. But the concierge kept on wagging his tail, though his hair still bristled,—saying as plainly as could be:

"My dear sir, do not blame me. I assure you that nothing in the world would give me more pleasure than to throw the whole house open to you; but consider for a moment. My master puts me here to see that nobody comes in but those he wishes to see, and that all other livestock, and most especially dogs, shall be kept out. (This with head bent on one side and neck arched.) Now, while I have the most distinguished consideration for your dogship (tail wagging violently), and would gladly oblige you, you must see that my honor is at stake (spine more rigid), and I feel assured that under the circumstances you will not press a request (low growl) which you must know would be impossible for me to grant."

And the strange dog did not. On the contrary, he lowered his tail as he listened, swaying it back and forth, until his interest increased it to a positive wag, ending in a sudden wheel and bound down the road,—convinced but not satisfied.

Then the concierge gravely settled himself once more on his haunches in his customary place, his eyes commanding the view up and down and across the road, where I sat still tilted back in my chair waiting for my cutlets,—his whole body at rest, his face expressive of that quiet content resultant upon duties performed and honor untarnished.

But the stranger had duties, too,—to answer the whistle, and find his master. So back he rushed to the concierge, looking up into his face, his eyes restless and anxious.

"If it was inconsistent with his honor to permit him to cross the threshold, was there any other way he could get into the coffee-room?" This last with a low whine of uneasiness, and a toss of head.

"Yes, certainly; why had he not mentioned it before? It would give him very great pleasure to show him the way to the side entrance," jumping to his feet, and away he went, everything wagging now, and stopped stock still at the corner, pointing with his nose to the closed door.

Then the stranger bounded down with a scurry and plunge, nervously edging up to the door, wagging his tail, crooning a low, anxious whine, springing to one side, his paws now on the sill, his nose at the crack until the door opened, and he dashed inside.

What happened in the coffee-room I do not know, for I could not see. I am willing, however, to wager that a dog of his loyalty, dignity, and sense of duty, did just what a dog of quality would do. No awkward springing at his master's chest with his dusty paws leaving marks on his vest front; no rushing around chairs and tables in mad joy at being let in, alarming waitresses and children. Only a low whine and gurgle of delight, a rubbing of his cold nose against his master's hand, a low, earnest look up into his face,—so frank, so trustful,—a look that carried no reproach for being shut out, and only gratitude for being let in. A moment more, and he was back again, head in air, sweeping in with a glance everything in the road, looking for his friend. Then a dash, and he was around by the archway, licking the concierge in the face, biting his neck, rubbing his nose under his forelegs, saying over and over again how deeply he thanked him,—how glad and proud he was of his acquaintance, and how delighted he would be if he came down to Vienna, or Milan, or wherever he came from, so that he might show him some attention, and make it pleasant for him.

Just here the landlord called out that the cutlets and coffee were ready, and, man like, I went in to breakfast.

F. Hopkinson Smith, "Another Dog." *Cosmopolitan: A Monthly Illustrated Magazine* 19, no. 1 (May 1895): 86–90.

Craig, an Appreciation (1916)

C.A.D.

"'Tis sweet to hear the watch-dog's honest bark bay deep-mouthed as you draw near home." The chap who wrote this was thinking only of his own dog and his own home. He did not think of the terror inspired in the heart of the stranger by this same baying. Being a lover of his own dog and a poet, instead of an ordinary mortal who is intent upon protecting his skin, he did not write about the feelings of fear and trepidation that seize the soul of the wayfarer who approaches the poet's domicile, and hears that "honest bark" for the first time.

The "honest bark" may be a warning to trespassers, or it may be the boisterous expression of exuberant welcome. In the case of Craig it is surely the latter. He is big enough to eat two or three children, and have plenty of room left for a chauffeur. His storage-capacity is great, but he belongs by birth and pedigree to the canine nobility. Behind his big hulk and deep-mouthed baying, there is the kindness of gentle breeding.

Craig is one of five canines, representing five different breeds of canine nobility, that guard the approaches to "Wayside," the beautiful country home of Mr. and Mrs. Robert W. Pomeroy, which lies about a mile from the city limits of Buffalo. He is a short-haired Newfoundland, and stands nearly five feet in his stockings. These five canine representatives of the "first families" constitute a reception committee that is always on the job—unless they happen to be incarcerated in the barn for the safety of the guests on some unusually festive occasion, when the ladies come handsomely gowned, and with white slippers and silk stockings. For Craig's welcome is effusive and boisterous. He makes up in physical energy what he lacks in power of articulate speech. He has been known to push over women and children in the exuberance of his gladness—not by the tumultuous impact of an impetuous greeting, but simply by the firm pressure of his mammoth body against said women and children. If a child of tender years gets in the way of his wagging tail it requires but one gentle oscillation to topple the little one over.

Once upon a time Craig found himself outside the French glass door which opens into the wide hall of the spacious mansion. The sight of good cheer and contentment at the family hearthstone inspired him with a desire to be a part of the family circle. Instead of waiting to be admitted in the regular way, he gently pushed in the glass. Why should a man-made door keep him from the companionship of those he loved? If a boy had pushed in the glass, he would have been promptly spanked and put to bed; in the case of Craig, however, he was promptly admitted, and Mrs. Pomeroy lost no time in making a suitable apology to his canine majesty.

The other dogs are just as pleased and just as happy over the arrival of guests, but they have to express their gladness in a different way. Craig is head of the "glad hand" department, and he knows his job. When he says his prayers at night he thanks his Maker that he does not have to live in the city. He knows that man made the city, and he fits naturally into the country that God made. He is a part of the landscape. All his ways are the ways of Nature. He is not a pervert. He keeps his digestion in good trim, and his liver is always in fine working order. He knows he is only a dog, and he knows his limitations. The large fur rugs that cover the floors of the home are a reminder of what might happen to him if he should suddenly forget to be a gentle, respectful dog. His morals are clean, and his habits above reproach. He looks with mute and compassionate scorn upon the ordinary vices of men. His table manners are perfect. He does not need a napkin tied under his chin to keep him from soiling his dinner coat—and he never changes his coat. He doesn't grumble at his bill of fare. If you pass him a morsel from the bountifully laden table, he takes it in such a way as not to hurt the hand that feeds him. When guests are feasting at the big round table in the wonderful oak dining-room, he sits on his haunches near the sideboard with an expression of patient resignation that becomes a dog of his breeding. Sitting in this position, his head is on a level with the top of the sideboard, and he could easily appropriate a hunk of Virginia ham, which he dearly loves, but there is nothing he enjoys so much as giving the assembled guests an example of self-restraint under great temptation. Sometimes the guests are entertained by a rough-and-tumble scrimmage on the floor participated by the five dogs. There is no biting, no snapping, no snarling or other evidences of bad temper, and the under dog takes his punishment good naturedly.

Craig enjoys the personal acquaintance of the leading families of Buffalo, but he makes no class distinctions. Being an aristocrat by birth, he is democratic in all his social relations. He has no use, however, for persons who do not love trees and flowers and birds. He roams with joyous abandon over every nook and corner of the wooded acres. He knows the name of every tree and bush in the Arboretum, and every vegetable and berry raised in the wonderful gardens—but he makes no unseemly display of his knowledge. He greets the first robin in the spring, and he knows the love-songs of the wren and the martin. He is generous to a fault, forgiving and kind. He is grateful for every human kindness, but, like all fine and sensitive souls, he is endowed with a certain strain of jealousy that leads him to manifest displeasure when too much affection is lavished by the children upon the pony, or other animals that inhabit the place.

Everybody is better, kinder, and more gentle, for having known Craig. Surely he presents a strong contrast to some human beings we know. He does not get on by pulling others down. He has no special pride of race, but he naturally looks down upon all curs of the short-legged variety. He did not want to sit for his photo, as there is no vanity in his make-up, and yet he is better looking than most humans. The photographer had to take him in one of his recumbent moments, without any fixing or fussing.

And for these gentle and human qualities that set him above most bipeds and quadrupeds that roam this mundane sphere, this appreciation is written, with the conviction that the world is made better by giving more than a passing thought to the moral stature and kingly behavior of a noble dog.

C. A. D., "Craig, an Appreciation." *Countryside Magazine and Suburban Life* 22 (March 1916): 160–61.

A Pleasant Instance of the Sagacity of a Dog (1781)

"ABRAHAM WEATHERWISE"

A Gentleman on the road to the house of a friend, was of a sudden seized by such an unexpected eruption of disorderly matter from the prison of his tormented bowels, as, an explosion from the mouth of Ætna, did the fatal business before he had warning to provide for his deliverance. His storm-blasted gall gaskins* were outrageously torn off, and were most inhumanly buried warm in the sepulcher of the next ditch, which were succeeded in the throne by a fresh pair from his portmantua.—All was appeased and easy: But mark the catastrophe! Scarce was he set down to the refreshments of a friendly dinner and engaging company, but the suffusion of a Tartarian vapour spread discord and insurrection all round the table, when the unfortunate gentleman casting his bewildered eyes to the earth, with the horrors of a guilty Macbeth discovered just under his chair an apparition of his evil genius, the ghastly spectre of his murdered breeches, which a careful spaniel, his attendant, in concern for the extravagance of his prodigal master, had brought as part of the baggage, and delivered to his custody. The sympathizing guests, in tears of laughter, pitied the confusion of the dismayed

---

*gall gaskins: colloquial English term for breeches

adventurer, and did not forget to reward honest Ranger's diligence with the remains of the feast, for his exemplary fidelity.

Abraham Weatherwise, "A Pleasant Instance of the Sagacity of a Dog." *Father Abraham's
New England Almanac, for the Year of Our Lord, 1782.* Hartford: Basil Webster, 1781, 23.

The Shepherd's Dog (1845)

J. S. SKINNER

The peculiar education of these dogs is one of the most important and interesting
steps pursued by the shepherd. His method is to select from a multitude of pups
a few of the healthiest and finest-looking, and to put them to a suckling ewe,
first depriving her of her own lamb. By force, as well as from a natural desire she
had to be relieved of the contents of her udder, she soon learns to look upon the
little interlopers with all the affection she would manifest for her own natural
offspring. For the first few days the pups are kept in the hut, the ewe suckling
them morning and evening only; but gradually, as she becomes accustomed to
their sight, she is allowed to run in a small enclosure with them, until she becomes so perfectly familiar with their appearance as to take the entire charge of
them. After this they are folded with the whole flock for a fortnight or so; they
then run about during the day with the flock, which after a while becomes so accustomed to them, as to be able to distinguish them from other dogs—even from
those of the same litter which have not been nursed among them. The shepherds
usually allow the slut to keep one of a litter for her own particular benefit; the
balance are generally destroyed.

"After the pups are weaned, they never leave the particular drove among
which they have been reared. Not even the voice of their master can entice
them beyond sight of the flock; neither hunger nor thirst can do it. I have been
credibly informed of an instance where a single dog having charge of a small
flock of sheep was allowed to wander with them about the mountains, while the
shepherd returned to his village for a few days, having perfect confidence in the
ability of his dog to look after the flock during his absence, but with a strange
want of foresight as to the provision of the dog for his food. Upon his return to
the flock, he found it several miles from where left, but *on the road leading to the
village,* and the poor faithful animal in the agonies of death, dying of *starvation,*
even in the midst of plenty; yet the flock had not been harmed by him. A reciprocal affection exists between them which may put to blush many of the human
family. The poor dog recognised them only as brothers and dearly-loved friends;

he was ready at all times to lay down his life for them; to attack not only wolves and mountain-cats, with the confidence of victory, but even the bear, when there could be no hope. Of late years, when the shepherds of New Mexico have suffered so much from Indian marauders, instances have frequently occurred where the dog has not hesitated to attack his human foes, and although transfixed with arrows, his indomitable courage and faithfulness have been such as to compel his assailants to pin him to the earth with spears, and hold him there until despatched with stones.

"In the above instance the starving dog could have helped himself to one of his *little brother* lambs, or could have deserted the sheep, and very soon have reached the settlements where there was food for him. But faithful even unto death, he would neither leave nor molest them, but followed the promptings of his instinct to lead into the settlement; their unconsciousness of his wants, and slow motions in travelling were too much for his exhausted strength.

"These shepherds are very nomadic in character. They are constantly moving about, their camp-equipage consisting merely of a kettle and bag of meal; their lodges are made in a few minutes, of branches, &c., thrown against cross-sticks. They very seldom go out in the daytime with their flocks, intrusting them entirely to their dogs, which faithfully return them at night, never permitting any straggling behind or lost. Sometimes different flocks are brought into the same neighbourhood, owing to scarcity of grass, when the wonderful instincts of the shepherd's dogs are most beautifully displayed; and to my astonishment, who have been an eye-witness of such scenes, if two flocks approach within a few yards of each other, their respective protectors will place themselves in the space between them, and as is very naturally the case, if any adventurous sheep should endeavour to cross over to visit her neighbours, her dog protector kindly but firmly leads her back, and as it sometimes happens, if many make a rush and succeed in joining the other flock, the dogs under whose charge they are, go over and bring them all out, but strange to say, under such circumstances they *are never opposed by the other dogs.* They approach the strange sheep only to prevent their own from leaving the flock, though they offer no assistance in expelling the other sheep. But they *never permit* sheep not under canine protection, nor dogs not in charge of sheep, to approach them. Even the same dogs which are so freely permitted to enter their flocks in search of their own are driven away with ignominy if they presume to approach them without that laudable object in view.

"Many anecdotes could be related of the wonderful instinct of these dogs. I very much doubt if there are Shepherd dogs in any other part of the world except

Spain, equal to those of New Mexico in value. The famed Scotch and English dogs sink into insignificance by the side of them. Their superiority may be owing to the peculiar mode of rearing them, but they are certainly very noble animals, naturally of large size, and highly deserving to be introduced into the United States. A pair of them will easily kill a wolf, and flocks under their care need not fear any common enemy to be found in our country."

In the same volume, honourable mention is made of a *tailless* breed of dogs employed in the care of sheep and cattle in England. We take room for the following extract, to impress as far as possible, on the mind of American farmers, the important aid to be derived from dogs of the proper blood, in extending our sheep-husbandry, hoping that when their value shall have been realized, measures will be taken by our legislatures to diminish the number of base sheep-killing curs, with which every part of the country is infested.

"Speaking of dogs, I think the Shepherd's dog the most valuable of his species, certainly for the farmer. Our dog Jack, a thorough-bred Scotch collie, has been worth $100 a year in managing our small flock of sheep, usually about 700 in number. He has saved us more than that in time in running after them. After sheep have been once broken in by, and become used to the dog, it is but little trouble to manage them; one man and the dog will do more than five men in driving, yarding, &c. Let any man once possess a good dog, he will never do without one again.

"The sagacity of the Shepherd's dog is wonderful; and if I had not seen so much myself, I could hardly credit all we read about them. It is but a few days since I was reading in a Scotch paper a wonderful performance of one of these collie dogs. It seems the master of the bitch purchased at a fair some 80 sheep, and having occasion to stay a day longer, sent them forward and directed his faithful collie to drive them home, a distance of about 17 miles. The poor bitch when a few miles on the road dropped two whelps; but faithful to her charge, she drove the sheep on a mile or two farther—then allowing them to stop, she returned for her pups, which she carried some two miles in advance of the sheep, and thus she continued to do, alternately carrying her own young ones, and taking charge of the flock, till she reached home. The manner of her acting on this occasion was gathered by the shepherd from various persons who had observed her on the road. On reaching home and delivering her charge, it was found that the two pups were dead. In this extremity the instinct of the poor brute was yet more remarkable; for, going immediately to a rabbit brae in the vicinity, she dug out of the earth two young rabbits, which she deposited on some straw in a barn, and continued to suckle them for some time, until they were unluckily killed by one of the farm tenants. It should be mentioned that the next day she set off to the place where she left her master, whom she met returning when about 13 miles from home.

"The anecdotes of their sagacity are innumerable, and truly wonderful.

"I purchased a bitch of the *tailless species,* known as the English drover dog, in Smithfield market, some two years ago. That species is much used up on the downs, and are a larger and fleeter dog than the collie. We raised two litters from her, got by Jack, and I think the cross will make a very valuable dog for all the purposes of the farmer. They learn easily, are very active, and so far they fully answer our expectations.

"A neighbour to whom we gave a bitch of the first litter would tell her to go into such a lot, and see if there were any stray cattle there; and she would go over the field, and if there were any there, detect them and drive them down to the house. He kept his cattle in the lot, and it was full 80 rods from the house. The dog was not then a year old. We had one of the same litter which we learned to go after cows so well, that we had only to tell him it was time to bring the cows, and he would set off for them from any part of the farm, and bring them into the yard as well as a boy. I think they would be invaluable to a farmer on the prairies. After raising two litters, we sent the bitch to Illinois. I hope farmers will take more pains in getting the Shepherd dog. There is no difficulty in training. Our old one we obtained when a pup, and trained him without any trouble, and without the help of another dog. Any man who has patience, and any *dog knowledge* at all, can train one of this breed to do all that he can desire of a dog."

About thirty years ago, Mr. Baudury, of Delaware, had the Spanish Shepherd's dog, which he thus described:

"The dog you inquire after is three times as large as the Shepherd's dog described by Buffon, but is endowed with the same good qualities: immense strength and great mildness in his usual deportment, though ferocious towards other dogs. I can say, without exaggeration, that at least twenty dogs have been killed in my barnyard, or on my farm, by my dog *Montague.*

"I annex a picture of Montague, with his dimensions: three feet eleven inches from his eyes to the root of his tail, and two feet eight inches high over the shoulders. He is a fine animal, *entirely white.* I prefer that colour in recollection of the story of old Jacob. In fact I had formerly a black dog, and many of my lambs were born black. Since I have Montague and his mother, I have very few black lambs.

"The natural instinct of this animal is to guard your sheep against wolves and dogs. No other training is required, but to keep them constantly with your flock, the moment they are from the litter, until they are grown."

Referring to this variety of the Shepherd's dog, G. W. Lafayette says, in a letter of the 31st of December, to the author of these sketches:—"It will be easy, my dear friend, to send you two good Shepherd's dogs, but very difficult to induce a shepherd to quit his village to go to the United States. French people, born in the country, in a certain position, are rather unenterprising, not having yet arrived at the point of venturing to emigrate, even where their interest would prompt them. To persuade one of our shepherds to go abroad, would require a pecuniary consideration out of proportion to any services that he could render, and even then I would not answer, that after arriving in America, he would not become homesick and wish to get back to France. But if you wish to have dogs, it is very easy to send you at the same time instructions, with their names, and particular destination when in use—for in general they are disciplined to guard the flock, one near at hand and the other far off, and I can assure you they will learn the English language in much less time than their masters would require to be taught a few words of it." Thus the sheep-growing interest is in a way to owe an important boon to one whose name is associated with all that is most glorious and conservative in the history of the country and the principles of the government, such at least as his father fought and bled to establish.

J. S. Skinner, "The Shepherd's Dog." In *The Dog and the Sportsman*. Philadelphia. Lea and Blanchard, 1845, 55–62.

When Eyes Were No Use (1920)

ALBERT PAYSON TERHUNE

"Yes, it's an easy trade to pick up," lectured Top-Sergeant Mahan, formerly of the regular army. "You've just got to remember a few things. But you've got to keep on remembering those few, all the time. If you forget one of 'em, it's the last bit of forgetting you're ever likely to do."

Top-Sergeant Mahan, of the mixed French-and-American regiment known as "Here-We-Come," was squatting at ease on the trench firing-step. From that professorial seat he was dispensing useful knowledge to a group of fellow-countrymen newly arrived from the base, to pad the "Here-We-Come" ranks, which had been thinned at the *Rache* attack.

"What sort of things have we got to remember, Sergeant?" jauntily asked a lanky Missourian. "We've got the drill pretty pat; and the trench instructions and—"

"Gee!" ejaculated Mahan. "I had no idea of that! Then why don't you walk straight ahead into Berlin? If you know all you say you do, about war, there's nothing more for you to learn. I'll drop a line to General Foch and suggest to him that you rookies be detailed to teach the game to us oldsters."

"I didn't mean to be fresh," apologized the jaunty one. "Won't you go ahead and tell us the things we need to remember?"

"Well," exhorted Mahan, appeased by the newcomer's humility, "there aren't so many of them, after all. Learn to duck, when you hear a Minnie grunt or a whizzbang cut loose; or a five-nine begin to whimper. Learn not to bother to duck when the rifles get to jabbering—for you'll never hear the bullet that gets you. Study the nocturnal habits of machine-guns and the ways of snipers and the right time not to play the fool. And keep saying to yourself: "The bullet ain't molded that can get *me!*" Mean it when you say it. When you've learned those few things, the rest of the war-game is dead easy."

"Except," timidly amended old Sergeant Vivier, the gray little Frenchman, "except when eyes are—are what you call it, no use." "That's right," assented Mahan. "In the times when eyes are no use, all rules fail. And then the only thing you can do is to trust to your Yankee luck. I remember—"

"'When eyes are no use?'" repeated the recruit. "If you mean after dark, at night—haven't we got the searchlights and the starshells and all that?"

"Son," replied Mahan, "we have. Though I don't see how you ever guessed such an important secret. But since you know everything, maybe you'll just kindly tell us what good all the lights in the world are going to do us when the filthy yellow-gray fog begins to ooze up out of the mud and the shell-holes, and the filthy gray mist oozes down from the clouds to meet it. Fog is the one thing that all the war-science won't overcome. A fogpenetrator hasn't been invented yet. If it had been, there'd be many a husky lad living today, who has gone West, this past few years, on account of the fogs. Fog is the boche's pet. It gives Fritzy a lovely chance to creep up or, us. It—"

"It is the helper of *us,* too," suggested old Vivier. "More than one time, it has kept me safe when I was on patrol. And did it not help to save us at *Rache,* when—"

"The fog may have helped us, one per cent, at *Rache,*" admitted Mahan. "But Bruce did ninety-nine per cent of the saving."

"A Scotch general?" asked the recruit, as Vivier nodded cordial affirmation of Mahan's words, and as others of the old-timers muttered approval.

"No," contradicted Mahan. "A Scotch collie. If you were dry behind the ears, in this life, you wouldn't have to ask who Bruce is."

"I don't understand," faltered the rookie, suspicious of a possible joke.

"You will soon," Mahan told him. "Bruce will be here to-day. I heard the K.O. saying the big dog is going to be sent down with some dispatches or something, from headquarters. It's his first trip since he was cut up so."

"I am saving him—this!" proclaimed Vivier, disgorging from the flotsam of his pocket a lump of once-white sugar. "My wife, she smuggle three of these to me in her last *paquet*. One I eat in my cafe noir; one I present to *mon* cher *vieux*, ce *bon* Mahan; one I keep for the grand dog what save us all that day."

"What's the idea?" queried the mystified rookie. "I don't—"

"We were stuck in the front line of the *Rache* salient," explained Mahan, eager to recount his dog-friend's prowess. "On both sides our supports got word to fall back. We couldn't get the word, because our telephone connection was knocked galley-west. There we were, waiting for a Hun attack to wipe us out. We couldn't fall back, for they were peppering the hillslope behind us. We were at the bottom. They'd have cut us to ribbons if we'd shown our carcasses in the open. Bruce was here, with a message he'd brought. The K.O. sent him back to headquarters for the reserves. The *boche* heavies and snipers and machine-guns all cut loose to stop him as he scooted up the hill. And a measly giant of a German police dog tried to kill him, too. Bruce got through the lot of them; and he reached headquarters with the *SOS* call that saved us. The poor chap was cut and gouged and torn by bullets and shell-scraps, and he was nearly dead from shell-shock, too. But the surgeon general worked over him, himself, and pulled him back to life. He—"

"He is a loved pet of a man and a woman in your America, I have heard one say," chimed in Vivier. "And his home, there, was in the quiet country. He was lent to the cause, as a patriotic offering, *ce brave!* And of a certainty, he has earned his welcome."

When Bruce, an hour later, trotted into the trenches, on the way to the "Here-We-Come" colonel's quarters, he was received like a visiting potentate. Dozens of men hailed him eagerly by name as he made his way to his destination with the message affixed to his collar.

Many of these men were his well-remembered friends and comrades. Mahan and Vivier, and one or two more, he had grown to like—as well as he could like any one in that land of horrors, three thousand miles away from The Place, where he was born, and from the Mistress and the Master, who were his loyally worshiped gods.

Moreover, being only mortal and afflicted with a hearty appetite, Bruce loved the food and other delicacies the men were forever offering him as a variation on the stodgy fare dished out to him and his fellow war-dogs.

As much to amuse and interest the soldiers whose hero he was, as for any special importance in the dispatch he carried, Bruce had been sent now to the trenches of the Here-We-Comes. It was his first visit to the regiment he had saved, since the days of the *Rache* assault two months earlier. Thanks to supremely clever surgery and to tender care, the dog was little the worse for his wounds. His hearing gradually had come back. In one shoulder he had a very slight stiffness which was not a limp, and a new-healed furrow scarred the left side of his tawny coat. Otherwise he was as good as new.

As Bruce trotted toward the group that so recently had been talking of him, the Missouri recruit watched with interest for the dog's joy at this reunion with his old friends. Bruce's snowy chest and black-stippled coat were fluffed out by many recent baths. His splendid head high and his dark eyes bright, the collie advanced toward the group.

Mahan greeted him joyously. Vivier stretched out a hand which displayed temptingly the long-hoarded lump of sugar. A third man produced, from nowhere in particular, a large and meat-fringed soup-bone.

"I wonder which of you he'll come to, first," said the interested Missourian.

The question was answered at once, and right humiliatingly. For Bruce did not falter in his swinging stride as he came abreast of the group. Not by so much as a second glance did he notice Mahan's hail and the tempting food.

As he passed within six inches of the lump of sugar which Vivier was holding out to him, the dog's silken ears quivered slightly, sure sign of hard-repressed emotion in a thoroughbred collie,—but he gave no other manifestation that he knew any one was there.

"Well, I'll be blessed!" snickered the Missourian in high derision, as Bruce passed out of sight around an angle of the trench. "So that's the pup who is such a pal of you fellows, is he? Gee, but it was a treat to see how tickled he was to meet you again!"

To the rookie's amazement none of his hearers seemed in the least chagrined over the dog's chilling disregard of them. Instead, Mahan actually grunted approbation.

"He'll be back," prophesied the Sergeant. "Don't you worry. He'll be back. We ought to have had more sense than try to stop him when he's on duty. He has better discipline than the rest of us. That's one of very first things they teach a courier-dog—to pay no attention to anybody, when he's on dispatch duty. When Bruce has delivered his message to the K.O., he'll have the right to hunt up his chums. And no one knows it better'n Bruce himself."

"It was a sin—a thoughtlessness—of me to hold the sugar at him," said old Vivier. "Ah but he is a so good soldier, *ce brave* Bruce! He look not to the left nor yet to the right, nor yet to the so-desired sugar-lump. He keep his head at attention! All but the furry tips of his ears. Them has not yet taught to be good soldiers. They tremble when he smell the sugar and the good soup-bone. They quiver like the little leaf. But he keep on. He—"

There was a scurry of fast-cantering feet. Around the angle of the trench dashed Bruce. Head erect, soft dark eyes shining with a light of gay mischief, he galloped up to the grinning Sergeant Vivier and stood. The dog's great plume of a tail was wagging violently. His tulip ears were cocked. His whole interest in life was fixed on the precious lump of sugar which Vivier held out to him.

From puppyhood, Bruce had adored lump sugar. Even at The Place, sugar had been a rarity for him, for the Mistress and the Master had known the damage it can wreak upon a dog's teeth and digestion. Yet, once in a while, as a special luxury, the Mistress had been wont to give him a solitary lump of sugar.

Since his arrival in France, the dog had never seen nor scented such a thing until now. Yet he did not jump for the gift. He did not try to snatch it from Vivier. Instead, he waited until the old Frenchman held it closer toward him, with the invitation:

"Take it, *mon vieux!* It is for you."

Then and then only did Bruce reach daintily forward and grip the grimy bit of sugar between his mighty jaws. Vivier stroked the collie's head while Bruce wagged his tail and munched the sugar and blinked gratefully up at the donor. Mahan looked on, enviously. "A dog's got forty-two teeth, instead of the thirty-two that us humans have to chew on," observed the Sergeant. "A vet' told me that once. And sugar is bad for all forty-two of 'em. Maybe you didn't know that, Monsoo Vivier? Likely, at this rate, we'll have to chip in before long and buy poor Brucie a double set of false teeth. Just because you've put his real ones out of business with lumps of sugar!"

Vivier looked genuinely concerned at this grim forecast. Bruce wandered across to the place where the donor of the soup-bone brandished his offering. Other men, too, were crowding around with gifts.

Between petting and feeding, the collie spent a busy hour among his comrades-at-arms. He was to stay with the "Here-We-Comes" until the following day, and then carry back to headquarters a reconnaissance report.

At four o'clock that afternoon the sky was softly blue and the air was unwontedly clear. By five o'clock a gentle India-summer haze blurred the world's sharper outlines. By six a blanket-fog rolled in, and the air was wetly unbreathable. The fog lay so thick over the soggy earth that objects ten feet away were invisible.

"This," commented Sergeant Mahan, "is one of the times I was talking about this morning—when eyes are no use. This is sure the country for fogs, in wartime. The cockneys tell me the London fogs aren't a patch on 'em."

The "Here-We-Comes" were encamped, for the while, at the edge of a sector from whence all military importance had recently been removed by a convulsive twist of a hundred-mile battle-front. In this dull hole-in-a-corner the new-arrived rivets were in process of welding into the more veteran structure of the mixed regiment.

Not a quarter-mile away—across No Man's Land and athwart two barriers of barbed wire—lay a series of German trenches. Now, in all probability, and from all outward signs, the occupants of this *boche* position consisted only of a regiment or two which had been so badly cut up, in a foiled drive, as to need a month of non-exciting routine before going back into more perilous service.

Yet the commander of the division to which the "Here-We-Comes" were attached did not trust to probabilities nor to outward signs. He had been at the front long enough to realize that the only thing likely to happen was the thing which seemed unlikeliest. And he felt a morbid curiosity to learn more about the personnel of those dormant German trenches.

Wherefore he had sent an order that a handful of the "Here-We-Comes" go forth into No Man's Land, on the first favorable night, and try to pick up a *boche* prisoner or two for questioning-purposes. A scouring of the doubly wired area between the hostile lines might readily harvest some solitary sentinel or some other man on special duty, or even the occupants of a listening-post. And the division commander earnestly desired to question such prisoner or prisoners. The fog furnished an ideal night for such an expedition.

Thus it was that a very young lieutenant and Sergeant Mahan and ten privates —the lanky Missourian among them—were detailed for the prisoner-seeking job. At eleven o'clock, they crept over the top, single file.

It was a night wherein a hundred searchlights and a million star-flares would not have made more impression on the density of the fog than would the striking of a safety match. Yet the twelve reconnoiterers were instructed to proceed in the cautious manner customary to such nocturnal expeditions into No Man's Land. They moved forward at the lieutenant's order, tiptoeing abreast, some twenty feet apart from one another, and advancing in three-foot strides. At every thirty steps the entire line was required to halt and to reestablish contact—in other words, to "dress" on the lieutenant, who was at the extreme right.

This maneuver was more time-wasting and less simple than its recital would imply. For in the dark, unaccustomed legs are liable to miscalculation in the matter of length of stride, even when shell-holes and other inequalities of ground do not complicate the calculations still further. And it is hard to maintain a perfectly straight line when moving forward through choking fog and over scores of obstacles.

The halts for realignment consumed much time and caused no little confusion. Nervousness began to encompass the Missouri recruit He was as brave as the next man. But there is something creepy about walking with measured tread through an invisible space, with no sound but the stealthy pad-pad-pad of equally hesitant footsteps twenty feet away on either side. The Missourian was grateful for the intervals that brought the men into mutual contact, as the eerie march continued.

The first line of barbed wire was cut and passed. Then followed an endless groping progress across No Man's Land, and several delays, as one man or another had trouble in finding contact with his neighbor.

At last the party came to the German wires. The lieutenant had drawn on a rubber glove. In his gloved hand he grasped a strip of steel which he held in front of him like a wand, fanning the air with it,

As he came to the entanglement, he probed the barbed wire carefully with his wand, watching for an ensuing spark. For the Germans more than once had been known to electrify their wires, with fatal results to luckless prowlers.

These wires, to-night, were not charged. And, with pliers, the lieutenant and Mahan started to cut a passageway through them.

As the very first strand parted under his pressure, Mahan laid one hand warningly on the lieutenant's sleeve, and then passed the same prearranged warning down the line to the left.

Silence—moveless, tense, sharply listening silence—followed his motion. Then the rest of the party heard the sound which Mahan's keener ears had caught a moment earlier—the thud of many marching feet. Here was no furtive creeping, as when the twelve Yankees had moved along. Rather was it the rhythmic beat of at least a hundred pairs of shapeless army boots—perhaps of more. The unseen marchers were moving wordlessly, but with no effort at muffling the even tread of their multiple feet.

"They're coming this way!" breathed Sergeant Mahan almost without sound, his lips close to the excited young lieutenant's ear. "And they're not fifty paces off. That means they're *boches*. So near the German wire, our men would either be crawling or else charging, not marching! It's a company—maybe a battalion —coming back from a reconnaissance, and making a gap in their own wire somewhere near here. If we lay low there's an off chance they may pass us by."

Without awaiting the lieutenant's order, Mahan passed along the signal for every man to drop to the earth and lie there. He all but forced the eagerly gesticulating lieutenant to the ground.

On came the swinging tread of the Germans. Mahan, listening breathlessly, tried to gauge the distance and direction. He figured, presently, that the break the Germans had made in their wire could only be a few yards below the spot where he and the lieutenant had been at work with the pliers. Thus the intruders, from their present course, must inevitably pass very close to the prostrate Americans—so close, perhaps, as to brush against the nearest of them, or even to step on one or more of the crouching figures.

Mahan whispered to the man on his immediate left, the rookie from Missouri:

"Edge closer to the wire—close as you can wiggle, and lie flat. Pass on the word."

The Missourian obeyed. Before writhing his long body forward against the bristly mass of wire he passed the instructions on to the man at his own left.

But his nerves were at breaking-point.

It had been bad enough to crawl through the blind fog, with the ghostly steps of his comrades pattering softly at either side of him. But it was a thousand times harder to lie helpless here, in the choking fog and on the soaked ground, while countless enemies were bearing down, unseen, upon him, on one side, and an impenetrable wire cut off his retreat on the other.

The Missourian had let his imagination begin to work; always a mistake in a private soldier. He was visualizing the moment when this tramping German force should become aware of the presence of their puny foes and should slaughter them against the merciless wires. It would not be a fair stand-up fight, this murder-rush of hundreds of men against twelve who were penned in and could not maneuver nor escape. And the thought of it was doing queer things to the rookie's overwrought nerves.

Having passed the word to creep closer to the wires, he began to execute the order in person, with no delay at all. But he was a fraction of a second too late. The Germans were moving in hike-formation with "points" thrown out in advance to either side—a "point" being a private soldier who, for scouting and other purposes, marches at some distance from the main body.

The point, ahead of the platoon, had swerved too far to the left, in the blackness—an error that would infallibly have brought him up against the wires, with considerable force, in another two steps. But the Missourian was between him and the wires. And the point's heavy-shod foot came down, heel first, on the back of the rookie's out-groping hand. Such a crushing impact, on the hand-back, is one of the most agonizing minor injuries a man can sustain. And this fact the Missourian discovered with great suddenness.

His too-taut nerves forced from his throat a yell that split the deathly stillness with an ear-piercing vehemence. He sprang to his feet, forgetful of orders intent only on thrusting his bayonet through the Hun who had caused such acute torture to his hand. Half way up, the rookie's feet went out from under him in the slimy mud. He caromed against the point, then fell headlong.

The German, doubtless thinking he had stumbled upon a single stray American scout, whirled his own rifle aloft, to dash out the brains of his luckless foe. But before the upflung butt could descend,—before the rookie could rise or dodge,—the point added his quota to the rude breaking of the night's silence. He screamed in panic terror, dropped his brandished gun and reeled backward, clawing at his own throat.

For out of the eerie darkness, something had launched itself at him— something silent and terrible, that had flown to the Missourian's aid. Down with a crash went the German, on his back. He rolled against the Missourian, who promptly sought to grapple with him.

But even as he clawed for the German, the rookie's nerves wrung from him a second yell—this time less of rage than of horror.

"Sufferin' cats!" he bellowed. "Why didn't anybody ever tell me Germans was covered with fur instead of clothes?"

The *boche* platoon was no longer striding along in hike-formation. It was broken up into masses of wildly running men, all of them bearing down upon the place whence issued this ungodly racket and turmoil. Stumbling, reeling, blindly falling and rising again, they came on.

Someone among them loosed a rifle-shot in the general direction of the yelling. A second and a third German rifleman followed the example of the first. From the distant American trenches, one or two snipers began to pepper away toward the enemy lines, though the fog was too thick for them, to see the German rifle-flashes.

The *boches* farthest to the left, in the blind rush, fouled with the wires. German snipers, from behind the Hun parapets, opened fire. A minute earlier the night had been still as the grave. Now it fairly vibrated with clangor. All because one rookie's nerves had been less staunch than his courage, and because that same rookie had not only had his hand stepped on in the dark, but had encountered something swirling and hairy when he grabbed for the soldier who had stepped on him!

The American lieutenant, at the onset of the clamor, sprang to his feet, whipping out his pistol; his dry lips parted in a command to charge—a command which, naturally, would have reduced his eleven men and himself to twelve corpses or to an equal number of mishandled prisoners within the next few seconds. But a big hand was clapped unceremoniously across the young officer's mouth, silencing the half-spoken suicidal order.

Sergeant Mahan's career in the regular army had given him an almost uncanny power of sizing up his fellowmen. And he had long ago decided that this was the sort of thing his untried lieutenant would be likely to do, in just such an emergency. Wherefore his flagrant breach of discipline in shoving his palm across the mouth of his superior officer.

And as he was committing this breach of discipline, he heard the Missourian's strangled gasp of:

"Why didn't anybody ever tell me Germans was covered with fur?"

In a flash Mahan understood. Wheeling, he stooped low and flung out both arms in a wide-sweeping circle. Luckily his right hand's fingertips, as they completed the circle, touched something fast-moving and furry.

"Bruce!" he whispered fiercely, tightening his precarious grip on the wisp of fur his fingers had touched. "Bruce! Stand still, boy! It's *you* who's got to get us clear of this! Nobody else, short of the good Lord, can do it!"

Bruce had had a pleasantly lazy day with his friends in the first-line trenches. There had been much good food and more petting. And at last, comfortably tired of it all, he had gone to sleep. He had awakened in a most friendly mood, and a little hungry. Wherefore he had sallied forth in search of human companionship. He found plenty of soldiers who were more than willing to talk to him and make much of him. But, a little farther ahead, he saw his good friend, Sergeant Mahan, and others of his acquaintances, starting over the parapet on what promised to be a jolly evening stroll.

All dogs find it hard to resist the mysterious lure of a walk in human companionship. True, the night was not an ideal one for a ramble, and the fog had a way of congealing wetly on Bruce's shaggy coat. Still, a damp coat was not enough of a discomfort to offset the joy of a stroll with his friends. So Bruce had followed the twelve men quietly into No Man's Land, falling decorously into step behind Mahan.

It had not been much of a walk, for speed or for fun. For the humans went ridiculously slowly, and had an eccentric way of bunching together, every now and again, and then of stringing out into a shambling line. Still, it was a walk, and therefore better than loafing behind in the trenches. And Bruce had kept his noiseless place at the Sergeant's heels.

Then—long before Mahan heard the approaching tramp of feet—Bruce caught not only the sound but the scent of the German platoon. The scent at once told him that the strangers were not of his own army. A German soldier and an American soldier—because of their difference in diet as well as for certain other and more cogent reasons—have by no means the same odor, to a collie's trained scent, nor to that of other breeds of war-dogs. Official records of dog-sentinels prove that.

Aliens were nearing Bruce's friends. And the dog's ruff began to stand up. But Mahan and the rest seemed in no way concerned in spirit thereby—though, to the dog's understanding, they must surely be aware of the approach. So Bruce gave no further sign of displeasure. He was out for a walk, as a guest. He was not on sentry-duty.

But when the nearest German was almost upon them, and all twelve Americans dropped to the ground, the collie became interested once more. A German stepped on the hand of one of his newest friends. And the friend yelled in pain. Whereat the German made as if to strike the stepped-on man.

This was quite enough for loyal Bruce. Without so much as a growl of warning he jumped at the offender.

Dog and man tumbled earthward together. Then after an instant of flurry and noise, Bruce felt Mahan's fingers on his shoulder and heard the stark appeal of Mahan's whispered voice. Instantly the dog was a professional soldier once more—alertly obedient and resourceful.

"Catch hold my left arm, Lieutenant!" Mahan was exhorting. "Close up, there, boys—every man's hand grabbing tight to the shoulder of the man his left! Pass the word. And you, Missouri, hang onto the Lieutenant! Quick, there! And tread soft and tread fast, and don't let go, whatever happens! Not a sound out of any one! I'm leading the way. And Bruce is going to lead me."

There was a scurrying scramble as the men groped for one another. Mahan tightened his hold on Bruce's mane.

"Bruce! He said, very low, but with a strength of appeal that was not lost on the listening dog. "Bruce! Camp! Back to *camp*! And keep *quiet*! Back to camp, boy! *Camp*!"

He had no need to repeat his command so often and so strenuously. Bruce was a trained courier. The one word "Camp!" was quite enough to tell him what he was to do.

Turning, he faced the American lines and tried to break into a gallop. His scent and his knowledge of direction were all the guides he needed. A dog always relies on his nose first and his eyes last. The fog was no obstacle at all to the collie. He understood the Sergeant's order, and he set out at once to obey it.

But at the very first step, he was checked. Mahan did not release that feverishly tight hold on his mane, but merely shifted to his collar.

Bruce glanced back, impatient at the delay. But Mahan did not let go. Instead he said once more:

"*Camp,* boy!"

And Bruce understood he expected to make his way to camp, with Mahan hanging on to his collar.

Bruce did not enjoy this mode of locomotion. It was inconvenient and there seemed no sense in it; but then there were many things about this strenuous war-trade that Bruce neither enjoyed nor comprehended, yet which he performed at command.

So again he turned campward, Mahan at his collar and an annoyingly hindering tail of men stumbling silently on behind them. All around were the Germans—butting drunkenly through the blanket-dense fog, swinging their rifles like flails, shouting confused orders, occasionally firing. Now and then two or more of them would collide and would wrestle in blind fury, thinking they had encountered an American.

Impeded by their own sightlessly swarming numbers, as much as by the impenetrate darkness, they sought the foe. And but for Bruce they must quickly have found what they sought. Even in compact form, the Americans could not have had the sheer luck to dodge every scattered contingent of Huns which starred the German end of No Man's Land—most of them between the fugitives and the American lines.

But Bruce was on dispatch duty. It was his work to obey commands and to get back to camp at once. It was bad enough to be handicapped by Mahan's grasp on his collar. He was minded to suffer further delay by running into any of the clumps of gesticulating and cabbage-reeking Germans between him and his goal. So he steered clear of such groups, making several wide detours in order to do so. Once or twice he stopped short to let some of the Germans grope past him, not six feet away. Again he veered sharply to the left—increasing his pace and forcing Mahan and the rest to increase theirs—to avoid a squad of thirty men who were quartering the field in close formation, and who all but jostled the dog as they strode sightlessly by. An occasional rifle-shot spat forth its challenge. From both trench-lines men were firing at a venture. A few of the bullets sang nastily close to the twelve huddled men and their canine leader. Once a German, not three yards away, screamed aloud and fell sprawling and kicking, as one such chance bullet found him. Above and behind, sounded the plop of star-shells sent up by the enemy in futile hope of penetrating the viscid fog. And everywhere was heard the shuffle and stumbling of innumerable boots.

At last the noise of feet began to die away, and the uneven groping tread of the twelve Americans to sound more distinctly for the lessening of the surrounding turmoil. And in another few seconds Bruce came to a halt—not to an abrupt stop, as when he had allowed an enemy squad to pass in front of him, but a leisurely checking of speed, to denote that he could go no farther with the load he was helping to haul.

Mahan put out his free hand. It encountered the American wires. Bruce had stopped at the spot where the part where the party had cut a narrow path through the entanglement on the outward journey. Alone, the dog could easily have passed through the gap, but he could not be certain of pulling Mahan with him. Wherefore the halt.

The last of the twelve men scrambled down to safety, in the American first-line trench, Bruce among them. The lieutenant went straight to his commanding officer, to make his report. Sergeant Mahan went straight to his company cook, whom he woke from a snoreful sleep. Presently Mahan ran back to where the soldiers were gathered admiringly around Bruce.

The Sergeant carried a chunk of fried beef, for which he had just given the cook his entire remaining stock of cigarettes.

"Here you are, Bruce!" he exclaimed. "The best in the shop is none too good for the dog that got us safe out of that filthy mess. Eat hearty!"

Bruce did not so much as sniff at the (more or less) tempting bit of meat. Coldly he looked up at Mahan. Then, with sensitive ears laid flat against his silken head, in token of strong contempt, he turned his back on the Sergeant and walked away.

Which was Bruce's method of showing what he thought of a human fool who would give him a command and who would then hold so tightly to him that the dog could hardly carry out the order.

Albert Payson Terhune, "When Eyes Were No Use." In *Bruce*. New York: Grossett and Dunlap, 1920, 110–40.

The Bar Sinister (1902)

RICHARD HARDING DAVIS

Part I

The Master was walking most unsteady, his legs tripping each other. After the fifth or sixth round, my legs often go the same way.

But even when the Master's legs bend and twist a bit, you mustn't think he can't reach you. Indeed, that is the time he kicks most frequent. So I kept behind him in the shadow, or ran in the middle of the street. He stopped at many public-houses with swinging doors, those doors that are cut so high from the sidewalk that you can look in under them, and see if the Master is inside. At night when I peep beneath them the man at the counter will see me first and say, "Here's the Kid, Jerry, come to take you home. Get a move on you," and the Master will stumble out and follow me. It's lucky for us I'm so white, for no matter how dark the night, he can always see me ahead, just out of reach of his boot. At night the Master certainly does see most amazing. Sometimes he sees two or four of me, and walks in a circle, so that I have to take him by the leg of his trousers and lead him into the right road. One night, when he was very nasty-tempered and I was coaxing him along, two men passed us and one of them says, "Look at that brute!" and the other asks "Which?" and they both laugh. The Master, he cursed them good and proper.

This night, whenever we stopped at a public-house, the Master's pals left it and went on with us to the next. They spoke quite civil to me, and when the Master tried a flying kick, they gives him a shove. "Do you want we should lose our money?" says the pals.

I had had nothing to eat for a day and a night, and just before we set out the Master gives me a wash under the hydrant. Whenever I am locked up until all the slop-pans in our alley are empty, and made to take a bath, and the Master's pals speak civil, and feel my ribs, I know something is going to happen. And that night, when every time they see a policeman under a lamp-post, they dodged across the street, and when at the last one of them picked me up and hid me under his jacket, I began to tremble; for I knew what it meant. It meant that I was to fight again for the Master.

I don't fight because I like it. I fight because if I didn't the other dog would find my throat, and the Master would lose his stakes, and I would be very sorry for him and ashamed. Dogs can pass me and I can pass dogs, and I'd never pick a fight with none of them. When I see two dogs standing on their hind-legs in the streets, clawing each other's ears, and snapping for each other's windpipes, or howling and swearing and rolling in the mud, I feel sorry they should act so, and pretend not to notice. If he'd let me, I'd like to pass the time of day with every dog I meet. But there's something about me that no nice dog can abide. When I trot up to nice dogs, nodding and grinning, to make friends, they always tell me to be off. "Go to the devil!" they bark at me; "Get out!" and when I walk away they shout "mongrel," and "gutter-dog," and sometimes, after my back is turned, they rush me. I could kill most of them with three shakes, breaking the back-bone of the little ones, and squeezing the throat of the big ones. But what's the good? They *are* nice dogs; that's why I try to make up to them, and though it's not for them to say it, I *am* a street-dog, and if I try to push into the company of my betters, I suppose it's their right to teach me my place.

Of course, they don't know I'm the best fighting bull-terrier of my weight in Montreal. That's why it wouldn't be right for me to take no notice of what they shout. They don't know that if I once locked my jaws on them I'd carry away whatever I touched. The night I fought Kelley's White Rat, I wouldn't loosen up until the Master made a noose in my leash and strangled me, and if the handlers hadn't thrown red pepper down my nose, I *never* would have let go of that Ottawa dog. I don't think the handlers treated me quite right that time, but maybe they didn't know the Ottawa dog was dead. I did.

I learned my fighting from my mother when I was very young. We slept in a lumber-yard on the river-front, and by day hunted for food along the wharfs. When we got it, the other tramp-dogs would try to take it off us, and then it was wonderful to see mother fly at them, and drive them away. All I know of fighting I learned from mother, watching her picking the ash-heaps for me when I was too little to fight for myself. No one ever was so good to me as mother. When it snowed and the ice was in the St. Lawrence she used to hunt alone, and bring me back new bones, and she'd sit and laugh to see me trying to swallow 'em whole. I was just a puppy then, my teeth was falling out. When I was able to fight we kept the whole river-range to ourselves. I had the genuine long, "punishing" jaw, so mother said, and there wasn't a man or a dog that dared worry us. Those were happy days, those were; and we lived well, share and share alike, and when we wanted a bit of fun, we chased the fat old wharf-rats: My! how they would squeal!

Then the trouble came. It was no trouble to me. I was too young to care then. But mother took it so to heart that she grew ailing, and wouldn't go abroad with me by day. It was the same old scandal that they're always bringing up against me. I was so young then that I didn't know. I couldn't see any difference between mother—and other mothers.

But one day a pack of curs we drove off snarled back some new names at her, and mother dropped her head and ran, just as though they had whipped us. After that she wouldn't go out with me except in the dark, and one day she went away and never came back, and though I hunted for her in every court and alley and back street of Montreal, I never found her.

One night, a month after mother ran away, I asked Guardian, the old blind mastiff, whose Master is the night-watchman on our slip, what it all meant. And he told me.

"Every dog in Montreal knows," he says, "except you, and every Master knows. So I think it's time you knew."

Then he tells me that my father, who had treated mother so bad, was a great and noble gentleman from London. "Your father had twenty-two registered ancestors, had your father," old Guardian says, "and in him was the best bull-terrier blood of England, the most ancientest, the most royal; the winning 'blue-ribbon' blood, that breeds champions. He had sleepy pink eyes, and thin pink lips, and he was as white all over as his own white teeth, and under his white skin you could see his muscles, hard and smooth, like the links of a steel chain. When your father stood still, and tipped his nose in the air, it was just as though he was saying, 'Oh, yes, you common dogs and men, you may well stare. It must be a rare treat for you Colonials to see a real English royalty.' He certainly was pleased with hisself, was your father. He looked just as proud and haughty as one of them stone dogs in Victoria Park—them as is cut out of white marble. And you're like him," says the old mastiff—"by that, of course, meaning you're white, same as him. That's the only likeness. But, you see, the trouble is, Kid—well, you see, Kid, the trouble is—your mother—"

"That will do," I said, for I understood then without his telling me, and I got up and walked away, holding my head and tail high in the air.

But I was, oh, so miserable, and I wanted to see mother that very minute, and tell her that I didn't care.

Mother is what I am, a street-dog; there's no royal blood in mother's veins, nor is she like that father of mine, nor—and that's the worst—she's not even like me. For while I, when I'm washed for a fight, am as white as clean snow, she—and this is our trouble, she—my mother, is a black-and-tan.

When mother hid herself from me, I was twelve months old and able to take care of myself, and, as after mother left me, the wharfs were never the same, I moved up-town and met the Master. Before he came, lots of other men-folks had tried to make up to me, and to whistle me home. But they either tried patting me or coaxing me with a piece of meat; so I didn't take to 'em. But one day the Master pulled me out of a street-fight by the hind-legs, and kicked me good.

"You want to fight, do you?" says he. "I'll give you all the *fighting* you want!" he says, and he kicks me again. So I knew he was my Master, and I followed him home. Since that day I've pulled off many fights for him, and they've brought dogs from all over the province to have a go at me, but up to that night none under thirty pounds, had ever downed me.

But that night, so soon as they carried me into the ring, I saw the dog was over-weight, and that I was no match for him. It was asking too much of a puppy. The Master should have known I couldn't do it. Not that I mean to blame the Master, for when sober, which he sometimes was, though not, as you might say, his habit, he was most kind to me, and let me out to find food, if I could get it, and only kicked me when I didn't pick him up at night and lead him home.

But kicks will stiffen the muscles, and starving a dog so as to get him ugly-tempered for a fight may make him nasty, but it's weakening to his insides, and it causes the legs to wabble.

The ring was in a hall, back of a public-house. There was a red-hot white-washed stove in one corner, and the ring in the other. I lay in the Master's lap, wrapped in my blanket, and, spite of the stove, shivering awful; but I always shiver before a fight; I can't help gettin' excited. While the men-folks were a-flashing their money and taking their last drink at the bar, a little Irish groom in gaiters came up to me and give me the back of his hand to smell, and scratched me behind the ears.

"You poor little pup," says he. "You haven't no show," he says. "That brute in the tap-room, he'll eat your heart out."

"That's what you think," says the Master, snarling. "I'll lay you a quid the Kid chews him up."

The groom, he shook his head, but kept looking at me so sorry-like, that I begun to get a bit sad myself. He seemed like he couldn't bear to leave off a-patting of me, and he says, speaking low just like he would to a man-folk, "Well, good-luck to you, little pup," which I thought so civil of him, that I reached up and licked his hand. I don't do that to many men. And the Master, he knew I didn't, and took on dreadful.

"What 'ave you got on the back of your hand?" says he, jumping up.

"Soap!" says the groom, quick as a rat. "That's more than you've got on yours. Do you want to smell of it?" and he sticks his fist under the Master's nose. But the pals pushed in between 'em.

"He tried to poison the Kid!" shouts the Master.

"Oh, one fight at a time," says the referee. "Get into the ring, Jerry. We're waiting." So we went into the ring.

I never could just remember what did happen in that ring. He give me no time to spring. He fell on me like a horse. I couldn't keep my feet against him, and though, as I saw, he could get his hold when he liked, he wanted to chew me over a bit first. I was wondering if they'd be able to pry him off me, when, in the third round, he took his hold; and I began to drown, just as I did when I fell into the river off the Red C slip. He closed deeper and deeper, on my throat, and everything went black and red and bursting; and then, when I were sure I were dead, the handlers pulled him off, and the Master give me a kick that brought me to. But I couldn't move none, or even wink, both eyes being shut with lumps.

"He's a cur!" yells the Master, "a sneaking, cowardly cur. He lost the fight for me," says he, "because he's a —— cowardly cur." And he kicks me again in the lower ribs, so that I go sliding across the sawdust. "There's gratitude fer yer," yells the Master. "I've fed that dog, and nussed that dog, and housed him like a prince; and now he puts his tail between his legs, and sells out, he does. He's a coward; I've done with him, I am. I'd sell him for a pipeful of tobacco." He picked me up by the tail, and swung me for the men-folks to see. "Does any gentleman here want to buy a dog," he says, "to make into sausage meat?" he says. "That's all he's good for."

Then I heard the little Irish groom say, "I'll give you ten bob for the dog."

And another voice says, "Ah, don't you do it; the dog's same as dead—mebby he is dead."

"Ten shillings!" says the Master, and his voice sobers a bit; "make it two pounds, and he's yours."

But the pals rushed in again.

"Don't you be a fool, Jerry," they say. "You'll be sorry for this when you're sober. The Kid's worth a fiver."

One of my eyes was not so swelled up as the other, and as I hung by my tail, I opened it, and saw one of the pals take the groom by the shoulder.

"You ought to give 'im five pounds for that dog, mate," he says; "that's no ordinary dog. That dog's got good blood in him, that dog has. Why, his father— that very dog's father—"

I thought he never would go on. He waited like he wanted to be sure the groom was listening.

"That very dog's father," says the pal, "is Regent Royal, son of Champion Regent Monarch, champion bull-terrier of England for four years."

I was sore, and torn, and chewed most awful, but what the pal said sounded so fine that I wanted to wag my tail, only couldn't, owing to my hanging from it.

But the Master calls out, "Yes, his father was Regent Royal; who's saying he wasn't? But the pup's a cowardly cur, that's what his pup is, and why—I'll tell you why—because his mother was a black-and-tan street-dog, that's why!"

I don't see how I get the strength, but some way I threw myself out of the Master's grip and fell at his feet, and turned over and fastened all my teeth in his ankle, just across the bone.

When I woke, after the pals had kicked me off him, I was in the smoking-car of a railroad-train, lying in the lap of the little groom, and he was rubbing my open wounds with a greasy, yellow stuff, exquisite to the smell, and most agreeable to lick off.

Part II

"Well—what's your name—Nolan? Well, Nolan, these references are satisfactory," said the young gentleman my new Master called "Mr. Wyndham, sir." "I'll take you on as second man. You can begin to-day."

My new Master shuffled his feet, and put his finger to his forehead. "Thank you, sir," says he. Then he choked like he had swallowed a fish-bone. "I have a little dawg, sir," says he.

"You can't keep him," says "Mr. Wyndham, sir," very short.

"'Es only a puppy, sir," says my new Master; "'e wouldn't go outside the stables, sir."

"It's not that," says "Mr. Wyndham, sir"; "I have a large kennel of very fine dogs; they're the best of their breed in America. I don't allow strange dogs on the premises."

The Master shakes his head, and motions me with his cap, and I crept out from behind the door. "I'm sorry, sir," says the Master. "Then I can't take the place. I can't get along without the dog, sir."

"Mr. Wyndham, sir," looked at me that fierce that I guessed he was going to whip me, so I turned over on my back and begged with my legs and tail.

"Why, you beat him!" says "Mr. Wyndham, sir," very stern.

"No fear!" the Master says, getting very red. "The party I bought him off taught him that. He never learnt that from me!" He picked me up in his arms, and to show "Mr. Wyndham, sir," how well I loved the Master, I bit his chin and hands.

"Mr. Wyndham, sir," turned over the letters the Master had given him. "Well, these references certainly are very strong," he says. "I guess I'll let the dog stay this time. Only see you keep him away from the kennels—or you'll both go."

"Thank you, sir," says the Master, grinning like a cat when she's safe behind the area-railing.

"He's not a bad bull-terrier," says "Mr. Wyndham, sir," feeling my head. "Not that I know much about the smooth-coated breeds. My dogs are St. Bernards." He stopped patting me and held up my nose. "What's the matter with his ears?" he says. "They're chewed to pieces. Is this a fighting dog?" he asks, quick and rough-like.

I could have laughed. If he hadn't been holding my nose, I certainly would have had a good grin at him. Me, the best under thirty pounds in the Province of Quebec, and him asking if I was a fighting dog! I ran to the Master and hung down my head modest-like, waiting for him to tell of my list of battles, but the Master he coughs in his cap most painful. "Fightin' dog, sir," he cries. "Lor' bless you, sir, the Kid don't know the word. 'Es just a puppy, sir, same as you see; a pet dog, so to speak. 'Es a regular old lady's lap-dog, the Kid is."

"Well, you keep him away from my St. Bernards," says "Mr. Wyndham, sir," "or they might make a mouthful of him."

"Yes, sir, that they might," says the Master. But when we gets outside he slaps his knee and laughs inside hisself, and winks at me most sociable.

The Master's new home was in the country, in a province they called Long Island. There was a high stone wall about his home with big iron gates to it, same as Godfrey's brewery; and there was a house with five red roofs, and the stables, where I lived, was cleaner than the aerated bakery-shop, and then there was the kennels, but they was like nothing else in this world that ever I see. For the first days I couldn't sleep of nights for fear someone would catch me lying in such a cleaned-up place, and would chase me out of it, and when I did fall to sleep I'd dream I was back in the old Master's attic, shivering under the rusty stove, which never had no coals in it, with the Master flat on his back on the cold floor with his clothes on. And I'd wake up, scared and whimpering, and find myself on the new Master's cot with his hand on the quilt beside me; and I'd see the glow of the big stove, and hear the high-quality horses below-stairs stamping in their straw-lined boxes, and I'd snoop the sweet smell of hay and harness-soap, and go to sleep again.

The stables was my jail, so the Master said, but I don't ask no better home than that jail.

"Now, Kid," says he, sitting on the top of a bucket upside down, "you've got to understand this. When I whistle it means you're not to go out of this 'ere yard. These stables is your jail. And if you leave 'em I'll have to leave 'em, too, and over the seas, in the County Mayo, an old mother will 'ave to leave her bit of a cottage. For two pounds I must be sending her every month, or she'll have naught to eat, nor no thatch over 'er head; so, I can't lose my place, Kid, an' see you don't lose it for me. You must keep away from the kennels," says he; "they're not for the likes of you. The kennels are for the quality. I wouldn't take a litter of them woolly dogs for one wag of your tail, Kid, but for all that they are your betters, same as the gentry up in the big house are my betters. I know my place and keep away from the gentry, and you keep away from the champions."

So I never goes out of the stables. All day I just lay in the sun on the stone flags, licking my jaws, and watching the grooms wash down the carriages, and the only care I had was to see they didn't get gay and turn the hose on me. There wasn't even a single rat to plague me. Such stables I never did see.

"Nolan," says the head-groom, "some day that dog of yours will give you the slip. You can't keep a street-dog tied up all his life. It's against his natur'."

The head-groom is a nice old gentleman, but he doesn't know everything. Just as though I'd been a street-dog because I liked it. As if I'd rather poke for my vittels in ash-heaps than have 'em handed me in a wash-basin and would sooner bite and fight than be polite and sociable. If I'd had mother there I couldn't have asked for nothing more. But I'd think of her snooping in the gutters, or freezing of nights under the bridges, or, what's worse of all, running through the hot streets with her tongue down, so wild and crazy for a drink, that the people would shout "mad dog" at her, and stone her. Water's so good, that I don't blame the men-folks for locking it up inside their houses, but when the hot days come, I think they might remember that those are the dog-days and leave a little water outside in a trough, like they do for the horses. Then we wouldn't go mad, and the policemen wouldn't shoot us. I had so much of everything I wanted that it made me think a lot of the days when I hadn't nothing, and if I could have given what I had to mother, as she used to share with me, I'd have been the happiest dog in the land. Not that I wasn't happy then, and most grateful to the Master, too, and if I'd only minded him, the trouble wouldn't have come again.

But one day the coachman says that the little lady they called Miss Dorothy had come back from school, and that same morning she runs over to the stables to pat her ponies, and she sees me.

"Oh, what a nice little, white little dog," said she; "whose little dog are you?" says she.

"That's my dog, miss," says the Master. "'Is name is Kid," and I ran up to her most polite, and licks her fingers, for I never see so pretty and kind a lady.

"You must come with me and call on my new puppies," says she, picking me up in her arms and starting off with me.

"Oh, but please, miss," cries Nolan, "Mr. Wyndham give orders that the Kid's not to go to the kennels."

"That'll be all right," says the little lady; "they're my kennels too. And the puppies will like to play with him."

You wouldn't believe me if I was to tell you of the style of them quality-dogs. If I hadn't seen it myself I wouldn't have believed it neither. The Viceroy of Canada don't live no better. There was forty of them, but each one had his own house and a yard—most exclusive—and a cot and a drinking-basin all to hisself. They had servants standing 'round waiting to feed 'em when they was hungry, and valets to wash 'em; and they had their hair combed and brushed like the grooms must when they go out on the box. Even the puppies had overcoats with their names on 'em in blue letters, and the name of each of those they called champions was painted up fine over his front door just like it was a public-house or a veterinary's. They were the biggest St. Bernards I ever did see. I could have walked under them if they'd have let me. But they were very proud and haughty dogs, and looked only once at me, and then sniffed in the air. The little lady's own dog was an old gentleman bull-dog. He'd come along with us, and when he notices how taken aback I was with all I see, 'e turned quite kind and affable and showed me about.

"Jimmy Jocks," Miss Dorothy called him, but, owing to his weight, he walked most dignified and slow, waddling like a duck as you might say, and looked much too proud and handsome for such a silly name.

"That's the runway, and that's the Trophy House," says he to me, "and that over there is the hospital, where you have to go if you get distemper, and the vet. gives you beastly medicine."

"And which of these is your 'ouse, sir?" asks I, wishing to be respectful. But he looked that hurt and haughty. "I don't live in the kennels," says he, most contemptuous. "I am a house-dog. I sleep in Miss Dorothy's room. And at lunch I'm let in with the family, if the visitors don't mind. They most always do, but they're too polite to say so. Besides," says he, smiling most condescending, "visitors are always afraid of me. It's because I'm so ugly," says he. "I suppose," says he, screwing up his wrinkles and speaking very slow and impressive, "I suppose I'm the ugliest bull-dog in America," and as he seemed to be so pleased to think hisself so, I said, "Yes, sir, you certainly are the ugliest ever I see," at which he nodded his head most approving.

"But I couldn't hurt 'em, as you say," he goes on, though I hadn't said nothing like that, being too polite. "I'm too old," he says; "I haven't any teeth. The last time one of those grizzly bears," said he, glaring at the big St. Bernards, "took a hold of me, he nearly was my death," says he. I thought his eyes would pop out of his head, he seemed so wrought up about it. "He rolled me around in the dirt, he did," says Jimmy Jocks, "an' I couldn't get up. It was low," says Jimmy Jocks, making a face like he had a bad taste in his mouth. "Low, that's what I call it, bad form, you understand, young man, not done in our circles—and—and low." He growled, way down in his stomach, and puffed hisself out, panting and blowing like he had been on a run.

"I'm not a street-fighter," he says, scowling at a St. Bernard marked "Champion." "And when my rheumatism is not troubling me," he says, "I endeavor to be civil to all dogs, so long as they are gentlemen."

"Yes, sir," said I, for even to me he had been most affable.

At this we had come to a little house off by itself and Jimmy Jocks invites me in. "This is their trophy-room," he says, "where they keep their prizes. Mine," he says, rather grand-like, "are on the sideboard." Not knowing what a sideboard might be, I said, "Indeed, sir, that must be very gratifying." But he only wrinkled up his chops as much as to say, "It is my right."

The trophy-room was as wonderful as any public-house I ever see. On the walls was pictures of nothing but beautiful St. Bernard dogs, and rows and rows of blue and red and yellow ribbons; and when I asked Jimmy Jocks why they was so many more of blue than of the others, he laughs and says, "Because these kennels always win." And there was many shining cups on the shelves which Jimmy Jocks told me were prizes won by the champions.

"Now, sir, might I ask you, sir," says I, "wot is a champion?"

At that he panted and breathed so hard I thought he would bust hisself. "My dear young friend!" says he. "Wherever have you been educated? A champion is a—a champion," he says. "He must win nine blue ribbons in the 'open' class. You follow me—that is—against all comers. Then he has the title before his name, and they put his photograph in the sporting papers. You know, of course, that *I* am a champion," says he. "I am Champion Woodstock Wizard III., and the two other Woodstock Wizards, my father and uncle, were both champions."

"But I thought your name was Jimmy Jocks," I said.

He laughs right out at that.

"That's my kennel name, not my registered name," he says. "Why, you certainly know that every dog has two names. Now, what's your registered name and number, for instance?" says he.

"I've only got one name," I says. "Just Kid."

Woodstock Wizard puffs at that and wrinkles up his forehead and pops out his eyes.

"Who are your people?" says he. "Where is your home?"

"At the stable, sir," I said. "My Master is the second groom."

At that Woodstock Wizard III looks at me for quite a bit without winking, and stares all around the room over my head.

"Oh, well," says he at last, "you're a very civil young dog," says he, "and I blame no one for what he can't help," which I thought most fair and liberal. "And I have known many bull-terriers that were champions," says he, "though as a rule they mostly run with fire-engines, and to fighting. For me, I wouldn't care to run through the streets after a hose-cart, nor to fight," says he; "but each to his taste."

I could not help thinking that if Woodstock Wizard III tried to follow a fire-engine he would die of apoplexy, and that, seeing he'd lost his teeth, it was lucky he had no taste for fighting, but, after his being so condescending, I didn't say nothing.

"Anyway," says he, "every smooth-coated dog is better than any hairy old camel like those St. Bernards, and if ever you're hungry down at the stables, young man, come up to the house and I'll give you a bone. I can't eat them myself, but I bury them around the garden from force of habit, and in case a friend should drop in. Ah, I see my Mistress coming," he says, "and I bid you good-day. I regret," he says, "that our different social position prevents our meeting frequent, for you're a worthy young dog with a proper respect for your betters, and in this country there's precious few of them have that." Then he waddles off, leaving me alone and very sad, for he was the first dog in many days that had spoken to me. But since he showed, seeing that I was a stable-dog, he didn't want my company, I waited for him to get well away. It was not a cheerful place to wait, the Trophy House. The pictures of the champions seemed to scowl at me, and ask what right had such as I even to admire them, and the blue and gold ribbons and the silver cups made me very miserable. I had never won no blue ribbons or silver cups; only stakes for the old Master to spend in the publics, and I hadn't won them for being a beautiful, high-quality dog, but just for fighting—which, of course, as Woodstock Wizard III says, is low. So I started for the stables, with my head down and my tail between my legs, feeling sorry I had ever left the Master. But I had more reason to be sorry before I got back to him.

The Trophy House was quite a bit from the kennels, and as I left it I see Miss Dorothy and Woodstock Wizard III walking back toward them, and that a fine, big St. Bernard, his name was Champion Red Elfberg, had broke his chain, and was running their way. When he reaches old Jimmy Jocks he lets out a roar like a grain-steamer in a fog, and he makes three leaps for him. Old Jimmy Jocks was about a fourth his size; but he plants his feet and curves his back, and his hair goes up around his neck like a collar. But he never had no show at no time, for the grizzly bear, as Jimmy Jocks had called him, lights on old Jimmy's back and tries to break it, and old Jimmy Jocks snaps his gums and claws the grass, panting and groaning awful. But he can't do nothing, and the grizzly bear just rolls him under him, biting and tearing cruel. The odds was all that Woodstock Wizard III was going to be killed. I had fought enough to see that, but not knowing the rules of the game among champions, I didn't like to interfere between two gentlemen who might be settling a private affair, and, as it were, take it as presuming of me. So I stood by, though I was shaking terrible, and holding myself in like I was on a leash. But at that Woodstock Wizard III, who was underneath, sees me through the dust, and calls very faint, "Help, you!" he says. "Take him in the hindleg," he says. "He's murdering me," he says. And then the little Miss Dorothy, who was crying, and calling to the kennel-men, catches at the Red Elfberg's hind-legs to pull him off, and the brute, keeping his front pats well in Jimmy's stomach, turns his big head and snaps at her. So that was all I asked for, thank you. I went up under him. It was really nothing. He stood so high that I had only to take off about three feet from him and come in from the side, and my long, "punishing jaw" as mother was always talking about, locked on his woolly throat, and my back teeth met. I couldn't shake him, but I shook myself, and every time I shook myself there was thirty pounds of weight tore at his windpipes. I couldn't see nothing for his long hair, but I heard Jimmy Jocks puffing and blowing on one side, and munching the brute's leg with his old gums. Jimmy was an old sport that day, was Jimmy, or, Woodstock Wizard III., as I should say. When the Red Elfberg was out and down I had to run, or those kennel-men would have had my life. They chased me right into the stables; and from under the hay I watched the head-groom take down a carriage-whip and order them to the right about. Luckily Master and the young grooms were out, or that day there'd have been fighting for everybody.

Well, it nearly did for me and the Master. "Mr. Wyndham, sir," comes raging to the stables and said I'd half-killed his best prizewinner, and had oughter be shot, and he gives the Master his notice. But Miss Dorothy she follows him, and says it was his Red Elfberg what began the fight, and that I'd saved Jimmy's life, and that old Jimmy Jocks was worth more to her than all the St. Bernards in the Swiss mountains—wherever they be. And that I was her champion, anyway. Then she cried over me most beautiful, and over Jimmy Jocks, too, who was that tied up in bandages he couldn't even waddle. So when he heard that side of it, "Mr. Wyndham, sir," told us that if Nolan put me on a chain, we could stay. So it came out all right for everybody but me. I was glad the Master kept his place, but I'd never worn a chain before, and it disheartened me—but that was the least of it. For the quality-dogs couldn't forgive my whipping their champion, and they came to the fence between the kennels and the stables, and laughed through the bars, barking most cruel words at me. I couldn't understand how they found it out, but they knew. After the fight Jimmy Jocks was most condescending to me, and he said the grooms had boasted to the kennel-men that I was a son of Regent Royal, and that when the kennel-men asked who was my mother they had had to tell them that too. Perhaps that was the way of it, but, however, the scandal was out, and every one of the quality-dogs knew that I was a street-dog and the son of a black-and-tan.

"These misalliances will occur," said Jimmy Jocks, in his old-fashioned way, "but no well-bred dog," says he, looking most scornful at the St. Bernards, who were howling behind the palings, "would refer to your misfortune before you, certainly not cast it in your face. I, myself, remember your father's father, when he made his début at the Crystal Palace. He took four blue ribbons and three specials."

But no sooner than Jimmy would leave me, the St. Bernards would take to howling again, insulting mother and insulting me. And when I tore at my chain, they, seeing they were safe, would howl the more. It was never the same after that; the laughs and the jeers cut into my heart, and the chain bore heavy on my spirit. I was so sad that sometimes I wished I was back in the gutter again, where no one was better than me, and some nights I wished I was dead. If it hadn't been for the Master being so kind, and that it would have looked like I was blaming mother, I would have twisted my leash and hanged myself.

About a month after my fight, the word was passed through the kennels that the New York Show was coming, and such goings on as followed I never did see. If each of them had been matched to fight for a thousand pounds and the gate, they couldn't have trained more conscientious. But, perhaps, that's just my envy. The kennel-men rubbed 'em and scrubbed 'em and trims their hair and curls and combs it, and some dogs they fatted, and some they starved. No one talked of nothing but the Show, and the chances "our kennels" had against the other kennels, and if this one of our champions would win over that one, and whether them as hoped to be champions had better show in the "open" or the "limit" class, and whether this dog would beat his own dad, or whether his little puppy sister couldn't beat the two of them. Even the grooms had their money up, and day or night you heard nothing but praises of "our" dogs, until I, being so far out of it, couldn't have felt meaner if I had been running the streets with a can to my tail. I knew shows were not for such as me, and so I lay all day stretched at the end of my chain, pretending I was asleep, and only too glad that they had something so important to think of, that they could leave me alone.

But one day before the Show opened, Miss Dorothy came to the stables with "Mr. Wyndham, sir," and seeing me chained up and so miserable, she takes me in her arms.

"You poor little tyke," says she. "It's cruel to tie him up so; he's eating his heart out, Nolan," she says. "I don't know nothing about bull-terriers," says she, "but I think Kid's got good points," says she, "and you ought to show him. Jimmy Jocks has three legs on the Rensselaer Cup now, and I'm going to show him this time so that he can get the fourth, and if you wish, I'll enter your dog too. How would you like that, Kid?" says she. "How would you like to see the most beautiful dogs in the world? Maybe, you'd meet a pal or two," says she. "It would cheer you up, wouldn't it, Kid?" says she. But I was so upset, I could only wag my tail most violent. "He says it would!" says she, though, being that excited, I hadn't said nothing.

So, "Mr. Wyndham, sir," laughs and takes out a piece of blue paper, and sits down at the head-groom's table.

"What's the name of the father of your dog, Nolan?" says he. And Nolan says, "The man I got him off told me he was a son of Champion Regent Royal, sir. But it don't seem likely, does it?" says Nolan.

"It does not!" says "Mr. Wyndham, sir," short-like.

"Aren't you sure, Nolan?" says Miss Dorothy.

"No, miss," says the Master.

"Sire unknown," says "Mr. Wyndham, sir," and writes it down.

"Date of birth?" asks "Mr. Wyndham, sir."

"I—I—unknown, sir," says Nolan. And "Mr. Wyndham, sir," writes it down.

"Breeder?" says "Mr. Wyndham, sir."

"Unknown," says Nolan, getting very red around the jaws, and I drops my head and tail. And "Mr. Wyndham, sir," writes that down.

"Mother's name?" says "Mr. Wyndham, sir."

"She was a—unknown," says the Master. And I licks his hand.

"Dam unknown," says "Mr. Wyndham, sir," and writes it down. Then he takes the paper and reads out loud: "Sire unknown, dam unknown, breeder unknown, date of birth unknown. You'd better call him the 'Great Unknown,'" says he. "Who's paying his entrance-fee?"

"I am," says Miss Dorothy.

Two weeks after we all got on a train for New York; Jimmy Jocks and me following Nolan in the smoking-car, and twenty-two of the St. Bernards, in boxes and crates, and on chains and leashes. Such a barking and howling I never did hear, and when they sees me going, too, they laughs fit to kill.

"Wot is this; a circus?" says the railroadman.

But I had no heart in it. I hated to go. I knew I was no "show" dog, even though Miss Dorothy and the Master did their best to keep me from shaming them. For before we set out Miss Dorothy brings a man from town who scrubbed and rubbed me, and sand-papered my tail, which hurt most awful, and shaved my ears with the Master's razor, so that you could most see clear through 'em, and sprinkles me over with pipe-clay, till I shines like a Tommy's cross-belts.

"Upon my word!" says Jimmy Jocks when he first sees me. "What a swell you are! You're the image of your grand-dad when he made his début at the Crystal Palace. He took four firsts and three specials." But I knew he was only trying to throw heart into me. They might scrub, and they might rub, and they might pipe-clay, but they couldn't pipe-clay the insides of me, and they was black-and-tan.

Then we came to a Garden, which it was not, but the biggest hall in the world. Inside there was lines of benches, a few miles long, and on them sat every dog in the world. If all the dog-snatchers in Montreal had worked night and day for a year, they couldn't have caught so many dogs. And they was all shouting and barking and howling so vicious, that my heart stopped beating. For at first I thought they was all enraged at my presuming to intrude, but after I got in my place, they kept at it just the same, barking at every dog as he come in; daring him to fight, and ordering him out, and asking him what breed of dog he thought he was, anyway. Jimmy Jocks was chained just behind me, and he said he never see so fine a show. "That's a hot class you're in, my lad," he says, looking over into my street, where there were thirty bull-terriers. They was all as white as cream, and each so beautiful that if I could have broke my chain, I would have run all the way home and hid myself under the horse-trough.

All night long they talked and sang, and passed greetings with old pals, and the home-sick puppies howled dismal. Them that couldn't sleep wouldn't let no others sleep, and all the electric lights burned in the roof, and in my eyes. I could hear Jimmy Jocks snoring peaceful, but I could only doze by jerks, and when I dozed I dreamed horrible. All the dogs in the hall seemed coming at me for daring to intrude, with their jaws red and open, and their eyes blazing like the lights in the roof. "You're a street-dog! Get out, you street-dog!" they yells. And as they drives me out, the pipe-clay drops off me, and they laugh and shriek; and when I looks down I see that I have turned into a black-and-tan.

They was most awful dreams, and next morning, when Miss Dorothy comes and gives me water in a pan, I begs and begs her to take me home, but she can't understand. "How well Kid is!" she says. And when I jumps into the Master's arms, and pulls to break my chain, he says, "If he knew all as he had against him, miss, he wouldn't be so gay." And from a book they reads out the names of the beautiful high-bred terriers which I have got to meet. And I can't make 'em understand that I only want to run away, and hide myself where no one will see me.

Then suddenly men comes hurrying down our street and begins to brush the beautiful bull-terriers, and Nolan rubs me with a towel so excited that his hands trembles awful, and Miss Dorothy tweaks my ears between her gloves, so that the blood runs to 'em, and they turn pink and stand straight and sharp.

"Now, then, Nolan," says she, her voice shaking just like his fingers, "keep his head up—and never let the Judge lose sight of him." When I hears that my legs breaks under me, for I knows all about judges. Twice, the old Master goes up before the Judge for fighting me with other dogs, and the Judge promises him if he ever does it again, he'll chain him up in jail. I knew he'd find me out. A Judge

"Bench Show. New England Kennel Club." Boston: The Forbes Co., ca. 1890.
Image courtesy of the Library of Congress, Prints and Photographs Division,
item# POS-US .Ao1, no. 176 (c size).

can't be fooled by no pipe-clay. He can see right through you, and he reads your
insides.

The judging-ring, which is where the Judge holds out, was so like a fighting-
pit, that when I came in it, and find six other dogs there, I springs into position, so that when they lets us go I can defend myself. But the Master smoothes
down my hair and whispers, "Hold 'ard. Kid, hold 'ard. This ain't a fight," says
he. "Look your prettiest," he whispers. "Please, Kid, look your prettiest," and
he pulls my leash so tight that I can't touch my pats to the sawdust, and my
nose goes up in the air. There was millions of people a-watching us from the
railings, and three of our kennel-men, too, making fun of Nolan and me, and
Miss Dorothy with her chin just reaching to the rail, and her eyes so big that I
thought she was a-going to cry. It was awful to think that when the Judge stood
up and exposed me, all those people, and Miss Dorothy, would be there to see
me driven from the show.

The Judge, he was a fierce-looking man with specs on his nose, and a red beard. When I first come in he didn't see me owing to my being too quick for him and dodging behind the Master. But when the Master drags me round and I pulls at the sawdust to keep back, the Judge looks at us careless-like, and then stops and glares through his specs, and I knew it was all up with me.

"Are there any more?" asks the Judge, to the gentleman at the gate, but never taking his specs from me.

The man at the gate looks in his book. "Seven in the novice-class," says he. "They're all here. You can go ahead," and he shuts the gate.

The Judge, he doesn't hesitate a moment. He just waves his hand toward the corner of the ring. "Take him away," he says to the Master. "Over there and keep him away," and he turns and looks most solemn at the six beautiful bull-terriers. I don't know how I crawled to that corner. I wanted to scratch under the sawdust and dig myself a grave. The kennel-men they slapped the rail with their hands and laughed at the Master like they would fall over. They pointed at me in the corner, and their sides just shaked. But little Miss Dorothy she presses her lips tight against the rail, and I see tears rolling from her eyes. The Master, he hangs his head like he had been whipped. I felt most sorry for him, than all. He was so red, and he was letting on not to see the kennel-men, and blinking his eyes. If the Judge had ordered me right out, it wouldn't have disgraced us so, but it was keeping me there while he was judging the high-bred dogs that hurt so hard. With all those people staring too. And his doing it so quick, without no doubt nor questions. You can't fool the judges. They see insides you.

But he couldn't make up his mind about them high-bred dogs. He scowls at 'em, and he glares at 'em, first with his head on the one side and then on the other. And he feels of 'em, and orders 'em to run about. And Nolan leans against the rails, with his head hung down, and pats me. And Miss Dorothy comes over beside him, but don't say nothing, only wipes her eye with her finger. A man on the other side of the rail he says to the Master, "The Judge don't like your dog?"

"No," says the Master.

"Have you ever shown him before?" says the man.

"No," says the Master, "and I'll never show him again. He's my dog," says the Master, "an' he suits me! And I don't care what no judges think." And when he says them kind words, I licks his hand most grateful.

The Judge had two of the six dogs on a little platform in the middle of the ring, and he had chased the four other dogs into the corners, where they was licking their chops, and letting on they didn't care, same as Nolan was.

The two dogs on the platform was so beautiful that the Judge hisself couldn't tell which was the best of 'em, even when he stoops down and holds their heads together. But at last he gives a sigh, and brushes the sawdust off his knees and goes to the table in the ring, where there was a man keeping score, and heaps and heaps of blue and gold and red and yellow ribbons. And the Judge picks up a bunch of 'em and walks to the two gentlemen who was holding the beautiful dogs, and he says to each "What's his number?" and he hands each gentleman a ribbon. And then he turned sharp, and comes straight at the Master.

"What's his number?" says the Judge. And Master was so scared that he couldn't make no answer.

But Miss Dorothy claps her hands and cries out like she was laughing, "Three twenty-six," and the Judge writes it down, and shoves Master the blue ribbon.

I bit the Master, and I jumps and bit Miss Dorothy, and I waggled so hard that the Master couldn't hold me. When I get to the gate Miss Dorothy snatches me up and kisses me between the ears, right before millions of people, and they both hold me so tight that I didn't know which of them was carrying of me. But one thing I knew, for I listened hard, as it was the Judge hisself as said it.

"Did you see that puppy I gave 'first' to?" says the judge to the gentleman at the gate.

"I did. He was a bit out of his class," says the gate-gentleman.

"He certainly was!" says the Judge, and they both laughed.

But I didn't care. They couldn't hurt me then, not with Nolan holding the blue ribbon and Miss Dorothy hugging my ears, and the kennel-men sneaking away, each looking like he'd been caught with his nose under the lid of the slop-can.

We sat down together, and we all three just talked as fast as we could. They was so pleased that I couldn't help feeling proud myself, and I barked and jumped and leaped about so gay, that all the bull-terriers in our street stretched on their chains, and howled at me.

"Just look at him!" says one of those I had beat. "What's he giving hisself airs about?"

"Because he's got one blue ribbon!" says another of 'em. "Why, when I was a puppy I used to eat 'em, and if that Judge could ever learn to know a toy from a mastiff, I'd have had this one."

But Jimmy Jocks he leaned over from his bench, and says, "Well done, Kid. Didn't I tell you so!" What he 'ad told me was that I might get a "commended," but I didn't remind him.

"Didn't I tell you," says Jimmy Jocks, "that I saw your grandfather make his debut at the Crystal—"

"Yes, sir, you did, sir," says I, for I have no love for the men of my family.

A gentleman with a showing leash around his neck comes up just then and looks at me very critical. "Nice dog you've got, Miss Wyndham," says he; "would you care to sell him?" "He's not my dog," says Miss Dorothy, holding me tight. "I wish he were."

"He's not for sale, sir," says the Master, and I was *that* glad.

"Oh, he's yours, is he?" says the gentleman, looking hard at Nolan. "Well, I'll give you a hundred dollars for him," says he, careless-like. "Thank you, sir, he's not for sale," says Nolan, but his eyes get very big. The gentleman, he walked away, but I watches him, and he talks to a man in a golf-cap, and by and by the man comes along our street, looking at all the dogs, and stops in front of me.

"This your dog?" says he to Nolan. "Pity he's so leggy," says he. "If he had a good tail, and a longer stop, and his ears were set higher, he'd be a good dog. As he is, I'll give you fifty dollars for him."

But, before the Master could speak, Miss Dorothy laughs, and says, "You're Mr. Polk's kennel-man, I believe. Well, you tell Mr. Polk from me that the dog's not for sale now any more than he was five minutes ago, and that when he is, he'll have to bid against me for him." The man looks foolish at that, but he turns to Nolan quick-like. "I'll give you three hundred for him," he says.

"Oh, indeed!" whispers Miss Dorothy, like she was talking to herself. "That's it, is it," and she turns and looks at me as though she had never seen me before. Nolan, he was gaping, too, with his mouth open. But he holds me tight.

"He's not for sale," he growls, like he was frightened, and the man looks black and walks away.

"Why, Nolan!" cries Miss Dorothy, "Mr. Polk knows more about bull-terriers than any amateur in America. What can he mean? Why, Kid is no more than a puppy! Three hundred dollars for a puppy!"

"And he ain't no thoroughbred neither!" cries the Master. "He's 'Unknown,' ain't he? Kid can't help it, of course, but his mother, Miss—"

I dropped my head. I couldn't bear he should tell Miss Dorothy. I couldn't bear she should know I had stolen my blue ribbon.

But the Master never told, for at that, a gentleman runs up, calling, "Three Twenty-Six, Three Twenty-Six," and Miss Dorothy says, "Here he is, what is it?"

"The Winner's Class," says the gentleman. "Hurry, please. The Judge is waiting for him."

Nolan tries to get me off the chain onto a showing leash, but he shakes so, he only chokes me. "What is it, Miss?" he says. "What is it?"

"The Winner's Class," says Miss Dorothy. "The Judge wants him with the winners of the other classes—to decide which is the best. It's only a form," says she. "He has the champions against him now."

"Yes," says the gentleman, as he hurries us to the ring. "I'm afraid it's only a form for your dog, but the Judge wants all the winners, puppy class even."

We had got to the gate, and the gentleman there was writing down my number.

"Who won the open?" asks Miss Dorothy.

"Oh, who would?" laughs the gentleman. "The old champion, of course. He's won for three years now. There he is. Isn't he wonderful?" says he, and he points to a dog that's standing proud and haughty on the platform in the middle of the ring.

I never see so beautiful a dog, so fine and clean and noble, so white like he had rolled hisself in flour, holding his nose up and his eyes shut, same as though no one was worth looking at. Aside of him, we other dogs, even though we had a blue ribbon apiece, seemed like lumps of mud. He was a royal gentleman, a king, he was. His Master didn't have to hold his head with no leash. He held it hisself, standing as still as an iron dog on a lawn, like he knew all the people was looking at him. And so they was, and no one around the ring pointed at no other dog but him.

"Oh, what a picture," cried Miss Dorothy; "he's like a marble figure by a great artist—one who loved dogs. Who is he?" says she, looking in her book. "I don't keep up with terriers."

"Oh, you know him," says the gentleman. "He is the Champion of champions, Regent Royal."

The Master's face went red.

"And this is Regent Royal's son," cries he, and he pulls me quick into the ring, and plants me on the platform next my father.

I trembled so that I near fall. My legs twisted like a leash. But my father he never looked at me. He only smiled, the same sleepy smile, and he still keep his eyes half-shut, like as no one, no, not even his son, was worth his lookin' at.

The Judge, he didn't let me stay beside my father, but, one by one, he placed the other dogs next to him and measured and felt and pulled at them. And each one he put down, but he never put my father down. And then he comes over and picks up me and sets me back on the platform, shoulder to shoulder with the Champion Regent Royal, and goes down on his knees, and looks into our eyes.

The gentleman with my father, he laughs, and says to the Judge, "Thinking of keeping us here all day, John?" but the Judge, he doesn't hear him, and goes behind us and runs his hand down my side, and holds back my ears, and takes my jaw between his fingers. The crowd around the ring is very deep now, and nobody says nothing. The gentleman at the score-table, he is leaning forward, with his elbows on his knees, and his eyes very wide, and the gentleman at the gate is whispering quick to Miss Dorothy, who has turned white. I stood as stiff as stone. I didn't even breathe. But out of the corner of my eye I could see my father licking his pink chops, and yawning just a little, like he was bored.

The Judge, he had stopped looking fierce, and was looking solemn. Something inside him seemed a troubling him awful. The more he stares at us now, the more solemn he gets, and when he touches us he does it gentle, like he was patting us. For a long time he kneels in the sawdust, looking at my father and at me, and no one around the ring says nothing to nobody.

Then the Judge takes a breath and touches me sudden. "It's his," he says, but he lays his hand just as quick on my father. "I'm sorry," says he.

The gentleman holding my father cries:

"Do you mean to tell me—"

And the Judge, he answers, "I mean the other is the better dog." He takes my father's head between his hands and looks down at him, most sorrowful. "The King is dead," says he, "long live the King. Good-by, Regent," he says.

The crowd around the railings clapped their hands, and some laughed scornful, and everyone talks fast, and I start for the gate so dizzy that I can't see my way. But my father pushes in front of me, walking very daintily, and smiling sleepy, same as he had just been waked, with his head high, and his eyes shut, looking at nobody.

So that is how I "came by my inheritance," as Miss Dorothy calls it, and just for that, though I couldn't feel where I was any different, the crowd follows me to my bench, and pats me, and coos at me, like I was a baby in a baby-carriage. And the handlers have to hold 'em back so that the gentlemen from the papers can make pictures of me, and Nolan walks me up and down so proud, and the men shakes their heads and says, "He certainly is the true type, he is!" And the pretty ladies asks Miss Dorothy, who sits beside me letting me lick her gloves to show the crowd what friends we is, "Aren't you afraid he'll bite you?" and Jimmy Jocks calls to me, "Didn't I tell you so! I always knew you were one of us. Blood will out, Kid, blood will out. I saw your grandfather," says he, "make his debut at the Crystal Palace. But he was never the dog you are!"

After that, if I could have asked for it, there was nothing I couldn't get. You might have thought I was a snow-dog, and they was afeerd I'd melt. If I wet my pats, Nolan gave me a hot bath and chained me to the stove; if I couldn't eat my food, being stuffed full by the cook, for I am a house-dog now, and let in to lunch whether there is visitors or not, Nolan would run to bring the vet. It was all tommy-rot, as Jimmy says, but meant most kind. I couldn't scratch myself comfortable, without Nolan giving me nasty drinks, and rubbing me outside till it burnt awful, and I wasn't let to eat bones for fear of spoiling my "beautiful" mouth, what mother used to call my "punishing jaw," and my food was cooked special on a gas-stove, and Miss Dorothy gives me an overcoat, cut very stylish like the champions', to wear when we goes out carriage-driving.

After the next show, where I takes three blue ribbons, four silver cups, two medals, and brings home forty-five dollars for Nolan, they gives me a "Registered" name, same as Jimmy's. Miss Dorothy wanted to call me "Regent Heir Apparent," but I was THAT glad when Nolan says, "No, Kid don't owe nothing to his father, only to you and hisself. So, if you please, Miss, we'll call him Wyndham Kid." And so they did, and you can see it on my overcoat in blue letters, and painted top of my kennel. It was all too hard to understand. For days I just sat and wondered if I was really me, and how it all come about, and why everybody was so kind. But, oh, it was so good they was, for if they hadn't been, I'd never have got the thing I most wished after. But, because they was kind, and not liking to deny me nothing, they gave it me, and it was more to me than anything in the world.

It came about one day when we was out driving. We was in the cart they calls the dog-cart, because it's the one Miss Dorothy keeps to take Jimmy and me for an airing. Nolan was up behind, and me in my new overcoat was sitting beside Miss Dorothy. I was admiring the view, and thinking how good it was to have a horse pull you about so that you needn't get yourself splashed and have to be washed, when I hears a dog calling loud for help, and I pricks up my ears and looks over the horse's head. And I sees something that makes me tremble down to my toes. In the road before us three big dogs was chasing a little, old lady-dog. She had a string to her tail, where some boys had tied a can, and she was dirty with mud and ashes, and torn most awful. She was too far done up to get away, and too old to help herself, but she was making a fight for her life, snapping her old gums savage, and dying game. All this I see in a wink, and then the three dogs pinned her down, and I can't stand it no longer and clears the wheel and lands in the road on my head. It was my stylish overcoat done that, and I curse it proper, but I gets my pats again quick, and makes a rush for the fighting. Behind me I hear Miss Dorothy cry, "They'll kill that old dog. Wait, take my whip. Beat them off her! The Kid can take care of himself," and I hear Nolan fall into the road, and the horse come to a stop. The old lady-dog was down, and the three was eating her vicious, but as I come up, scattering the pebbles, she hears, and thinking it's one more of them, she lifts her head and my heart breaks open like someone had sunk his teeth in it. For, under the ashes and the dirt and the blood, I can see who it is, and I know that my mother has come back to me.

I gives a yell that throws them three dogs off their legs.

"Mother!" I cries. "I'm the Kid," I cries. "I'm coming to you, mother, I'm coming."

And I shoots over her, at the throat of the big dog, and the other two, they sinks their teeth into that stylish overcoat, and tears it off me, and that sets me free, and I lets them have it. I never had so fine a fight as that! What with mother being there to see, and not having been let to mix up in no fights since I become a prizewinner, it just naturally did me good, and it wasn't three shakes before I had 'em yelping. Quick as a wink, mother, she jumps in to help me, and I just laughed to see her. It was so like old times. And Nolan, he made me laugh too. He was like a hen on a bank, shaking the butt of his whip, but not daring to cut in for fear of hitting me.

"Stop it, Kid," he says, "stop it. Do you want to be all torn up?" says he. "Think of the Boston show next week," says he. "Think of Chicago. Think of Danbury. Don't you never want to be a champion?" How was I to think of all them places when I had three dogs to cut up at the same time. But in a minute two of 'em begs for mercy, and mother and me lets 'em run away. The big one, he ain't able to run away. Then mother and me, we dances and jumps, and barks and laughs, and bites each other and rolls each other in the road. There never was two dogs so happy as we, and Nolan, he whistles and calls and begs me to come to him, but I just laugh and play larks with mother.

"Now, you come with me," says I, "to my new home, and never try to run away again." And I shows her our house with the five red roofs, set on the top of the hill. But mother trembles awful, and says: "They'd never let the likes of me in such a place. Does the Viceroy live there, Kid?" says she. And I laugh at her. "No, I do," I says; "and if they won't let you live there, too, you and me will go back to the streets together, for we must never be parted no more." So we trots up the hill, side by side, with Nolan trying to catch me, and Miss Dorothy laughing at him from the cart.

"The Kid's made friends with the poor old dog," says she. "Maybe he knew her long ago when he ran the streets himself. Put her in here beside me, and see if he doesn't follow."

So, when I hears that, I tells mother to go with Nolan and sit in the cart, but she says no, that she'd soil the pretty lady's frock; but I tells her to do as I say, and so Nolan lifts her, trembling still, into the cart, and I runs alongside, barking joyful.

When we drives into the stables I takes mother to my kennel, and tells her to go inside it and make herself at home. "Oh, but he won't let me!" says she.

"Who won't let you?" says I, keeping my eye on Nolan, and growling a bit nasty, just to show I was meaning to have my way.

"Why, Wyndham Kid," says she, looking up at the name on my kennel.

"But I'm Wyndham Kid!" says I.

"You!" cries mother. "You! Is my little Kid the great Wyndham Kid the dogs all talk about?" And at that, she, being very old, and sick, and hungry, and nervous, as mothers are, just drops down in the straw and weeps bitter.

Well, there ain't much more than that to tell. Miss Dorothy, she settled it.

"If the Kid wants the poor old thing in the stables," says she, "let her stay."

"You see," says she, "she's a black-and-tan, and his mother was a black-and-tan, and maybe that's what makes Kid feel so friendly toward her," says she.

"Indeed, for me," says Nolan, "she can have the best there is. I'd never drive out no dog that asks for a crust nor a shelter," he says. "But what will Mr. Wyndham do?"

"He'll do what I say," says Miss Dorothy, "and if I say she's to stay, she will stay, and I say—she's to stay!"

And so mother and Nolan, and me, found a home. Mother was scared at first—not being used to kind people—but she was so gentle and loving, that the grooms got fonder of her than of me, and tried to make me jealous by patting of her, and giving her the pick of the vittles. But that was the wrong way to hurt my feelings. That's all, I think. Mother is so happy here that I tell her we ought to call it the Happy Hunting Grounds, because no one hunts you, and there is nothing to hunt; it just all comes to you. And so we live in peace, mother sleeping all day in the sun, or behind the stove in the head-groom's office, being fed twice a day regular by Nolan, and all the day by the other grooms most irregular. And, as for me, I go hurrying around the country to the bench-shows; winning money and cups for Nolan, and taking the blue ribbons away from father.

Richard Harding Davis, "The Bar Sinister." 1902. In *The Bar Sinister and Other Stories*. New York: Charles Scribner's Sons, 1919, 3–55.

That Spot (1908)

JACK LONDON

I don't think much of Stephen Mackaye any more, though I used to swear by him. I know that in those days I loved him more than my own brother. If ever I meet Stephen Mackaye again, I shall not be responsible for my actions. It passes beyond me that a man with whom I shared food and blanket, and with whom I mushed over the Chilcoot Trail, should turn out the way he did. I always sized Steve up as a square man, a kindly comrade, without an iota of anything vindictive or malicious in his nature. I shall never trust my judgment in men again. Why, I nursed that man through typhoid fever; we starved together on the headwaters of the Stewart, and he saved my life on the Little Salmon. And now, after the years we were together, all I can say of Stephen Mackaye is that he is the meanest man I ever knew.

We started for the Klondike in the fall rush of 1897, and we started too late to get over Chilcoot Pass before the freezeup. We packed our outfit on our backs part way over, when the snow began to fly, and then we had to buy dogs in order to sled it the rest of the way. That was how we came to get that Spot. Dogs were high and we paid one hundred and ten dollars for him. He looked worth it. I say looked, because he was one of the finest appearing dogs I ever saw. He weighed sixty pounds, and he had all the lines of a good sled animal.

We never could make out his breed. He wasn't husky, nor Malemute, nor Hudson Bay; he looked like all of them and he didn't look like any of them, and on top of it all he had some of the white man's dog in him, for on one side, in the thick of the mixed yellow-brown-red-and-dirty-white that was his prevailing color, there was a spot of coal black as big as a water bucket. That was why we called him Spot.

He was a good-looker, all right. When he was in condition his muscles stood out in bunches all over him, and he was the strongest-looking brute I ever saw in Alaska, also, the most intelligent looking. To run your eyes over him, you'd think he could out pull three dogs of his own weight. Maybe he could, but I never saw it. His intelligence didn't run that way. He could steal and forage to perfection; he had an instinct that was positively gruesome for divining when work was to be done and for making a sneak accordingly, and for getting lost and not staying lost he was nothing short of inspired. But when it came to work, the way that intelligence dribbled out of him and left him a mere clot of wobbling, stupid jelly would make your heart bleed.

There are times when I think it wasn't stupidity. Maybe, like some men I know, he was too wise to work. I shouldn't wonder if he put it all over us with that intelligence of his. Maybe he figured it all out and decided that a licking now and again and no work was a whole lot better than work all the time and no licking. He was intelligent enough for such a computation. I tell you, I've sat and looked into that dog's eyes till the shivers ran up and down my spine and the marrow crawled like yeast. What of the intelligence I saw shining out? I can't express myself about that intelligence. It is beyond mere words; I saw it, that's all. At times it was like gazing into a human soul to look into his eyes, and what I saw there frightened me and started all sorts of ideas in my own mind of rein-carnation and all the rest. I tell you I sensed something big in that brute's eyes;

there was a message there, but I wasn't big enough myself to catch it. Whatever it was (I know I'm making a fool of myself)—whatever it was, it baffled me. I can't give an inkling of what I saw in that brute's eyes; it wasn't light, it wasn't color; it was something that moved away back when the eyes themselves weren't moving. And I guess I didn't see it move, either; I only sensed that it moved. It was an expression—that's what it was—and I got an impression of it. No, it was different from a mere expression, it was more than that. I don't know what it was, but it gave me a feeling of kinship just the same. Oh, no, not sentimental kinship. It was, rather, a kinship of equality. Those eyes never pleaded like a deer's eyes. They challenged. No, it wasn't defiance. It was just a calm assumption of equality, and I don't think it was deliberate. My belief is that it was unconscious on his part. It was there because it was there, and it couldn't help shining out. No, I don't mean shine. It didn't shine, it moved.

I know I'm talking rot, but if you'd looked into that animal's eyes the way I have, you'd understand. Steve was affected the same way I was. Why, I tried to kill that Spot, once—he was no good for anything—and I fell down on it. I led him out into the brush, and he came along slowly and unwillingly. He knew what was going on. I stopped in a likely place, put my foot on the rope, pulled my big Colt's, and that dog sat down and looked at me. I tell you he didn't plead. He just looked, and I saw all kinds of incomprehensible things moving, yes, moving in those eyes of his. I didn't really see them move; I thought I saw them, for, as I said before, I guess I only sensed them, and I want to tell you right now that it got beyond me. It was like killing a man, a conscious, brave man who looked calmly into your gun as much as to say, "Who's afraid?" Then, too, the message seemed so near that, instead of pulling the trigger quick, I stopped to see if I could catch the message. There it was right before me, glimmering all around in those eyes of his. And then it was too late. I got scared. I was trembly all over, and my stomach generated a nervous palpitation that made me seasick. I just sat down and looked at that dog and he looked at me, till I thought I was going crazy. Do you want to know what I did? I threw down the gun and ran back to camp with the fear of God in my heart. Steve laughed at me, but I notice that he led Spot into the woods a week later for the same purpose and that he came back alone, while a little later Spot drifted back, too.

At any rate, Spot wouldn't work. We paid a hundred and ten dollars for him from the bottom of our sack and he wouldn't work; he wouldn't even tighten the traces. Steve spoke to him, the first time we put him in harness, and he sort of shivered, that was all—not an ounce on the traces. He just stood still and wobbled like so much jelly. Steve touched him with the whip. He yelped, but not an ounce. Steve touched him again a bit harder and he howled—the regular long, wolf howl, then Steve got mad and gave him half a dozen and I came on the run from the tent.

I told Steve he was brutal with the animal, and we had some words—the first we'd ever had. He threw the whip down in the snow and walked away mad. I picked it up and went to it. That Spot trembled and wobbled and cowered before ever I swung the lash and with the first bite of it he howled like a lost soul, next he lay down in the snow. I started the rest of the dogs and they dragged him along while I threw the whip into him. He rolled over on his back and bumped along, his four legs waving in the air, himself howling as though he were going through a sausage machine. Steve came back and laughed at me and I apologized for what I'd said.

There was no getting any work out of that Spot, and to make up for it, he was the biggest pig-glutton of a dog I ever saw. On top of that, he was the cleverest thief. There was no circumventing him—many a breakfast we went without our bacon because Spot had been there first, and it was because of him that we nearly starved to death up the Stewart. He figured out the way to break into our meat cache, and what he didn't eat, the rest of the team did, but he was impartial—he stole from everybody. He was a restless dog, always very busy snooping around or going somewhere, and there was never a camp within five miles that he didn't raid. The worst of it was that they always came back on us to pay his board bill, which was just, being the law of the land; but it was mighty hard on us, especially that first winter on the Chilcoot when we were busted, paying for whole hams and sides of bacon that we never ate. He could fight, too, that Spot. He could do everything but work. He never pulled a pound, but he was the boss of the whole team. The way he made those dogs stand around was an education. He bullied them, and there was always one or more of them fresh-marked with his fangs, but he was more than a bully. He wasn't afraid of anything that walked on four legs, and I've seen him march single-handed into a strange team without any provocation whatever, and put the "kibosh" on the whole outfit. Did I say he could eat? I caught him eating the whip, once. That's straight. He started in at the lash and when I caught him he was down to the handle and still going.

But he was a good-looker. At the end of the first week we sold him for seventy-five dollars to the mounted police. They had experienced dog drivers, and we knew that by the time he'd covered the six hundred miles to Dawson he'd be a good sled dog. I say we knew, for we were just getting acquainted with that Spot. A little later we were not brash enough to know anything where he was concerned. A week later we woke up in the morning to the dangdest dog fight we'd ever heard. It was that Spot, come back and knocking the team into shape. We ate a pretty depressing breakfast, I can tell you; but cheered up two hours afterward when we sold him to an official courier, bound in to Dawson with government dispatches. That Spot was only three days in earning back, and as usual, celebrated his arrival with a rough house.

We spent the winter and spring, after our own outfit was across the pass, freighting other people's outfits, and we made a fat stake. Also, we made money out of Spot. If we sold him once, we sold him twenty times. He always came back and no one asked for their money. We didn't want the money; we'd have paid handsomely for anyone to take him off our hands for keeps. We had to get rid of him, and we couldn't give him away for that would have been suspicious; but he was such a fine looker that we never had any difficulty in selling him. "Unbroke," we'd say, and they'd pay any old price for him. We sold him as low as twenty-five dollars, and once we got a hundred and fifty for him. That particular man returned him in person, refused to take his money back, and the way he abused us was something awful. He said it was cheap at the price to tell us what he thought of us, and we felt he was so justified that we never talked back. But to this day I've never quite regained all the old self-respect that was mine before that man talked to me.

When the ice cleared out of the lakes and river, we put our outfit in a Lake Bennett boat and started for Dawson. We had a good team of dogs and, of course, we piled them on top the outfit. That Spot was along—there was no losing him, and a dozen times the first day, he knocked one or another of the dogs overboard in the course of fighting with them. It was close quarters, and he didn't like being jostled.

"What that dog needs is space," Steve said the second day. "Let's maroon him." We did, running the boat in at Caribou Crossing for him to jump ashore. Two of the other dogs, good dogs, followed him, and we lost two whole days trying to find them. We never saw those two dogs again, but the quietness and relief we enjoyed made us decide, like the man who refused his hundred and fifty, that it was cheap at the price. For the first time in months Steve and I laughed and whistled and sang. We were as happy as clams; the dark days were over; the nightmare had been lifted—that Spot was gone.

Three weeks later, one morning, Steve and I were standing on the river bank at Dawson. A small boat was just arriving from Lake Bennett. I saw Steve give a start and heard him say something that was not nice and that was not under his breath. Then I looked, and there, in the bow of the boat, with ears pricked up, sat Spot. Steve and I sneaked immediately, like beaten curs, like cowards, like absconders from justice. It was this last that the lieutenant of police thought when he saw us sneaking. He surmised that there were law officers in the boat who were after us. He didn't wait to find out, but kept us in sight and in the M and M saloon got us in a corner. We had a merry time explaining, for we refused to go back to the boat and meet Spot, and finally he held us under guard of another policeman while he went to the boat. After we got clear of him we started for the cabin and when we arrived there was that Spot sitting on the stoop waiting for us. Now, how did he know we lived there? There were forty thousand people in Dawson that summer, and how did he savvy our cabin out of all the cabins? How did he know we were in Dawson, anyway? I leave it to you; but don't forget what I have said about his intelligence and that immortal something I have seen glimmering in his eyes.

There was no getting rid of him any more. There were too many people in Dawson who had bought him up on Chilcoot, and the story got around. Half a dozen times we put him on board steamboats going down the Yukon, but he merely went ashore at the first landing and trotted back up the bank. We couldn't sell him, we couldn't kill him (both Steve and I had tried) and nobody else was able to kill him. He bore a charmed life. I've seen him go down in a dog fight on the main street with fifty dogs on top of him and when they were separated he'd appear on all his four legs, unharmed, while two of the dogs that had been on top of him would be lying dead.

I saw him steal a chunk of moose meat from Major Dinwiddie's cache so heavy that he could just keep one jump ahead of Mrs. Dinwiddie's squaw cook who was after him with an ax. As he went up the hill, after the squaw gave up, Major Dinwiddie himself came out and pumped his Winchester into the landscape. He emptied his magazine twice and never touched that Spot; then a policeman came along and arrested him for discharging firearms inside the city limits. Major Dinwiddie paid his fine and Steve and I paid him for the moose meat at the rate of a dollar a pound, bones and all. That was what he paid for it. Meat was high that year.

I am only telling what I saw with my own eyes. And now I'll tell you something else. I saw that Spot fall through a water-hole. The ice was three and a half feet thick and the current sucked him under like a straw. Three hundred yards below was the big water hole used by the hospital. Spot crawled out of the hospital water hole, licked off the water, bit out the ice that had formed between his toes, trotted up the bank, and whipped a big Newfoundland belonging to the Gold Commissioner.

In the fall of 1898, Steve and I poled up the Yukon on the last water, bound for Stewart river. We took the dogs along, all except Spot. We figured we'd been feeding him long enough. He'd cost us more time and trouble and money and grub than we'd got by selling him on the Chilcoot—especially grub; so Steve and I tied him down in the cabin and pulled our freight. We camped that night at the mouth of Indian river, and were pretty facetious over having shaken him. Steve was a funny cuss, and I was just sitting up in the blankets and laughing when a tornado hit camp. The way that Spot walked into those dogs and gave them what-for was hair-raising. Now how did he get loose? It's up to you—I haven't any theory. And how did he get across the Klondike river? That's another facer. Anyway, how did he know we had gone up the Yukon? You see, we went by water and he couldn't smell our tracks. Steve and I began to get superstitious about that dog; he got on our nerves, too, and between you and me, we were just a mite afraid of him.

The freezeup came on when we were at the mouth of Henderson creek, and we traded him off for two sacks of flour to an outfit that was bound up White river after copper. Now that whole outfit was lost. Never trace nor hide nor hair of men, dogs, sleds, or anything was ever found. They dropped clean out of sight. It became one of the mysteries of the country. Steve and I plugged away up the Stewart and six weeks afterward that Spot crawled into camp. He was a perambulating skeleton and could just drag along, but he got there. And what I want to know is who told him we were up the Stewart? We could have gone a thousand other places. How did he know? You tell me, and I'll tell you.

No losing him. At the Mayo he started a row with an Indian dog. The buck who owned the dog took a swing at Spot with an ax, missed him, and killed his own dog. Talk about magic and turning bullets aside—I, for one, consider it a blamed sight harder to turn an ax aside with a big buck at the other end of it, but I saw him do it with my own eyes. That buck didn't want to kill his own dog. You've got to show me.

I told you about Spot breaking into our meat cache. It was nearly the death of us. There wasn't any more meat to be killed and meat was all we had to live on. The moose had gone back several hundred miles and the Indians with them. There we were—spring was on and we had to wait for the river to break. We got pretty thin before we decided to eat the dogs, and we decided to eat Spot first. Do you know what that dog did? He sneaked. Now how did he know our minds were made up to eat him? We sat up nights laying for him, but he never came back and we ate the other dogs. We ate the whole team.

And now for the sequel. You know what it is when a big river breaks up and a few billion tons of ice goes out, jamming and milling and grinding. Just in the thick of it, when the Stewart went out, rumbling and roaring, we sighted Spot out in the middle. He'd got caught as he was trying to cross up above somewhere. Steve and I yelled and shouted and ran up and down the bank, tossing our hats in the air. Sometimes we'd stop and hug each other, we were that boisterous, for we saw Spot's finish. He didn't have a chance in a million. He didn't have any chance at all. After the ice-run we got into a canoe and paddled down to the Yukon, and down the Yukon to Dawson, stopping to feed up for a week at the cabins at the mouth of Henderson creek. And as we came in to the bank at Dawson, there sat that Spot, waiting for us, his ears pricked up, his tail wagging, his mouth smiling, extending a hearty welcome to us. Now how did he get out of that ice? How did he know we were coming to Dawson, to the very hour and minute, to be out there on the bank waiting for us?

The more I think of Spot, the more I am convinced that there are things in this world that go beyond science. On no scientific grounds can that Spot be explained. It's psychic phenomena, or mysticism, or something of that sort, I guess, with a lot of theosophy thrown in. The Klondike is a good country. I might have been there yet and become a millionaire if it hadn't been for Spot. He got on my nerves. I stood him for two years altogether, and then I guess my stamina broke. It was the summer of 1899 when I pulled out. I didn't say anything to Steve—I just sneaked; but I fixed it up all right. I wrote Steve a note, and enclosed a package of "rough-on-rats," telling him what to do with it. I was worn down to skin and bone by Spot, and I was that nervous that I'd jump and look around when there wasn't anybody within hailing distance; but it was astonishing the way I recuperated when I got quit of him. I got back twenty pounds before I arrived in San Francisco, and by the time I'd crossed the ferry to Oakland I was my old self again, so that even my wife looked in vain for any change in me.

Steve wrote to me once, and his letter seemed irritated. He took it kind of hard because I'd left him with Spot. Also, he said he'd used the "rough-on-rats," per directions, and that there was nothing doing. A year went by. I was back in the office and prospering in all ways—even getting a bit fat. And then Steve arrived. He didn't look me up. I read his name in the steamer list, and wondered why, but I didn't wonder long. I got up one morning and found Spot chained to the gatepost and holding up the milkman. Steve went north to Seattle, I learned, that very morning. I didn't put on any more weight. My wife made me buy Spot a collar and tag, and within an hour he showed his gratitude by killing her pet Persian cat.

There is no getting rid of Spot. He will be with me until I die for he'll never die. My appetite is not so good since he arrived and my wife says I am looking peaked. Last night that Spot got into Mr. Harvey's hen house—Harvey is my next door neighbor—and killed nineteen of his fancy bred chickens. I shall have to pay for them. My neighbors on the other side quarreled with my wife and then moved out. Spot was the cause of it, and that is why I am disappointed in Stephen Mackaye. I had no idea he was so mean a man.

Jack London, "That Spot." *Sunset* 20, no. 4 (February 1908): 371–76.

PART 2

Sporting Dogs

The tenth sign, which belonged to the tenth day of the month, was Itzcuintli, which means Dog. This sign was held to be fortunate and happy. Those born under it were omened bliss and felicity. They were to be courageous, generous, likely to ascend in the world, men with many children, overflowing with plenty, lavish, prodigal, fond of having enough to give away, enemies of poverty, friends to those who ask favors, always willing to comply.

> Fray Diego Durán, *Book of the Gods and Rites*
> *and the Ancient Calendar,* ca. 1576–79

Archeologists agree that somewhere about twelve thousand years ago, at the end of the Paleolithic period and at roughly the beginning of the Neolithic or New Stone Age, our ancestors began to live in stable communities. They experimented with planting indigenous crops for food, and they made the earliest attempts at domesticating wild animals. There is little doubt that the dog, or what then was a smaller and less aggressive strain of native wolf, was the first domestic animal whose use as an aid to the hunt dramatically improved the efficiency of societies whose survival still depended heavily on their million-year identities as hunters. The transition from hunter-gatherers to domestic farmers was far from rapid and instantaneous, and the wolves and jackals that had begun to associate themselves with scattered settlements, perhaps lured as much by the warmth of the tribal fires as by the scraps of food they found there, may have approached our prehistoric ancestors themselves instead of being captured and tamed. Abandoned or orphaned pups, raised by early women alongside their human offspring and then selectively bred for useful or endearing traits, pose another plausible explanation for the eventual development of *Canis familiars*—the domestic dog.

While historical evidence of the lives of Paleolithic peoples remains limited, it is certain that from its earliest development as a hunting, meat-eating species, *Homo erectus* always had to deal with the principal problem of the hunt: the absence of game he was seeking at the very time that he wanted to find it. As Jorge Ortega y Gasset tells us in his *Meditations on Hunting:* "[the game's] instincts for hiding make his being absent the greatest problem that the venatic act has to solve."* And so it remains today. However, one morning in that long-ago past,

*Jorge Ortega y Gasset, *Meditations on Hunting,* Howard B. Westcott, trans. (New York: Scribner, 1972), 88.

a Paleolithic hunter had an inspiration. What he realized was the relationship between the dogs that had begun to form a part of his camp and this central, enduring problem of all hunters, past and present. His dogs were already skilled hunters, so he asked them for their help in discovering the hiding places of his elusive quarry. The dog was therefore introduced into the human hunting pageant and raised it to its highest level. The sporting dog's love for his work and his eagerness for the chase have served to endear him to his masters ever since.

Today, where sport hunting has become more of a ritualistic privilege than a daily necessity, rare indeed is the hunting dog who spends more than a small fraction of his life actually pursuing game. Instead, while the various breeds of hunting dogs may occasionally help their masters locate birds and animals, they mostly provide companionship and protection as living liaisons between their prehistoric identities as hunters and the modern world of today. As Elizabeth Thurston has reminded us in *The Lost History of the Canine Race:* "For many of us, canines are our one and only link to the natural world that has shaped the human psyche for eons."* In the memoirs of the sporting dogs that follow, over and again we see that the dogs used for hunting have retained their native instincts, if somewhat refined or cultivated by us. They have also adopted many qualities they share with their humans, not the least of which are friendship and love.

*Elizabeth Thurston, *The Lost History of the Canine Race* (Kansas City, Mo.: Andrews and McMeel, 1996), x.

The Setter, an Aristocrat among Dogs (1920)

*While His Rightful Role Is in the Hunting Field, He Is Also Well
Adapted to Serve as a Trusted and Loyal Member of the Household*

ROBERT S. LEMMON

They are called setters because they "set" or "point" game birds—a curious impulse which causes them to stand stock-still in a semi-cataleptic state when their
highly developed sense of smell tells them that they are close to the quarry which
both they and their masters are seeking. While this tendency to point is present
to some degree in nearly every breed of dog, it reaches such a state of development in the setters that it can almost be termed an instinct. In many individuals
it occurs without any training, although a course of lessons is necessary to make
the dogs entirely subservient and useful to their owners in the finding and shooting of game.

Different Kinds of Setters

There are several varieties of setters, just as there are of spaniels or terriers. The
Irish is a mahogany-red dog, the Gordon black with tan points, and the English
shows different combinations of tan, orange, lemon or black on a white ground.
All three have the same general size and form, but the differences in their disposi-
tions are such as to make the English the most worthy of consideration as a dog
fitted in every way to become a member of the household.

It would seem inevitable that a dog which for generation after generation has
been bred and trained for so highly specialized a life work as hunting would be
lost when taken out of his own particular field of activity. Such is not the case
with the setter, however, probably because his long and close companionship
with man has developed a peculiarly keen intelligence and sympathy with man's
ways. It may be too much to assert that a good setter consciously and with the
purpose of mutual success cooperates with his owner in the pursuit of game, but
I have often suspected that such is the case.

In the English setter, then, we have a dog which fits admirably into the family life of the household. He is unusually affectionate and reliable in disposition,
robust and healthy, courageous and yet tractable when properly trained. His
size makes him capable of adequate protection of hearth and home, and in the

matter of beauty he is second to none. There is something innately well-bred about the appearance and character of an English setter which puts him at once in the gentleman class; and it goes without saying that his intelligence comes as close to being human as that of any four-footed animal can come.

His Adaptability

From a somewhat extended experience with English setters I can say confidently that they can fill the double role of hunting ally and family friend. Many a one is "shot over" for days or weeks every autumn, and yet is a playmate for the children during the rest of the year. In the latter part you need not fear his losing his temper under teasing or mauling treatment, for he is essentially good natured.

Three points only would I especially urge you to bear in mind when deciding upon one of these dogs. First, do not get one at all unless you can give him plenty of exercise in the open air, for by birth and breeding he needs this. Second, get only a well-bred dog (advice, by the way, which is apropos no matter what kind of canine you are seeking). Third, avoid the extremely high-strung, nervous "field trial" dogs, for they have been so specialized in blood and training to find birds speedily in competition with other dogs that they are too much racing machines to be entirely satisfactory around the average house. Many thoroughbred, pedigreed setters are to be had which have not the extreme nervous development of those of field trial stock, and it is from among these that your selection should be made. The Llewellyn strain is a good one, and dogs with a fair percentage of Laverack blood in their veins are also excellent. Many setters are of Gladstone stock, than which none is better.

In conclusion, treat your setter with due regard for his physical as well as mental nature. Remember that he is a dog which needs exercise, good food and wholesome surroundings in order to be at his best. A pine tree from the mountain top will not thrive in a mushroom cellar, nor will an English setter with an ancestry of open-air hunters succeed in a boudoir atmosphere of sachet powder and steam heat.

Robert S. Lemmon, "The Setter, an Aristocrat among Dogs." *House and Garden* 38 (August 1920): 45, 58.

Memoir of a Celebrated Setter Dog (1831)

Philadelphia, May 26, 1830.

Mr. Editor:

As your Magazine is a proper place of record for all interesting facts connected with Natural history, and is beautifully interspersed with memoirs of many of our most valuable horses, I thought I would pen a brief memoir, as forming a variety in your publication, of a valuable setter dog which I formerly possessed.

This dog I purchased in June 1822, when about six months old; at which age, he shewed the predominant features which distinguish this description of dogs from all others in such a remarkable degree, that from the first moment I saw him I did not rest satisfied until he became my property; nor was I disappointed.

In detailing some instances of his remarkable sagacity I will pass over the more common qualities of bottom, a good nose, fine ranging, standing and backing, for these he possessed equal to any of his contemporaries; but those which I will mention may be considered as *extra*, and are not witnessed by many sportsmen.

In the first place, in windy weather when the birds were restless and would run before him, he would trail them until he could get the sportsman as nigh as the birds would suffer him to approach, and if he still found the birds moving off, would instantly, and with great rapidity make a half circle to the leeward, and coming up immediately in front, would bring them to a sudden stop. By this finesse he would enable the sportsman to get to a desirable situation, when nothing else would avail; for birds when running from their feeding ground to cover in windy weather, are almost certain to rise at too great a distance, if the noise which occurs in their wake seems to approach them very close; on the contrary a sudden transit from that to almost any other situation will have the effect of stopping them; this, the sagacity of this dog found out, and he would invariably practice it whenever the occasion offered, yet I never knew him but once to flush a covey, and this occurred in miserable cover. It certainly was interesting to see the manner and spirit with which he controlled the actions of the birds in order to contribute to the pleasures of his master.

I have several times known "Thorn"* to point a live bird with a dead one in his mouth. On one occasion while hunting in company with two other gentlemen

---

*This was his name.

on the extensive farm belonging to S. H. in Evesham, N.J. I had an excellent opportunity to witness this remarkable trait, in his character.—I had just shot a partridge in a small copse, and while reloading my empty barrel, missed my favourite dog, but on looking behind me I discovered him at a point with the bird in his month that I had just shot; friend S. H. who before that day had never seen dogs point game, was so enamoured with it, that he followed us nearly the whole day for no other purpose than to see the dogs hunt; and thinking perhaps that he never would have another opportunity of seeing a dog situated as mine was at that moment, I beckoned him to me, and after shewing him the dog, and explaining to him the cause of his acting thus, I flushed and shot the bird; thus giving the most palpable evidence of the fact that was possible to give; and as the like circumstance very rarely occurs (and I know of but two instances on record, the one I believe is in Daniels' Rural Sports, and the other in your Magazine,) I should like to know how often sportsmen have witnessed the same action in dogs of their own or those belonging to their friends.

This dog was so perfectly acquainted with his duty that he has been known to evince the greatest displeasure when another dog in company committed an error.—An instance of this kind I will mention as related to me by some gentlemen, who had him with them on an excursion in the neighbourhood of Holmesburg near this city. They were hunting him in company with another dog, which was very headstrong and disobedient, and although he would find and stand game very well, would not back another dog that had found it, nor suffer another dog to back him, but would in both cases invariably flush the game, having on this day exercised this disposition in several instances to the great displeasure of the company. At length he pointed a covey in some bushes, and my dog being near him at the time, backed him without moving from the spot; but the former dog hearing the noise of the sportsmen approaching from behind, caused him to turn his head, when he no sooner discovered that he was backed by another dog, than he sprang upon the covey and flushed them. Thorn, whose patience I suppose was exhausted, as well as the sportsmen at such conduct, immediately seized the offender by the throat, with that degree of ferocity, as not only to punish him severely, but to leave those impressions upon him, which he remembered the rest of the day.

He was a favourite dog with three very respectable and experienced sportsmen of this city, Mr. H., Mr. C. and Mr. L., and perhaps no three gentlemen could be found of better judgment and greater experience in sporting concerns; and as, Mr. Editor, I lend my dog, and gun also, (especially to experienced sportsmen, who I am convinced will always take care of that which is committed to their trust,) it was the prime consideration of these gentlemen (as they always hunted together,) when preparing for a gunning excursion, to secure the services of this dog, for he was their Alpha, and was always rated by them as a dog of the highest order, and indeed as possessing some properties, which their experience had never before witnessed. These gentlemen informed me that on one occasion after partridges, he suffered three shots to be fired over him, before he broke from his point, and upon another occasion while they were on an excursion after woodcock in the lower part of New Jersey, one of the party fired at, and supposed wounded a bird, but as the majority were against his opinion, he made no further research, but gave it up. The day being warm, and they wishing to change their ground, thought it advisable first to go to a tavern, about one fourth of a mile distant from them for some refreshment, where they remained about half an hour. On preparing to renew their hunt, they called their dogs, but Thorn was in default; this excited much uneasiness amongst them. They then commenced hallooing and whistling, and using such other means to find their absent friend as the emergency of the case required; they were however soon relieved from all unpleasant feelings on the subject, for they discovered his approach through a cornfield, with a woodcock in his mouth, supposed to be the identical bird fired at last and wounded by one of the party.—It appears, as stated by a boy who watched the dog, that after following the party some distance towards the house, he suddenly turned about and made directly for the thicket into which the bird had flown, and where no doubt he had seen it settle, and that finding the bird, pointed it, and remained so until he heard them calling at the house, when he sprang upon the bird and caught it.

Another interesting case occurred with Mr. H, a young gentleman of this city, who has related it several times, with a great degree of pleasure. Himself and his father were desirous of spending a short time in the country, and although not being sportsmen, were nevertheless desirous of taking with them guns and a dog, in order to break in upon the monotony that a stay in the country presents to a citizen; they accordingly procured my dog, and the next morning after having reached their new abode, they determined to spend in hunting; accordingly all things prepared they set out on their excursion, but the day waxing warm, the father became tired, and returned. The son, not yielding to fatigue so soon, and unwilling to return without some trophy of his perseverance, continued his pursuit for several hours. During this period, after flushing a covey of partridges, the dog found and pointed several scattered birds, at which our young sportsman fired without success. The dog discovering the kind of master he had to work for, became utterly regardless of the game, and would run over every bird instead of pointing them. Discouraged at his ill success, our young friend concluded to return home with but one bird, (which the dog pointed and caught in the act of rising,) disposed to impute the blame to the dog as the cause of his disappointment; but on relating the circumstance to his father became soon convinced where the error was, by an anecdote of the same nature being related to him, of two celebrated pointer dogs the property of a nobleman in England, having left the field and returned home, because the gentleman who was hunting with them, being a stranger, and having missed the three first shots at birds which they had found and pointed for him. And it is here worthy to remark, that good dogs will uniformly act in concert with good shots, and become indifferent in performing their duty, in proportion to the inferiority of the master they are serving.

There was perhaps no dog superior to this for finding and bringing shot game; he could be directed any course you wished by simply throwing a stone, and he seldom returned without the object he was sent for, even in the most difficult, and, to the sportsmen, inaccessible places; such as swamps, marshes, briers, and swimming broad streams, &c. and I knew him once to swim into a mill pond 150 yards and bring to land a duck, from the midst of an innumerable quantity of stumps and dead tree tops.

This remarkable dog was taken from my yard about two years since by an acquaintance, who was going after woodcock, whilst I was absent from the city, and was lost by him the same evening, since which period he has not been heard of—it is supposed he fell a sacrifice to our dog laws, then in force, or was taken to a distance, the former, however, is the most probable.

In England the performances of dogs are regarded with nearly as much interest as of horses, and peculiar instances of sagacity are recorded with such zeal as sufficiently proves how much higher value English sportsmen place upon these companions of their toil and pleasure, than do the sportsmen of this country. Surely we have dogs which will bear as good a comparison in their qualities, with any dogs in Europe, as do our horses with those of England; and the privilege being given in the Turf Register and Sporting Magazine, to all sportsmen, to record interesting facts which may come under their notice.

I hope to see its pages graced with more anecdotes than have yet appeared, of this description. Beside affording amusement to those who know but little of the character of the dog, those narrations interest those who are intimately acquainted with the history of this animal—for, a man who is fond of any subject or creature, delights in every thing which embellishes the character, or gives interest to the object of his admiration; and thus to the sportsman would it also prove a source of entertainment, because these little reminiscences forcibly recall to him many forgotten incidents of his life, while in the enjoyment of his dogs

and gun, whether on the plain, the mountain, or the valley, and bring to the remembrance of the more aged, the scenes of those early days in whose retrospection he gains new fire, and becomes refreshed with all the vigour of youth.
D.

"Memoir of a Celebrated Setter Dog." *American Turf Register* 2, no. 5 (January 1831): 221.

Dog Knew a Sportsman (1906)

Setter That Gave Up in Disgust and Went Home

"I was visiting some relatives in North Carolina last fall during the quail season," said a Washington man. "Game was plentiful on the plantation, but as I am a poor hunter and a worse marksman, I didn't participate in the daily shooting. One fine day, however, my uncle insisted that I should take his gun and his crack setter, Belle, and go over to the game preserves, a mile or so back of the house, and try my hand at the quail, which, he said, were so plentiful there that if I shut my eyes and let the charge go haphazard, with Belle's assistance I would be bound to come home with the game bag filled.

"He handed me his gun, with a lot of cartridges, called Belle from the shade of a convenient tree and, pointing to me, talked to her as if the dog understood every word he said, winding up his instructions to her by saying that he relied upon her to pilot me right and to bring me home again with lots of birds. From the way the setter looked from her master's face into mine, yawned, blinked her intelligent eyes and barked a couple of affirmative yelps, I am free to say that I believe she understood every word of the talk as well as either of us.

"At any rate, the dog started for the field with every manifestation of joy, piloted me through the pines and the brush, and evinced the liveliest interest in me all the way over to the quail field. Here Belle was the lady on the spot for sure, for the birds flew up in all directions. I followed two or three flocks over the field and banged away at the birds right and left, but not one could I bring down. During this fusillade I noticed that Belle would stop her work frequently and look at me in an inquiring way. Once or twice she even came up to me, looked up into my face, gave a little bark or two, and then started back and worked at flushing the birds with renewed vigor.

"Finally, just as I had about expended all my ammunition without hitting a single bird, I saw Belle suddenly stop, take a long look in my direction, as though some dog idea of hers had been confirmed. Then she bounded toward me, gave a few barks when she got near, which were undoubtedly expressive of the deepest dog disgust for me as a sportsman, and away she scampered as tight as she could go, over the fields and through the woods to the house.

"I followed a little later, very much crestfallen. From that hour Belle never paid the slightest attention to me during the remainder of my visit, and no cajolling on my part nor commands of her master could make that intelligent and discriminating setter even so much as look at me. She just reasoned it out that I was a fraud so far as a sportsman was concerned, and was in consequence beneath her notice. Ever since then I have believed in the discriminating intelligence of dogs."

Washington Star.

"Dog Knew a Sportsman." *Life* 48, no. 1253 (November 1, 1906): 477.

That First Bird Dog (1913)

FRED O. COPELAND

Dogs may come and dogs may go, but the memory of that first bird dog will go on forever, influencing me in every future purchase. First impressions do strike in deep and when I think of the many devout sportsmen struggling with their first bird dogs my heart goes out to them in their many disappointments wishing them success as by faith their see their pupil freeze to a point just behind the birds on many a future October morning. Nearly all lovers of the grouse and woodcock have at times longed for a dog. The dog is a positive necessity, for the prowler of the woodcock coverts and the lonely partridge hunter must needs look to his dog for his only sign of activity for long stretches of woodland. It would be interesting to know what per cent. of sportsmen train their own dogs. I hope it would reach into the high figures, for certainly such a man making the purchase of a trained dog in after days is in a far better position to work and take care of it. Moreover, nearly anyone will admit that a little pointer or setter pup will bring the sunshine into the darkest room. No doubt in the light of other days, if I am permitted to walk the autumn woods for a goodly number of years, I shall look back on these "words of wisdom" with a smile, yet I feel sure some may read these lines and gain a little comfort and satisfaction thereby.

For years I had played the role of the lonely partridge hunter. Not lonely in the full sense of the word, for many birds have fallen to my lot and the autumn days are never lonely, but there came a day one Fall when I accompanied a friend and his pointer and it opened a new world to me. Many a day since I have stood with thumping heart and bulging eyes, knowing well a bird lay a few feet ahead in a little corner and have seen that trembling form of liver and white creep forward to a point. Knowing well that the sport was in the quality rather than the quantity, I resolved to buy a dog.

For two months every mail out and into my town carried a letter to or from a seller of bird dogs. For no reason at all I wanted a black and white English setter, and expected, of course, I could get one. It gradually dawned on me that if I could get anything in the way of a dog at all I would be lucky. I was getting so I could call off every dog owner in New England by their first names much as a baseball fan enjoys leaning back and running off the major league players without a second's hesitation. During this time I could stand up anywhere, night or day, and quote passages from the four or five best books on training hunting dogs. I was getting so I would follow a dog no matter what the breed as far as it would let me. Withal, the whole kingdom of canines interested me greatly.

At last I ran down a little lady puppy in one of our New England states. I could have the pedigree if I wanted it. I didn't. I wanted a companion on the hunt. Of course, she would find birds—hadn't her blood been kept pure for time out of mind? I was finally advised she was six months old, of the small breed of pointers, liver and white, and would be shipped on a certain morning and would reach me dead or alive the following day before time had a good firm grip on it. The great day arrived. Needless to say, I was on hand, and hardly had the train snorted in when I was hammering at the express car for my dog. I was looking for a crate larger than a grape basket. There was no dog, that was plain to be seen, but as I turned away disappointed a hail brought me back, and sure enough there was a shivering little object in a tiny crate looking up at me with great brown eyes asking for help if there was any of that commodity still left in this big round world. After "words on both sides" the company would deliver the dog before sending out each parcel. In the meantime the object made it plainly understood she wanted freedom or death. She was an American.

I had been warned to have a piece of corn bread in hand when I took her out of the crate that she might come to me. I must not go to her, and thereafter she would always look on me as her master. Therefore with a piece of corn bread in one hand and a hammer in the other I stood in my cellar and saluted the crate. I let the dog out of the box; she came to me, accepted the bread, acknowledged me as master according to directions, and went on a still hunt of the cellar. I had also been warned not to let her get frightened at anything. In an evil moment, as she was on her nine hundredth round of the cellar, she ran afoul of an old iron poker hanging on a post and, although she only brushed it slightly, it let out a sad clang. The dog shinned to the top of the cellar stairs, and, lifting one paw, sent up to high heaven a series of screams that would lift the hair on any human. I tasted lemon just as you will when a piece of chalk makes an off-key noise on a blackboard. I was learning. Surely the pointer breed of dogs was as full of riddles as a fiddle of tunes, and this I verified again and again as long as I owned her.

I christened her "Biddie." She soon won my heart with her winning ways, and many were the romps we had together during the winter months on the south slopes where the ground lay bare and the birds came out to enjoy the warmth. One Spring day we came to a railroad track. I had supposed she had forgotten her long ride when she was shipped to me, but she had seen the enemy, she placed her tail where it would be least in the way, heaven lent her wings, and the way she used them must have made her donor sigh for a like pair to take him to the celestial patent office. I wended my way home, found the dog overjoyed that I had not been killed by the Montreal express. Together we went back and had a good long look at the track, so long, in fact, that I contracted a cold that I would have given the price of the dog to be rid of. This was charged up to dog training.

In the late Spring "Biddie" developed distemper. I won't describe it. Let me say right here my next dog will be guaranteed against that. Only careful nursing and better food than I was eating pulled her through. It was late Summer before the weakness left her stern propellers.

I had chosen a good book on training. It was clear, straight to the point and made training a pleasure. I really think the dog enjoyed a large part of it after she had learned a command or two. By the middle of September "Biddie" would "heel" anywhere, stop to order in the woods on the instant, "go on" at the word, "down" (I preferred it to "charge") in the woods or out; moreover, she had roaded old birds to a point and seemed anxious to hunt. I had taught her to retrieve by the "force system," and she enjoyed hunting out and bringing me anything I might hide. She had grown handsome and attracted attention wherever she went. She was nearly all white, with the exception of a dark liver patch over each eye and ear, a small diamond on the forehead, a small patch between the shoulders and one at the root of the tail. One would think I was on the border of fairyland with the bird season just opened and a trim young pointer to work the virgin cover for me, but such as not the case. Gun-shy in red letters was written all over that dog. She was of such a shy disposition she dreaded the strong light of day like a grass widow. I had done everything to prevent it. I had walloped a large wash boiler with a piece of hard wood till the nails started from the side of the house; she liked it and got so she wouldn't eat unless I fired off a cap pistol as a sort of a blessing and sign to begin the feast. A twenty-two caliber made her sit down a long way off, a twelve-gauge turned her into a wooden dog or a high-powered projectile. Yet at home she cared nothing about the sight of a gun or the report. Perhaps because she had nowhere to run, she was already home.

I will never forget the day that marked the beginning of the end. Late one warm September afternoon we set out for as pretty a little corner of cover as sportsmen ever gunned. It held a flock of young grouse. They were scattered and as one flushed wild I endeavored to show the dog how easy it is to kill one of these ghosts. That shot which wouldn't have made her wink at home turned her into a wooden dog. I finally had to carry her bodily twenty rods from the scene before she would move a muscle. Still shivering with fright, she tried to thank me for delivering her from unknown death. I have no reason to doubt but that she would have stood motionless a week had I not helped her out. All bird sense left her after this. Not only that, but when she struck scent in after days she would leave the woods, and on several occasions when a bird flushed unexpectedly she almost turned wrongside out to be out of the vicinity. I always let her follow me to the woods and by the same sign she always left me once I was safely there, whether I had a gun or not. The greatest kindness had always been shown her even in the most provoking moments.

Someone was found who wanted to try to break her of gunshyness more than I did. I made sure they would be kind to her and in her new surroundings I understand she is doing a little better, although she tore off a Marathon the first time the new owner took her to the woods.

I am not discouraged. I learned more than I taught. This experience was one in a hundred, for I know of many cases where young dogs started right off as good dogs without yard breaking of any kind. As a sign of the faith that is in me I already have another pointer and am as confident he will love the birds as I am that "Biddie" tried to, for she gave me the best that was in her and I have nothing but admiration for the affectionate little lady. Perhaps that love which

—hath power to tame a savage,
Break a rock and cook a cabbage,

may make her a dog hard to equal in the days to come. If so, I want the first chance to shake hands with her trainer.

Fred O. Copeland, "That First Bird Dog." *Field and Stream* 81, no. 25 (December 20, 1913): 766.

A Lesson in Faithfulness (1919)

The Tale of a Man and His Dog on the Lonely, Windswept Marshes
of the Chesapeake Where Wildfowl Fill the Air with Swish of Wings

A. A. HUTTON

The December moon, nearly full, and well risen, was pouring a flood of silver light down over the old city of Annapolis. A light snow, which had fallen the day before, lay glistening on the roofs, along walls and in scant soiled ridges in the streets. The air was sharp and frosty, and off in the west there lingered a faint glow against which the bare branches of the trees showed in a lacy fret-work.

Two men carrying guns and accompanied by a dog, were walking briskly along Duke of Gloucester street toward the bridge over Spa creek where the street terminates. They were bound for the shore of the bay where they hoped to find wild geese, the marshes along the Chesapeake being the haunt of many wildfowl at this season. These men had a hut on the shore a mile or two from the city, where they could have shelter at times while waiting for a chance at the birds, and this hut was their immediate destination.

The man who owned the dog was Ned Hunter, his companion's name was Jim Ryerson, and the dog himself was a splendid specimen of a special breed known as "Chesapeake Bay dogs," a large water-spaniel, bred expressly for this kind of sport. This dog, Tony by name, was the size and build of the ordinary Newfoundland, not over-large, and of a perfect dead grass color from the tip of his nose to the end of his tail.

"We ought to be having good sport tonight," remarked Jim as they struck the bridge. "It's as clear as a bell."

"Yes," replied Hunter, glancing up and down the wide creek, "but there's lots of broken ice. A man on the wharf—came in a little while ago with Tibbs' oyster pungy—says the bay's full of it. However, we'll get 'em if we find 'em, won't we, Tony boy?"

Tony cocked an intelligent eye at his master and ambled along with a cheerful air.

"That dog has never failed me yet," continued Ned; "he always brings in a shot bird."

"They do get lost sometimes, though, where no dog can find 'em," said Jim.

"Well, of course, one might drop too far out for him to see, but if Tony gets a bird he never lets go. I've known him to stay a half-hour out in broken ice, but he always brings in the bird if it's *there.*"

With such conversation they beguiled the way and were soon leaving the suburb on the opposite bank of the creek, and striking out into the open country. Here there was more snow, crunching crisply underfoot, clinging in light masses to pine and cedar, and piled delicately on every weed and spray. Over all the magic radiance of moonlight. Here, the shadows sharp and dark upon the snow, beyond, along field and wood, by hollow and hillside, soft mysterious gray and purple, and afar, growing clearer as they neared it, a line of silver that meant the bay. Soon the cabin they were bound for stood in full view, somewhat off the road, the path leading to it curving on gently down a slope to the water's edge. Over to the left lay a marsh, on the right the shore line ended abruptly in irregular, steep bluffs.

"Here we are," remarked Jim, and presently they were inside the cabin which consisted of a single room with one window and a fireplace; and contained a few pieces of rough furniture. Hunter struck a match and lighted a lantern which he took down from a nail, placing it on the table, and beside it several parcels which he took from his coat pockets.

"There," he said, "that will do for later on when we have a fire. Now we are ready for action."

Extinguishing the lantern they stepped out into the moonlight again, and took the path down the slope. Skirting the marsh they proceeded cautiously and some ten minutes later caught sight of birds at a little distance.

"They're getting up," said Jim in a whisper, raising his gun. Both men fired at the same moment and three birds fell as the flock rose with a mighty whirr and were out of range before Jim's gun cracked again, vainly.

"Bring 'em in, Tony," said Ned and the dog sprang out on the frozen marsh, returning presently, dragging a great bird. He laid it at his master's feet and plunged back again among the reeds.

"Swan," said Ned, picking up the bird. "A whopper, isn't he? Here comes Tony with another."

"The third one was only wounded," said Jim; "there it is out on the ice fluttering along. We'll lose that one, I reckon."

"Not much," replied Ned. "The dog will get it. Here, Tony, go bring it in."

The dog just depositing the second bird, glanced up at his master, then following the direction of his hand toward the water, saw the fluttering bird and was off like a shot. The bird was on the broken ice in-shore, but as the dog approached fluttered on and on, the dog pursuing. The two men walked on down to the little strip of beach which ended on the right at the foot of a bluff. Here they stood intently watching the chase, which drew farther and farther away until both dog and bird were finally lost sight of behind the bluff. Up and down they walked, talking while they waited. Twenty minutes passed; a half-hour.

"Where do you s'pose he is?" asked Jim at length. "Think he's made shore below there?"

"He can't make it for about six miles down," replied Hunter. "I know this shore like my own back yard, and there isn't a landing place except just this side the Ridge. He'll come back this way if the current and wind aren't too strong for him. The wind's getting up."

He buttoned his coat up close to his throat, stuck his hands into his pockets, and again they tramped up and down. Another half-hour passed, there was no sign of the dog and Ryerson was growing steadily more disgruntled.

"Why the devil didn't he give it up and come back?" he grumbled. "Then we could have followed the birds up the marsh and had some sport. The chances are now he'll never make shore. He'll get swamped out there in that great pack of floating ice."

"Oh, he'll get in, I guess, sometime," said Ned slowly. "Anyway, I won't give him up. I tell you what, we'll go up to the cabin and make a fire and have some coffee. Then if he isn't back by that time, you can light out for home if you like, and I'll wait for him."

Jim agreed to the proposal, and was soon silting by a crackling blaze in the cabin while Ned heated some coffee he had brought, and opened a package of sandwiches.

"Well," said Jim at last with a yawn, "it's nearly twelve, and I think I'll make a break for town. You'd better come along. If the dog makes shore at all he'll follow on home."

"No," said Ned, "I'll wait. You take your pick of the two birds, and I'll go out and rustle up some more fuel."

They parted outside the cabin, Jim making for the road while Ned took the path to the beach. The moon was well past the meridian, the shadows had shifted around the bluff, and the outspread marsh had taken on a new aspect. The icy wind soughing among the reeds, the water lapping on the beach, and the grating of broken ice were the only sounds to break the stillness. The low line of the farther shore across the bay was a mere melting shadow, and occasionally, far out, a deeper, moving shadow and twinkling light revealed some vessel making up to port. The compelling beauty of it all held the man as he gazed awhile. Then the chilling wind brought him to action, and collecting an armful of driftwood he returned to the cabin.

Thus the night wore on. He dozed a little by the fire, rousing now and then to throw on another stick, or to go to the door and look out, or to stroll about outside and bring in more firewood. He fell asleep finally, his head on his arms folded upon the table, and waked at last with a start. The lantern was flickering out, the fire had died out to a few red coals, and there was a chill in the air. He threw on some wood and by the blaze looked at his watch. It was nearly four. Then he went to the door and looked out. In the west the moon was sinking behind the trees that edged the road, which looked dim in the paling light and lengthening shadows. He swept the scene with a disheartened glance, there was no living thing visible.

"Not much use waiting longer," he thought as he shut the door and went back to the fire. He sat awhile gazing gloomily into it. Until now he had not known how much he really loved the dog. Perhaps Jim was right and he had been swamped in the floating ice, worn out by the vain effort to effect a landing. The thought caught him in the throat and choked him, and made him restless. He got up and went outside, pacing to and fro with his eyes on the road. After all these hours that was the only way the dog could have come. Reluctantly at last he turned again toward the cabin and paused at the threshold for a last searching gaze. Was that—*could* that be a *moving* shadow by the bush where the path and road met?

He took a sudden step forward and waited. Yes, surely it moved, turning slowly into the path, advancing slowly. Yes, it *was* the dog.

"Tony!" he shouted excitedly. The dog quickened his pace a little, hampered as he was, and as his master reached him laid down the great dead bird, and looked up for approval. Ned was down on his knees, a hand on each shaggy ice-covered ear, shaking the big head slowly as he half-sobbed:

"Why, Tony, old boy, good old boy."

Later, in the cabin, having eagerly devoured the remaining sandwiches, Tony lay before the fire gnawing the ice from his shaggy legs and paws, and finally stretched himself for slumber, while the ice that entirely covered his thick coat, slowly melted in the heat and formed puddles around him. Underneath that icy cover the soft, fine, close hair next the skin was warm and dry.

Ned sat and watched him, pondering deeply. Visions rose before him of the long hours of battling for life and duty in that icy water, and of weary travel after landing. Six miles fully by the road, he knew it well, and more by the shore-line. A lesson in faithfulness surely! Time wore on; again the fire died down and an intense chill crept into the little room. The dog was growing restless in his sleep. Ned roused him with a word, then raking out the fire he made all safe and left the cabin. The moon had set, the wind had died, and in the weird stillness and grayness of approaching dawn the man and dog took their homeward way.

A. A. Hutton, "A Lesson in Faithfulness." *Forest and Stream: A Journal of Outdoor Life, Travel, Nature Study, Shooting, Fishing, Yachting* 89, no. 3 (March 1919): 123, 143.

A Walt Whitman Grouse (1916)

ARCHIBALD RUTLEDGE

It was in mellow October, and the tinted woods were sifting red and yellow
  leaves,
As we walked up the old logging-road, my faithful setter and I.
Far-off we heard a soft reverberant drumming; insistent. Penetrant, challenging;
It was the proud cock-grouse, standing upon his favorite mossy log (so I
  supposed),
And drumming his challenge—for it was too late to be a call of mating and
  love.
And I said to my dog, "Let us find him, this high-souled woodland prince,
For he is one of the noblest patricians of the North American wilds.
His lineage is lofty and far-descended from the best blood of the past;
He carries armorial bearings of the ancient forest-world;
His 'scutcheon is gorgeous with wood-symbols and thrilling wood mysteries;
His arms are the beauties of virginal woodlands and of powerful silent
  mountains,
And of dusky laurelled gorges, glimmering, luring the heart away.
If we see him, we shall have seen the very soul of wild beauty,
The heart of the magical lonely woods, the spirit of solitude, the source of life."
And my dog listened to me and understood me; I am very sure he understood
  me;
For he looked at me with clear, faithful eyes, accepting my words and
  approving.
He is more intelligent and affectionate than many men I know;
He will follow me to the death; his greatest grief is when I must leave him.
So we stepped quietly forward on the wonderful glowing leaves,
Alert, expectant of the radiant apparition of a presence of glory.
And the tattered gold of the yet-unfallen leaves, hanging gorgeous and ruinous,

Seemed screens to veil a miracle, or arras marginal to mystery.
We were very careful—my dog more careful than I. He did not trail or point,
But he stepped tense and ghostlike, his noble eyes ready for the vision.
Then, thro a vista, shimmering far with sad and beautiful autumnal lights,
Proud on a mossy log, unconscious of us, yet superbly wary, valiant and brave,
Stood the cock-partridge!
His fan-tail was spread; his wings were lowered; he was strutting.
The soft gleaming of woodland lights was on his plumage. I could see the ruff,
The prince's black ruff, quiver in the stress of a challenger's emotions.
All this my dog saw—and perhaps he saw more than I. He was fast to a point.
—A man, a dog, a cock-grouse. . . . We had no gun. . . . And did we regret it?
No. For once we were not sorry, though we were hunters and lovers of sport.
For we had seen the heart of the beautiful lonely woods,—
And we left it beautiful and unbroken.

Archibald Rutledge, "A Walt Whitman Grouse." *Recreation* 55, no. 10 (October 1916): 154.

Sportsmen's Dogs—the Setters (1897)

ED. W. SANDYS

At this late day we need not bother about the exact origin of the setter. Suffice it to say that he was originally a spaniel, and was known as "sitter," because he would sit down or crouch, and wait for the sportsman's approach, after locating the game. Records tell of the work of these sitting spaniels in 1515, and even prior to that date, but the dust is so deep upon those ancient tomes, and the setter of today is so unlike his spaniel ancestor, that we may well skip several chapters of musty history.

From the term "sitter," of course, came the name setter, and the expression, "to *set* game." The latter is now seldom heard, for our modern setters are not encouraged to adopt the true setting, or crouching, position when on game. Fashion has decreed that the more upright *point* of the pointer is *the* thing for the setter, and the jauntier and bolder the pose, the better it is liked.

Only twenty years ago the term "set" was in general use. A sportsman, especially an old timer, when a setter paused on game, would then say, "There's a *set!*" while if the same man were following a pointer he would say, "There's a *point!*" when the dog stiffened. Some old fellows stuck so rigidly to these little distinctions that they would chaff one of the younger school who was careless in his use of the two terms, but gradually the "set" was dropped until "point" (the better term) came into universal usage. This was hastened by the professional handlers at field trials, for these gentry were given to bawling, "Point!" at every possible, and for that matter, impossible excuse. The bawlers, too, were mighty sharp about certain other *points,* with which, however, we have nothing to do.

The modern setter is an "improvement" of a grand old stock. Some field performers that I have seen have suggested the idea that the improvement (?) has been carried too far, yet most of our modern dogs are better for the work required of them than their ancestors would be. In this respect the setter is a curious illustration of man's ability to alter, by what we may term "artificial selec- tion," the characteristics of any breed of animals. Field-trials and bench-shows have been powerful factors in the improvement of the dogs; and had the breeders of the past fifteen years been wise enough to have bred to a uniform type, and striven to produce the best field qualities without losing beauty, there would be more useful and handsome dogs, and we should have been spared much bitter feeling and endless, wearisome discussions of "field-type" and "show-type."

Good as are the modern dogs, some of the unimproved old-timers were, perhaps, their superiors as all-round workers, and especially as companions for gentlemen sportsmen. The old-fashioned dogs were heavier and slower than the latter-day crack-a-jack, but they were stout, stanch, brainy and frequently very beautiful. They had "bird-sense" a-plenty, were great stayers, if not lightning go- ers, and they admirably suited the conditions then existing. In the days of the muzzle-loader matters afield moved more slowly than they do now, and stanch- ness and obedience were of the utmost importance. With the breechloader came more rapid action (in more ways than one); ejectors hurried things still more, until at present the flying American types of dogs and men fairly *rush* their sport.

I have no objection to this field-trial style of taking one's pleasure. I can shoot as fast, load as fast, and tramp as fast as any sportsman should be expected to do. Yet I sometimes sigh for the somewhat staider, better controlled, more pic- turesque and much more enjoyable sport of a couple of decades ago, before the Improver introduced the hurricane method now so much in vogue.

Were those slow, old potterers any use? Aye! that they were, my friend, and the days they helped one to enjoy were wondrous pleasant. Those dogs—peace be to their ashes!—the dear old orange-and-whites, lemon-and-whites, head- strong Irishmen, heavy Gordons, Campbells, "natives," *et al.* were *workers!* They were intelligent, willing and systematic; they dropped to shot, and to wing; they stood like rocks, they backed freely and they heeded commands. Many of them were very stylish, and while few of them would be deemed at all fast today, yet they were free rangers and quartered their ground with a systematic thorough- ness which made them most efficient. All day and every day was their style. The end of the week found them "going yet"—a trifle foot-sore at starting, a bit raw as to end of stern, a bit pink on the flanks, but "going yet," running the soreness out and facing cover with a courage that seldom failed. They had good noses, too, had those old-fashioned dogs, and many of them were fine retrievers, wet or dry. Such a dog was Llewellin's famous Dan, a slashing worker, which any sportsman of today might be glad to follow.

Now, to consider the different breeds of setters. These include the two strains of English setter proper, known as the Llewellin and the Laverack, the red Irish setter, and the black-and-tan Gordon setter. An all-black strain some years ago had many admirers, and specimens of it may yet be found, some of them cracking good dogs too, but they and other minor strains need not be dwelt upon.

The Gordon setter, true to type, is a large, handsome dog, comparatively easily trained, and a stout, reliable worker. In nose, intelligence, and general field qualities he is excellent, yet he has only a limited number of admirers—perhaps for reasons which I shall mention later on. The original Gordon was a black, tan and white dog, but modern breeders dislike the white and prefer a coat without even a tuft of white upon the breast. The standard coat is marked as in the black-and-tan terrier. The black cannot be too deep and glossy, while the best shade of tan is a warm mahogany-red, showing in a spot above each eye, on lips, cheek and throat; upon the forelegs about to the elbows, upon the hindlegs to the stifles, and for a short distance upon the underside of the tail, or flag, the longer hairs of which should be entirely black. A good coat is not so very common, and when in fine condition it is a pretty thing to look upon.

One of the faults of the Gordon is a superabundance of bone and beef, causing more or less heaviness and clumsiness; there is also a heaviness of head and nose which is not either so sprightly in expression or so pleasing in general effect as the cleaner cut heads of the other breeds. The handsome coat, too, is an undesirable feature for field-work in a country like ours, where a large proportion of the shooting is done in cover. There the black-and-tan blends too well with the surroundings, and an obstinately stanch dog may frequently get on a point and cause a lot of delay, trouble and perhaps lost opportunities, while his owner is making a row trying to get him in, or locate him.

Some admirers of Gordons may object to my statements and point to the show-bench and ask, "Where are the bone, beef and clumsiness?" I'll admit that many dogs shown of late are somewhat of the Llewellin model—but then they are not Gordons, unless we dub them improved Gordons. In the original home of the breed, the heavy, sedate, moderate-paced fellows suited the conditions, and the coat was not such a drawback, owing to the nature of the shooting grounds; but, unless they are to be preserved here for some extraordinary quality, or qualities, which the English setter lacks, why not keep them true to type? The Gordon has no advantages over the English in any quality of excellence for field-work, or as a companion, and nothing desirable is to be gained by departing from the original type and producing an imitation of an English setter in a beautiful, but from the field-work point of view, undesirable coat.

The red Irish setter, or "Irishman," as he is affectionately dubbed, is a handsome animal, with considerable of the "divil," and perhaps the "laste taste in de wurruld" of Hibernian recklessness in his affectionate nature. He ranks next to the typical Gordon in size, "an' he's a darlin', God bless 'im!" Keen-nosed, lean, sinewy, ragged-hipped, he can show them all how to cover the country. His methods are full of vim and dash, he has any amount of pluck, he is excitable, but he can stay to the end and can fight "wid the best av thim"—in fine, he's—I-r-i-s-h!

His best coat, which he is so ready to trail in the mud, water, or any old place, for sport or for war, is of a deep mahogany-red, with frequently a small spot of white upon the breast. Personally, I prefer a coat without a white hair in it. The eyes match the coat. The nose is chocolate-color. The typical Irish head is a thing of beauty, while it looks like "business." Long, lean, domed skull, pronounced stop and occipital protuberance, low-set, close-hanging ears, lean cheek and muzzle—clean-cut best describes it. It well suits the wiry, tireless machinery behind it.

A dog of this type must needs be a fast, high-headed and courageous worker, and when thoroughly broken and given plenty to do, there is no better dog on earth. He is also a delightful comrade, even for a man who does not shoot.

His coat is open to the same objection noted in connection with the Gordon. His other faults are a hilarious tendency to raise the deuce upon the slightest excuse, a general excitability of temperament, and an objection to being firmly controlled. Of all our sporting dogs the Irishman requires most work, most training and most whip. He sometimes has to be practically re-broken at the opening of each season, but this is apt to be partially the fault of his owner. An excitable sportsman should never own an Irish setter; nor will a dog of this breed answer for the sportsman who himself breaks shot, chases, and does other things which men who value their dogs never think of attempting. The Irishman is only too ready to take advantage of any carelessness on the part of his handler.

Once I met a man in the field who had just had trouble with his Irishman. "What do you think of it?" he roared. "I paid one hundred dollars to have that brute trained, and here he goes and raises hob the first time I try him!"

"I think the dog will shortly need rebreaking as badly as you yourself now need *breaking*," I replied, and it just about covered the case.

The reader will readily guess that the Irishman is not the dog for a novice to buy, yet, when handled by a cool, practical experienced man, the red fellow's work is up to the highest standard. It is true that English setters have beaten him when both have been handled by skilled professionals, but that signifies little. Much more attention has been paid to the development of the English strains, breeders have been at liberty to choose sires at will, while the total number of well-bred Irish setters in the country is comparatively very small.

If many of the complaints of the dog's being too headstrong were carefully gone into, it would be found that he, instead of being to blame, had merely got into the wrong hands. Not one of our sportsmen out of twenty, more likely not one in fifty, knows how to break a dog or how to keep him in form after he has been broken by a professional.

Give me a well-broken Irishman, and I will guarantee to get good work out of him; and so might any other man who can shoot well enough to keep a dog steady, who knows what a dog should do, how he should do it, what he should not do, and the proper course to pursue when the dog runs riot. The Irishman has plenty of brains, and like any clever dog, he mighty soon discovers when he is with a man who is firmly kind, but who will stand no shenanigan.

I like the dog well. He is a great bird-finder, and will face thorns and cold water without hesitation; he is lithe and active as a cat, is a noted stayer, and I have yet to see one with a poor nose. As a rule, too, his feet are good, while for his size he is so light and springy that he can get over almost anything without pounding himself when landing, as heavier-bodied dogs are apt to do. The only objection I have to him is his color, one of the very worst for cover, before, and while the leaves are coming down. So soon as the snow has come, his coat is a decided advantage, and he is a rare good one in rough weather. It is not my intention to claim that he is a better all-round dog than the Llewellin setter. No dog out-ranks the latter for all-round work, but Llewellin men are given to digging at the Irishman, whose many sterling qualities should instead command the respect of all who know anything about dogs. The Llewellin has something the best of it, but none too much. Lest the reader may think that I am a crank on the Irish question, let me state that my favorite dog really is the pointer. Now a word about the English setter.

Prior to 1870 the most prominent bench-show setters in England were of a strain known as the Laverack, their breeder being Mr. Edward Laverack, who had kept the same strain without out-crossing for about half a century. The fountainhead of this breed was the union of Ponto and Old Moll. While Mr. Laverack may have been fond enough of a good dog to pat the bark on a tree, he was not much of a trainer, and the dogs owned by him did not distinguish themselves in field-trials or even in ordinary field-work. They were, however, very pretty and almost unbeatable on the show-bench. Mr. Laverack did this much for the English setter: he established a type, he demonstrated that hardly any amount of inbreeding would cause a strain to deteriorate, and he supplied beautiful and well-bred material for others to experiment with, and to develop further in the line of field-work. The Laveracks, as he bred them, were a bit too chunky and short-timbered to suit modern taste, but their heads and coats were handsome enough to please all critics.

I have not had much to do with the Laverack. The fad for the pure strain was not long lived in this country, for in a few years breeders appeared to find that the Llewellin was the better strain. Champion Thunder, an excellent type of Laverack, imported Moll, Lady Thunder, and a few others were all that I can form an opinion by. Two puppies, Boz and Sport, by Thunder ex Moll, I handled for a friend, and the amount of trouble bestowed upon them would, perhaps, have produced more gratifying results upon something else. The Laveracks, as I know them, while very handsome, are what I may term a bit too soft all over—more like pets than hard, dashing workers for the field. None of the dogs I have seen had good feet. I have no intention of decrying the strain, as many of them must have done clinking good work, but I speak of the few I know as they proved to be.

Perhaps to Mr. R. L. Purcell Llewellin, more than to Mr. Laverack, we owe thanks for the grand field performances of today. He was practical all through, and after he had secured Prince, Countess and Nellie (Laveracks), he put the ladies through a course of sprouts which ultimately developed brilliant though erratic working qualities.

The Llewellin strain originated in this way. Mr. Llewellin had a brace of English setters, Dan and Dora, by Field's Duke out of Slatter's Rhoebe. Dan, of evergreen memory, was a slashing big fellow, very handsome, and a grand worker, as is attested by his winning three stakes in the Shrewsbury trials of 1871.

Dan was bred to Countess and Nellie, while his sister, Dora, was mated to Prince. The progeny of both crosses proved so good that breeders here became greatly interested. In March, 1874, Mr. L. H. Smith, of Strathroy, Ontario, imported Dart (Prince-Dora), the first of the strain to cross the water. Dora was afterwards brought over by a Boston gentleman. Leicester, Druid, Queen Mab and others followed. Mr. Smith was very successful as a breeder; his famous dog Paris was as handsome a specimen of his race as ever stood upon feet.

The late Mr. Arnold Burgess, of Michigan, imported Druid and Queen Mab, both magnificent specimens. Druid I knew through some of his progeny—the Druid-Stars. Star was bred by Mr. Smith and sold, as a puppy, to my friend,

Mr. W. B. Wells, of Chatham, Ontario. In time Star, a good one in the field, was bred to Druid, and Mr. Wells made a record with this nick. Most of the puppies of this cross were handsome and excellent workers. Other crosses, too, have brought satisfaction to this kennel. Upon its roll of honor are, among other names, those of Dido I., Dido II., Mingo, Cambriana, Ticky-Tack, Luke, and a dozen others which have won upon the bench and in the field.

Of course, in a paper of limited length, it is impossible to even mention the famous Llewellins of America, and I have no intention of trying to do so. From the earlier importations have come the best dogs of today, and each succeeding generation has bravely upheld the family reputation for speed, courage, endurance, and all-round field qualities. The point which I desire to bring up is this, and I have mentioned the Druid-Star cross because it will excellently serve as an example. Paris, sire of Star, was an unusually handsome dog, having the typical long, narrow head, prominent skull, pronounced stop, square muzzle, and long, thin ear, set very low. He also had the characteristic low body and beautiful coat of the Laverack. Druid, too, was even handsomer than Paris, while Star had her fair share of her sire's good looks. The Druid-Star puppies were handsome and good workers. Next we will notice Mr. Wells's famous Dido II., which the late Dr. Rowe and other good judges pronounced to be the best bitch of her year, an opinion confirmed at the important shows. She was young when Mr. Wells sold her, and I do not know how far her field education was carried after that, but I know that if she did not develop into a crack-a-jack she should have done so. In the field she was very fast, stylish, and a stayer; in fact, just about as promising a youngster as a man could wish to see.

Now, the point is this. All these dogs were beautiful, and their beauty did not interfere with their field qualities. Yet one would have to search, perhaps, far and wide to find a few dogs as good as they were and of their types. Dido's was not the Laverack type, but something between it and today's Llewellin type. Mr. Wells's best dog, at present, of a dozen or more, is probably Luke (Toledo Blade-Cambriana)—nothing at all like his old type; indeed, Luke, in form, more nearly resembles a good Southern foxhound than a Laverack. He is a clinking good dog, too, stout, fast and intelligent, as his work in trials has proved; but his beauty is seriously incommoded by limits.

What has been done in this case has been done in kennels all over the country, and the result is a lot of fast trial-machines, all of one general family, some handsome, some homely, and representing half a dozen or more different types. I believe that a handsome good dog is better than an ugly good one, and I do not believe in "show-type," and "field-type" being necessary for a breed of dogs that is supposed to be for shooting purposes above all other things. A tip-topper among Llewellins should be good enough to win upon the bench and at trials; and, in justice to all concerned, breeders should decide upon what may be termed the standard type.

Not long ago, at Madison Square Garden, I devoted some time to Cactus and Maid Marian. Here we find a good deal of the old type, though not quite so taking, in my opinion, as the Druid and Paris cast. These dogs won along the line, and very nice dogs they are, but no judges who fancied the racing Llewellin type would approve of them; and *vice versa.* They are Laveracks out and out, in heads, coats, and everywhere, dogs that Edward Laverack himself would have considered to fill the bill. Dogs at all resembling the crack Dido II., good old Cambriana, who won many a time in her day, or, in fact, any animal of what may be called the modern Llewellin type, would stand no chance whatever under a judge who admired the Laverack pattern, as exemplified in Cactus and Maid Marian. These latter, too, under some Llewellin men whom I know, might as well keep out of the ring. Such a state of affairs is hardly likely to foster the best interests of the English setter. We should have a recognized type to breed to, keep as close as possible to it, and then let conformation, coat, and condition decide where the ribbons should go.

The trouble with breeders appears to be that the moment a dog of any type, or of no recognized type, wins an important trial, there is a desire to breed to him because he is a winner, and not because he is by blood, conformation and disposition the best dog to be mated with the bitches sent to him.

The typical English setter is not only a handsome dog, but he is admirably suited to his work. As he must be both fast and enduring his form shows a blending, or happy medium, between the speedy lines of the greyhound and the endurance model of the foxhound. The best type of head is as follows: skull, long and rather narrow; the muzzle long, medium in width and deep, end square; nose large with open nostrils; eyes, medium fulness, bright and mild; ears, long, thin, placed low on the head and close-hanging. The neck is moderately long, clean and graceful. The dog's body and legs should be strong enough for endurance without being too clumsy for speed. The chest is deep, ribs well spring, without any suggestion of barrel-shape, and well-ribbed back. The feet may either what is termed "harefoot," or "catfoot," so long as there is plenty of hair between the toes; for in this hairy foot lies the setter's sole advantage over the pointer as a worker in severe weather and over ice, frozen, or other trying ground. The tail is of medium length, strong at root and tapering to a point; it is carried with a moderate curve, and it should be well feathered.

The coat of the English setter varies in color, but it is always rather silky, close-lying, abundant and free from curl. Unpopular colors are orange and white, lemon and white, liver and white, roan and all black. One or more of these, however, may crop out now and then in litters of the best Llewellin blood. It indicates a throwback to the old stock, and the off-colored puppy may or may not be the best one of the litter, exactly as though he were of the most fashionable markings.

Some English setter coats are marvels of beauty. The favorite color is some combination of black, white and tan; next we may rank what is termed the "blue belton," white and black flecked, in which the black shows with a slaty-blue effect; and thirdly, black and white in large markings, without any tan. The black, white and tan, if evenly laid on, certainty is attractive, but it is not always as evenly distributed as though an artist had done the work. The handsomest coat I have ever seen was a blue belton, in which white predominated. The oddest coat I have seen was in the case of a Laverack-Llewellin bitch called Lady Patch. She had one side of the top of her head liver and the other jet black, two black ears, and a white body with a few small black marks.

Ed. W. Sandys, "Sportsmen's Dogs—the Setters." *Outing* 29, no. 5 (February 1897): 479–87.

Mac

The Story of a Dog of Honor (1920)

TRAVERS D. CARMAN

He was a wee, small pup when he arrived in his crate, a gift from the State Comptroller of New Jersey. As he was lifted out by the scruff of his neck he landed squarely on all four stocky legs, barked once in open defiance of all the world, and then, in recognition of the outstretched hand that brought him a message of masterly love, his tongue did penance for the hostile greeting of a moment before, and Mac, an English setter puppy, had found his lifelong master.

Puppy Days

His puppyhood was not unlike that of many other dogs—distended belly and all was well in a world of contentment and sunshine; an empty stomach and a land of darkness and gloom. And yet there was throughout even his early youth this distinguishing characteristic of a dog of pedigree—loyalty and real love for his master alone, tolerance of those his master loved, and calm indifference to all others.

Born in April, the following fall he was taken out in company with a seasoned dog and made his first point, in all awkwardness to be sure, when trembling legs knew not how to behave, and tail was limply outstretched in uncertain arch—but a point nevertheless, and stanchly held while the old dog, in rare condescension, ranged up in silent contempt and "backed" with hauteur the lucky pup who was "on the birds."

As the quail whirred away his master shot with deliberate and particular care, that he might kill a quail with his first shot and thereafter identify the report of a gun in the puppy's mind with the amazing delight of the scent of a dead quail held near his nose.

Since his master at that time lived a comparatively lonely life in the country, the puppy was permitted to sleep in the house, and thus became his master's constant companion when at home. His master, the editor of a horticultural and farm paper, was forever fussing with plants, vegetables, grains, and flowers, marking some with different colored strings, tying others carefully up in paper bags, in fact doing many amazing things that puzzled the puppy as he sat and watched him with quizzical glance and head cocked inquiringly on one side. But it was his master who did it, and so it must be right—his master who, night after night, snuggled him up in his arms in front of the sputtering logs and caused those delightful sensations behind his ears.

The days followed in such rapid succession that no puppy could keep track of them—each with some thrilling experience, often a catastrophe; a daily lesson from the master full of new puzzling words and commands which slowly separated in his mind to become associated with things he was to do. To come in at the sound of a certain whistle was the first lesson learned; to charge and heel were soon mastered. But there were other commands less easily understood and most bewildering. When running ahead of his master, he could not remember what he was to do when a hand was waived to one side or the other or directly overhead. He did not see why, when he had run and caught a ball, he should bring it back to his master, who had just thrown it away. But he tried his utmost, and gradually the meaning of all things became clear.

"The Ways of the Transgressor Are Hard"

His master kept a prize flock of Indian Game chickens, and in jealous charge of the hens strutted with pride the Indian Game cock; ever watchful of the approach of danger, with massive breadth of chest, a cruelly efficient bill, and spurs as sharp as a needle-point. The puppy with playful longing had often watched them through the picket fence and barked for the joy of seeing them scatter with discordant cackling and utter confusion. And then had come the day when, to his delight, he had discovered an opening under one of the bottom boards of the chicken-run and through it he squeezed. As the hens fluttered out of his way with squawks of alarm, the puppy sprang at the one nearest, to grab only a mouthful of feathers and to be ferociously attacked the next minute by the Indian Game cock, who came valiantly to the rescue. In the act of jumping over the puppy the cock struck him with one of his spurs and sent him reeling. As he struggled to his feet he was again laid low, and as often as he attempted to rise he met a similar fate, until, in panic and acute distress, besmeared with blood and dirt, he found at last his exit, and sought the comfort of the cold earth under the hydrangea bushes, to repent at leisure for his misdeeds and lick his wounds, a sadder but wiser dog. He had learned two things of value to the hunting dog: first, to leave chickens alone; and, second, not to chase a feathered creature fluttering however temptingly ahead of him.

It seemed that the gardener had been an amused spectator of the tragic comedy and reported it to Mac's master upon his return from the city that night, who smiled with keen appreciation at the lesson the puppy had so effectively though painfully learned.

But his evil genius was not yet content, for upon the following day, through the carelessness of the housekeeper, he absent-mindedly wandered into the pantry, where the smell of cookies proved irresistible. Cautiously raising himself up on his hind legs, he brought his fore paws down on what he supposed to be the edge of the lower shelf of the pantry, only to turn loose upon his unsuspecting head the wrath of the pantry gods in the shape of the contents of a huge pan of curdled milk, which covered him from the tip of his nose to the end of his tail. Then, too, the pan set in motion some particularly sticky sheets of fly-paper, which sailed down in time to make connection with his hind feet. Tragedy begets tragedy in puppydom, and the stage was well set for the villain. Shocked by his sudden milk bath, with increasing terror beclouding his sanity, spurred on by the flapping of the fly-paper on his feet, in a mad retreat of panic he started for the kitchen door and came in violent contact with a leg of the intervening table, which promptly reared up, tottered in its mild protest, and fell on its side, taking with it to the floor jar after jar of recently made jelly. Goaded on afresh by the new catastrophe, that inflicted all of the nerve shock of shells bursting over the trenches, he dashed wildly through the closed kitchen screen door, taking most of the screen with him. His dirt wallow under the hydrangea bushes soothed in time his injured pride and screen-scratched nose, and the lesson of keeping out of the kitchen was wisely remembered without further experiment.

His Second Campaign

The bite of the air in the morning brought to him the memories of the year previous. With puppy ways forever cast aside, broad of forehead and of chest, and intelligent of eye, he watched with growing impatience for some sign from his master that the hunting season had come.

He had been dozing by the fire one evening after a particularly generous supper that the housekeeper, due to special orders, had begrudgingly given him, when he awoke with a start to find his master gone. The door leading into his master's room was open, with a light shining brightly out into the hall as his guide, and there he found his master and the joyous news that he had so impatiently awaited. The master was overhauling his hunting clothes, cartridge vest, boots, and quail gun, and around all still clung that most wonderful of smells, the quail scent. With a low whine and with love and pleading in his eyes, he crawled to his master's feet and, trembling from head to foot, raised a paw in supplication. A pat, a low word of hunting command, the well-imitated rallying cry of quail when scattered, such was his greeting from his master; and, responding with a wild, joyous bark of delirious anticipation, Mac knew that the following dawn would usher in another hunting season.

All night long he lay by his master's bedside, shaking in his excitement, incapable of sleep, but too well trained to stir until his master awoke at dawn.

The next day Mac won his commission as a hunting dog. A lazy sun discovered him and his master well on their way to the nearest buckwheat stubble, the frost outlining in silver the delicate tracery of the grass and woods. The solemn dropping of an occasional leaf as it haltingly dipped to earth from near-by trees, the flutter of small birds along the roadside hedge, the smell of the fall in the air, and the brilliant contrasts in the changing foliage—all attested to the ideal hunting day.

The buckwheat field soon reached, the dog was ordered on, and with superb restraint he held a steady pace as he quartered right and left in glad response to the wave of his master's hand. At the end of fifteen minutes, the field thoroughly covered and no birds found, he returned to his master for further orders. The dog was motioned to heel, and they too, in perfect understanding, with love and respect for the other, struck out for a cornfield nearby. And so the day was spent in silent reverence for God's own out-of-doors, and with due regard for nature's need of game conservation. A bird was shot here and there and proudly retrieved by the young setter; luncheon was shared by them both beside a sparkling spring where purple asters and goldenrod proudly stood sentinel, then upon the return in the afterglow the memories of the day were treasured by dog and master.

An Unusual Nose

Rarely has a dog possessed the nose or bird sense that Mac developed in his second season. Hunting up wind or down, he never flushed birds, stopping often so suddenly when he came unexpectedly upon a covey of quail that he would, with back hunched and all four feet braced, slide to a sudden stop.

Perhaps the incident for which he was most justly famous occurred in his third hunting season. He had found a covey of quail; his master and a friend with him had each shot a bird as they rose, and the party moved on to hunt for single birds. At the edge of a young growth of birch Mac pointed, a single quail flushed, and was shot by his master's companion, falling well inside the thicket. Mac was ordered to retrieve the dead bird, was plainly heard working into the cover, and then suddenly vanished and all was quiet. As Mac failed to return and ignored his master's whistle, the gunners started into the thicket in the direction the bird was seen to fall. One hundred yards ahead, Mac was found with the dead quail carefully held in his mouth and pointing another bird! As the hunters moved up the quail flushed and was shot by his master. Here then was a problem for Mac. Should he first retrieve the bird in his mouth, or attempt to retrieve them both at the same time? He decided in favor of the latter, and proudly returned holding each bird by a wing for fear of doing them injury by careless mouthing.

A Significant Lesson

In the instance of one man, a never-to-be-forgotten lesson was taught him by Mac. A thorough gentleman in all other ways, when on the hunting field he invariably claimed all birds at which he shot. Mac's master knew through mutual friends of this yellow streak, and I think purposely invited him to hunt, anticipating the lesson that Mac, through his loyalty, might silently administer.

Not till well on in the forenoon were quail found. Hidden behind an old log on a southern exposure at the edge of a swale were the birds, and Mac was in the act of jumping over the log when he caught the scent. Clutching at the log with all brakes set, and maintaining a balance with difficulty on top of the log, he pointed as best he could, seeming to realize his loss of dignity in the absurd position he was compelled to assume. The gunners came up, and in response to a noise of a branch purposely broken by one of the hunters, the quail got up. Somewhat rattled, the invited guest shot his right barrel as he was bringing his gun to his shoulder and the second barrel at a bird that had already started to fall as a result of the master's first shot.

The guest plainly showed his irritation over his obviously premature first shot, and remarked with emphasis that he was glad he had scored with his "left."

His companion looked amused and dryly remarked, "Suppose we leave it to Mac as to who shot the bird," and the faithful dog proudly and promptly retrieved it to his master in no uncertain manner.

The guest was man enough to accept the dog's apparent rebuke, apologized handsomely, and later told his friends: "Mac made me feel like the tin-horn sport that I was, and taught me what a game-hog I have been."

A Remarkable Point

Mac's stanchness on point was early indicated, but soon became developed to a remarkable degree. The spring following his third hunting season he discovered after breakfast one morning an English snipe in the open meadow behind the barn. Wild as the English snipe usually are, this particular bird evidently was wing-weary from a long flight the night before, and to the delight of Mac did not flush. Carefully working up to the bird, he came to point, nostrils dilated and eyes blazing in his excitement. The head gardener reported the fact that Mac was pointing, "one of them snipes, sir, on the north meadow, sir." The master, absorbed in the writing of an important article, dismissed the gardener with a word of thanks and promptly forgot Mac and the snipe. At twelve o'clock, upon coming down to his early luncheon, the master's housekeeper, with ill-concealed rebuke in her voice, said: "The gardener, sir, says as how Mac's still a-pointing, sir, in the north meadow—he's been that way since nine this mornin', he says." Conscience-smitten, the master grabbed his gun and a shell or two, and was soon striding up behind the faithful setter. At his spoken "Good dog" Mac's tail "broke point" for a moment in a joyous wag of welcome, and the dog once more became a statue of stone.

The bird, flushed by the disturbance, started upon its erratic, zigzag course, to fall forty yards away at the first shot, and was duly retrieved with dignity; but the reaction from the long strain under which Mac had suffered all morning was too much for him, and with grown-up manners cast to the four winds, he barked and capered about his master in all the abandonment of his joy and relief. I believe it was from that moment that his master realized that Mac was destined to become a truly great dog.

Mac Takes A Trip

That summer his education was enlarged by a most interesting and at times dismaying trip to a farm on Long Island owned by his master's father. The arrival of the puffing engine at the station, the dog's abrupt introduction into the baggage car, and the jerk of the train as it started, struck terror to his stalwart heart. Had it not been for the presence of a *blasé* bulldog, who eyed him with amused scorn from the further end of the car, poor Mac would have howled. Appeasing his own outraged feelings with a low whine of self-pity, he managed meanwhile to glare insultingly back at the bulldog and grudgingly settled himself with the philosophy of a stoic for whatever fate the trip had in store. Recovering his poise by the time the ferry was reached, and fortified by a wonderful ham sandwich, he succeeded without effort in walking, stiff-legged and with back hair bristling ferociously, in front of a panic-stricken sky-terrier that a woman had hastily taken up in her arms at his approach.

The journey ended, Mac, whose fame had preceded him, was welcomed as the guest of honor, and condescendingly accepted the homage given him. To his master alone did he show plainly that he was only putting on airs and enjoying the situation to its uttermost.

Lonely Days

And then strange days befell Mac and all was not well with him. There arrived at the farm a beautiful lady, soft of voice, kind of eye, who reminded Mac in some way of sweet clover in blossom. And what was more worthy of observation, his master appeared pleased with her, and as the friendship ripened, spent hours at a time in her company on long walks lasting into the afterglow of the day. At such times the dog, seeking to please his master and secure his favor, searched most diligently for quail, without in any way securing the attention he so deeply craved, and his heart ached. Yet the bigness of the dog showed in his attitude to the girl his master honored. In spite of the jealousy arising from his master's strange neglect of him through devotion to the lady, he loyally extended his friendship to one who found favor in his master's eye. It was well that it was so, for dire days, full of sorrow, soon befell Mac. His master was obliged to remain in town throughout each week, leaving him on the farm to await with ill-concealed impatience his arrival each week-end. Through the lonely days to be endured during his master's absence he was wont to go forlornly up to his master's room and there lie down upon some discarded coat his master had worn, indifferent to the possible delights each day had to offer, yearning only for the one he loved. It was there, lying on his master's coat, that the lady found him, and in time, as they grew to understand the bond between them, the dog was persuaded to leave his sanctuary and seek comfort in the presence of his master's lady. The two soon became inseparable, and waited, each with a love that few men are worthy to inspire, the return of the absent one, vying each with the other in the welcome extended to him upon his arrival.

Now it came about that the wonderful lady was greatly embarrassed upon one occasion by the dog's keen nose. Returning from town one mid-week day, she was greeted by the family assembled, who soon were seeking without success to conceal their amusement over the discovery of a profound secret that Mac so ingenuously made apparent to all. The lady had that day, as ladies will forever and a day, met, without undue publicity, the man of her heart and choosing. And what is more, horror of great horrors, had lunched with him unbeknown to his family, and, shocking as it may seem, had even walked in Central Park with him after the luncheon.

The fullness of the skirts in the courting days of yesterday made the contact of skirts and trousers well-nigh unavoidable for those who walked and talk of things most intimate each to the other. The dog had discovered, in the presence of the master's family, the scent of his master on the hem of the wonderful lady's skirts. With a low whine of heart-hungry longing, Mac capered about her, sniffing her skirts in ecstasy, until the mother, with a teasing smile, said, "Daughter of mine to be, Mac confirms your guilty though becoming blushes. How is that son of mine?"

The years rolled on until we come to the latter days of Mac's life, in which he performed an act of love and heroism that inspires even to-day the master's children, now grown, with a memory of great reverence for the dog who taught all with whom he came into contact a mighty lesson in loyalty, devotion, and service.

A Tragedy with a Happy Ending

A baby girl arrived to bless his master and mistress, and, although regarded at first by old Mac with suspicion, was soon accepted by him as a responsibility that he must assume. Plague him as she might, he patiently suffered her baby attentions with no sign of protest or annoyance. It was well-nigh a daily sight, and the fitting end of a strenuous afternoon of baby play, to find the little lady fast asleep with her head on Mac's stomach and the dog not daring to move lest he disturb his charge, diplomatically feigning sleep until a member of the family appeared to relieve the faithful nurse. And then came a tragic day. The little lady had disappeared, no one knew where; night was approaching, and the chill of the fall evenings made exposure at night for a youngster of three fatal beyond doubt. Mac had followed the carriage to the station to welcome his master from the city, and therefore offered no comforting thought of the possibility of his having wandered off with the child to protect it from harm. House, barn, carriage-house, and grounds had been frantically searched. Mother, gardeners, and housekeeper were wild with terror and awaited heart-broken the return and help of the father. Grasping the situation upon his arrival, he instinctively called Mac to him, who seemed to sense the terror that was upon them all. Reminded, at thought of him, of Mac's wonderful nose that had never failed him in the hunting-field, the master caught up a little jacket belonging to his daughter. Holding it out for the dog to see and smell, he said, "Go find her, Mac!" With an eager whine the dog was off to search the familiar parts of the estate where dog and girl had been accustomed to play. Some distance from the house, he suddenly raised his head, stood motionless for a moment sniffing the air, and then with nose near the ground he unhesitatingly followed a trail that led off back of the barn and along an old pasture road. Stopping uncertainly at a stone wall, the dog again picked up the trail, which led into the dark of the woods nearby. Stumbling on as best he could, the stricken father heard at last the wild barking of Mac, a mile away, deep in the tangle of the thick woods. And there the little lady was found, Mac licking her tear-stained face and barking with all his might in his joy at finding the maiden bold, who had wandered off to catch the sunset that the forest hid from view each night.

Another winter passed, with Mac's advancing years foretelling the end. Rejoicing in the arrival of early summer's warmth and sunshine, he sought the comfort of his favorite spot beneath the hydrangea bushes, and there asleep he peacefully crossed the great divide into the happy hunting-grounds beyond. There too he was buried with a headstone marking the grave, and inscribed upon it were the words: "Mac, a dog with heart and soul, a mighty hunter, beloved by those whose lives he shared and held in honored memory by his master whom he served so faithfully."

Travers D. Carman, "Mac: The Story of a Dog of Honor" *Outlook* (November 3, 1920): 416–19.

"Setter indicating a woodcock." Thomas W. Knox. *Dog Stories and Dog Lore.*
New York: Cassell and Company, 1887. Image courtesy of Special
Collections and Archives, James B. Duke Library, Furman University.

Some Dogs That I Have Owned (1901)

W. C. CLARKE

Manchester, N.H.

My interest in wing shooting began in 1883 in a somewhat singular way. I was out hunting for gray squirrels one afternoon with a squirrel dog, when I almost stepped upon a partridge in an oak thicket. I snapped my gun to my shoulder, or, at least, attempted to do so, but did not succeed, for when it was waist high, in my excitement I pulled the trigger and the gun went off. Imagine my astonishment when I heard a partridge fluttering in the brush not over five rods away. The dog heard the noise, too, for he pounced upon the bird and would have torn her to pieces if I had not released his hold. In my pride at shooting a partridge on the wing I imagined that the art of wing shooting was not such a very difficult one after all, and at once made up my mind that my way to becoming a proficient wing-shot was easy. In the years of apprenticeship that I served afterward I learned differently. I brought my bird home in triumph, had it stuffed and roasted, and never before nor since has a partridge tasted half so sweet. The only partridge I had ever before killed was in the Dunlap woods while still-hunting. The bird had been pruning and was shaking the dust from herself when I fired. She fell, and although she was apparently mortally wounded, she fluttered so hard that I felt sure she would get away, so I gave her the second barrel at a distance of not over six rods.

Max.

But to return to the subject of wing shooting. My first bird dog was Max. He was seven or eight years old when I got him. He came from Springfield, Mass., and was a descendant of Ethan Allen's famous strain of blue beltons. He was a medium sized black and white setter, well ticked, with a good feathered tail and fairly large silky ears, much like those of a spaniel. Indeed, his pedigree showed away back a spaniel cross. He had rather a pointed head and a sharp nose, yet in the quality of scent his nose was as good as anybody's dog's. He was sturdily built and in his prime could hunt from daylight to darkness and repeat day after day. He was a tireless worker, extremely ambitious, and as staunch as a rock on a point. Partridges were his favorite game. He worked well on woodcock and quail, but was happiest when on the trail of an old partridge. So fond was he of trailing one of these birds that I frequently had to call him off, especially in the season of woodcock, as he was liable to pass by birds in his desire to work out a trail.

I never knew him to flush a bird intentionally. He had one fault that I practically broke him of, yet I always had to keep close watch to see that he did not commit it. When I first got him he would "break at shot" and chase. After various reprimands he got over this mean notion, though, as I have before said, it was not safe to always let him have his own way, for he was a very headstrong dog and sometimes a trifle willful. Another habit he had that he would indulge in in spite of all I could do was that of squeezing his birds in retrieving them. He had a hard mouth, and though he received many corrections for using it, I could not wholly cure him of the habit, but got around it by compelling him for the most part to point dead birds. After one full season's hunting I had learned his ways and he mine, and we got along first rate together. He was a good bird finder, and as I was lucky enough to be one of a party that included some first-class shots, a lot of birds were killed over Max.

At his best, after we had hunted together a few years, Max was a good enough dog for anybody. He found birds well, pointed them staunchly, and was true and steady on a trail. He never quit whether those behind him shot poorly or well. He always did his part, generally better than I did, for he was my first bird dog, and his experience and knowledge of the game was vastly superior to mine. I allowed him to teach me at the beginning, and I tried to profit by my early lessons. I have seen Max pick a live woodcock off from a sunken log in a dried-up brook and again lift a live partridge from a position near the trunk of a tree where he had pointed her so close that she was afraid to fly. He was naturally a fast dog, and kept the man working him and the man on the outside busy, when birds were plenty. At this writing, December, 1899, when I am on the lookout for a bird dog for next season's shooting, I am free to say that I would be satisfied with a dog as good and serviceable as was Max in his prime.

In his old age Max became quite cross toward strangers, and had to be carefully guarded. He was naturally a sharp watch dog, and for a setter of his pounds could put up a good stiff scrap. He always managed to take care of himself whether in the city or country. If he was possessed of much affection he seldom showed it, and for this reason was rather an unsociable companion, except when engaged in hunting. In this respect he was not unlike many hounds.

In the fall of 1887 I thought Max was going back on me, and I took steps toward securing a new dog. Ira Moore and I went out Sept. 1, and about the middle of the afternoon Max showed such unmistakable signs of playing out that although we were in a good woodcock cover where there were birds left, Ira and I decided that it was good judgment to let up on the dog, so we stopped hunting with eight birds in our basket, with the prospect of increasing the string to an even dozen if the dog had been able to go on. I felt a good deal disappointed as I drove home, for I had believed that Max would certainly last another season. Ira said he might come around all right when the weather got cooler, but I felt that having hunted birds for three (?) years I knew more than did Ira, who had been following them for twenty-five (?) years.

Burke.

The upshot of the whole matter was that I got a new dog, once more through the recommendation of my former teacher, William W. Colburn, of Springfield, Mass. This time Mr. Colburn took somebody's "say so," and while he sent me a beautiful individual, I got a dog that knew scarcely more than a pup about partridges, and nothing at all about woodcock. Burke, for that was the dog's name, was a dark, rich, handsome red Irish setter, a son of Dr. Jarvis' noted show dog and field trial winner, Elcho, Jr. He was a dog of marked intelligence, perfect manners, and had I desired a canine companion only I could scarcely have found a more lovable or congenial one than Burke. But I wanted a hunting dog that I could kill game over, and as Burke was not that kind of a dog I sold him the following year.

Sept. 21 Gil Moore and I left by wagon for the north. At first I intended to take the new dog only, but after talking with Gil we both thought it good judgment to put Max in the wagon, too, and we did, most happily for us as it turned out. On the first day out we started in with Max, and he worked as slick as a whistle. After lunch I felt that I wanted to see the new dog work, so Max was tied in the barn and the aristocratic Burke was cut loose. And he did cut loose with a vengeance. He smashed into a flock of partridges like a line backer on a football eleven the first crack out of the box, sending the birds helter skelter in all directions, and not until he had chased them out of the county did he come back to me.

"What kind of a dog have you got there?" exclaimed Gil.

"A treer, I guess," I replied. Well, after a little more experimenting with the "red cuss" he was exchanged for Max, and we began doing business at the old stand again. We killed that day twelve birds—ten partridges and two woodcock —and during the three days we were away we shot thirty-two birds—twenty-two partridges and ten woodcock—all over old reliable Max, that, after getting seasoned up, worked as fine as silk and all day long.

After returning home I gave Burke a few more trials, on which I killed some birds, but he was erratic and unreliable, and made hunting very unsatisfactory. The first woodcock I shot with him I flushed, and he did not know what kind of a bird it was when I brought him to it. I don't think he had ever seen a woodcock before. Certainly he never would point one for me. Burke had a defective nose, and I might add that I never hunted with a red Irish setter bird dog that had a true nose.

Belle.

It was apparent when September of 1888 came in that Max would not be able to do my hunting. He had become very deaf and was fast going by, so I began looking for a younger dog to take his place. I inspected several, and finally on Sept. 12 bought of Nathaniel Wentworth, of Hudson Center, N.H., the liver and white pointer bitch Belle, then four years old. No sweeter piece of canine flesh ever lived than Belle, and we had many a good day together, until her untimely death on Feb. 15, 1890.

Belle was small in body and light in limb, and her style was the embodiment of beauty and grace. When she walked, trotted or ran it was as if her little legs were treading upon cushions. She had the most expressive and human-like pleading eyes that I ever saw set in a dog's head. She was timid almost to a fault, and one had to be extremely careful in correcting her for a wrong. Wherever I went with her she attracted the attention of every lover of a dog by reason of her marked beauty and grace.

Belle was not of a bench show type. Her nose was rather too pointed for that; otherwise she would have stood criticism. She had a fine, slim, straight tail and a sleek coat. Indeed, her coat was too fine for rough hunting, and she herself was almost too fine in her make-up to stand some kinds of hunting late in the fall, when the weather was very bleak. And to add to her other qualities of fineness, her nose was fine, "almost too fine," as her former owner often expressed himself to me. She did not exactly "potter" on scent, but she was so afraid of making a mistake that she frequently halted on old trails. Her nose was by no means poor, yet it was not always as true a nose as that Max had. She was a fair retriever, yet she was sometimes guilty of pinching her birds, especially a wing-tipped partridge. Belle was the easiest dog to work I ever hunted with. She kept in close, obeyed a call or a low whistle instantly, and made as delightful a companion in the brush as any man would wish for.

A lot of birds were killed over her in the two seasons I was permitted to hunt her. She was a member of a party that bagged nineteen partridges out from Manchester, Oct. 25, 1888, and on several other occasions she did her part in securing some big strings of birds. On account of her small size she was very handy to carry in a wagon. She was a perfect house dog, and was loved by every member of the family. Her sex did not give me the slightest trouble, yet it was her sex that ultimately was the cause of her death. It was my intention to breed her to Sime Young's pointer Prince, but I never got the chance. The cross would have produced some first-class stock.

Sweet little Belle lies buried at the farm beneath an overhanging apple tree whose white blossoms fall softly upon her grave every springtime. Beside her sleeps dear Mattie, the sweetest and loveliest piece of horseflesh that it has ever been my lot to see. Strangely enough, each met a sudden death at a time when her true value was being so much enjoyed and appreciated.

Prince.

I now approach with some misgivings concerning my ability to properly describe what in my opinion was the greatest bird dog I ever saw. Of course my friends know I refer to Prince, "the noblest Roman of them all." In my mind he was a monarch among dogs. What other bird dogs could do he accomplished, only, as a rule, better. If there ever lived a perfect partridge, quail and woodcock dog, that dog was Prince. Such old and experienced bird hunters as Gil Moore, Sime Young and Walter Leach have said that he would find more birds than any dog they ever saw. His ability as a bird finder was wonderful. He was a very fast dog when I got him—too fast for comfortable hunting—yet with his great speed he rarely flushed a bird, and never with the intention of doing so. On account of his speed and marvelous nose we were enabled to cover an immense amount of ground in a day's hunting. When he struck a cover containing no birds he was not long finding it out and telling us so. This made it possible for us to hunt many covers in a day. When he found birds he worked slowly and carefully. So absolutely true was he when he came to a rigid point that I can truthfully say that I never knew him to make a single mistake, nor did I ever see him make a false point. This, I know, is a strong statement to make, and one that some sportsmen might be inclined to doubt, but none of the men who have hunted with Prince and who knew him thoroughly will doubt the truth of it one moment.

Prince had a habit, when he got a strong whiff of scent, of stopping, chiefly, I think, as a warning to the man behind him to be on the lookout, and for the purpose of waiting until his handler had got within easy distance of him. At such times there was a slight wiggle of the tail, indicating that he was suspicious of game ahead. When he went on if he stopped again and that wiggle of the tail had ceased, it was a dollar to a cent piece that he had a bird nailed. When he "froze up" it meant business. So implicit was my confidence in Prince that had he come to a point in the paved streets of Manchester I should have expected a bird to rise. He never deceived me, and after I had hunted him one season I knew just what to expect from his every action.

His style on the three kinds of game birds found in our Northern covers was entirely different—so different that I always knew what kind of game he was following or pointing. Prince was the only dog I ever hunted with except Dick Lynch's setter Dash, that put up his own birds at the command, "Go on." As a rule he did all of the bouncing, which, of course, was a big advantage to me in my shooting. When he had a stiff point on a bird it was my practice to select the best possible opening and then send him on. He worked entirely for the man behind him, with no thought of any outsider. So tactful was he that I have seen him repeatedly, when in a bad place for me to shoot, back away from his point and approach the bird on the opposite side so that he might drive her my way.

I hunted with Prince a lot alone, and whenever he pointed a bird near the outside of a cover I always circled around and got on to the outside so as to get a better shot. At such times I either clucked to him (meaning for him to go on) or tossed a small object (generally an apple or a stone, or when hard pressed a cartridge) directly in front of him. The latter method never failed to start him, while when very close to a bird the words "Go on" sometimes failed to make him move. Any birds that Prince bounced came out of the cover; they never had a chance to "skin" back over his head. He did this kind of work as he did everything, in a practical and business-like fashion. He would hold a point as long as any dog I ever knew. In fact, he would hold one as long as a bird would lie for him.

I remember before I bought him having Sime call Gill and me up from a run to a side hill to surround an old partridge that he had pointed under a thick, heavy hemlock with big overhanging branches. It was at least fifteen minutes before Gil and I reached the spot, for we had to thread our way through a pile of thick slash where there had been a cut off. When we got to Sime we found him sitting on a rock smoking his pipe, while the end of Prince's tail could just be seen under a hemlock branch. Sime positioned us around the tree, and then told the old dog to go on. And he did go on, and out boiled the partridge to Gil, who killed her. Sime from his position never saw her at all, but I did, and should have fired had not Gil dropped the bird.

Instances without number of Prince's cunning and woodcraft might be related. I think I am justified in saying that on the whole he could outwit and outgeneral more birds than were able to deceive him. He delighted in following up a wild old partridge that would not lie for him. Then he was in his element, and so sure was he of eventually making such a bird stay for a point that it was a sure thing in the end if the bird kept out of a tree. When we got on to one of these "wild devils" I used frequently to send a charge of shot after the bird, often out of gun range, for the purpose of making the bird lie and the experiment generally worked successfully. When Prince got his mouth on to one of these birds he was immensely pleased. Ordinarily he manifested no especial pleasure in bringing in a dead bird. He retrieved, as he did other things, in a matter of fact way, but when he secured one of his old favorites he would circle around me two or three times as proud as a peacock, and if I reached for the bird he would turn his head the other way and avoid my hand. After about the third strut he would yield the bird up and start hunting again. He knew well enough that he had done his part toward capturing an old "skinner," for on no other occasion did he hesitate about giving up a dead bird.

After Prince had hunted a cover a few times he knew exactly where birds in it were usually to be found, and his generalship in working them to the best advantage for good shots was remarkable. If he was sent into an edge while I was following along on the outside, he invariably entered the cover at the further side so as to keep any bird that might be there between him and me. These tactics frequently resulted in some excellent easy outside shots. Pages might be written about Prince and what he had accomplished, but I will not add more, for many of his life deeds are firmly fixed; they will last as long as memory holds, and will be recalled in after years as I read again the diary of events contained in this unpretentious volume, compiled from data that I kept and entered after each hunt in a scrap book.

After Prince died in February, 1896, I gave up hunting, not resuming it until the fall of 1899, when I went out for a few times. It was pitiful to me to see Prince try to hunt in the fall of 1895, when he was so badly used up with rheumatism, lameness and a blood disorder that he could scarcely get around. His nose remained true to the last, but the Prince of old as I shall always remember him, had departed. That grand dog that seemed to rise supreme to our greatest of Northern game birds, the ruffed grouse, whose masterful ability in every department of the sport of bird hunting known to dog kind was a revelation, at last failed under increasing years, and the covers of New Hampshire and Massachusetts in which he achieved his great triumphs will know him no more. Good-by, old man! You were always faithful, honest, loyal, tender and true, and no master ever had a better friend.

In appearance Prince was a rugged type of an old-fashioned English pointer. He looked the grand old hero that he was. Everything about him denoted great strength. He weighed in usual flesh 73 pounds; in hunting time he got down around 60 pounds. His legs were massive, his body powerful and his head large and square cut at the nose. He had a long, coarse tail, his only defect. His color was liver and white in about equal proportions. A strip of white ran down between his eyes, spreading out at the nose, which was finely ticked. He had very expressive, intelligent eyes. Prince, while a very affectionate dog, rarely displayed his affection in a lavish manner. He was content with a quiet devotion. To his credit when he died, Prince had a record of very close to 2,500 woodcock, quail and partridges.

W. C. Clarke, "Some Dogs That I Have Owned." *Forest and Stream* 56, no. 19 (May 11, 1901): 365.

Do Dogs Dream? (1882)

C.B.A.

I am led to ask this question from a circumstance which came under my personal observation. While out in the country a few days ago with my setter dog I noticed a number of meadow larks in a field adjoining the road. Merely to give him a little exercise, I bade him "find 'em!" He ranged and quartered beautifully, and stood two birds fully thirty feet from the tip of his nose. Becoming somewhat excited, he afterward flushed another, for which I lightly boxed his ears. He is a very sensitive dog, and a flogging causes him to "drop to heel" and remain there. A slight reprimand has always been sufficient to correct any indiscretions, but on this occasion he seemed to fear that I was holding the flogging in reserve, and that the chastisement he had received was only a forerunner of what he might expect. The birds had by this time become very wild, and wound up and away before he could catch a scent. The dog's actions plainly showed that he considered the condition of affairs all his fault; he hunted slowly and carefully, but it was of no use. No more points were had. I called him in, and as he approached me with downcast head and drooping tail his appealing look seemed to plead for mercy. I patted him and otherwise gave him evidence of my forgiveness, but his cheerfulness had departed for that day.

After returning home in the evening I sat down to read; the dog came up to me, wagged his tail and dropped at my feet. In the course of half an hour I took my eyes from the paper and happened to look at him. He was asleep: his breathing seemed labored, broken occasionally by a piteous whine. Suddenly he jumped up, every muscle in his body stiffened, his tail betokened that he had found game, and there he was, fast asleep, staunchly pointing an imaginary bird. A close scrutiny revealed the fact that he was in a somnambulistic state. I touched him; he awoke with a start, appeared very much confused, turned around two or three times and went out into the yard.

I fully believe the dog had been dreaming of the incidents of the day, and that his conduct having so worked on his mind, actually dreamed he had found a bird, and, as a matter of course, must point it.

Now the question arises: Do dogs dream? I can see no reason why they should not. They are certainly the most highly organized animals of the brute creation. Will not some of the close observers of dogs give an opinion on this point?

C.B.A.

[Most certainly dogs do dream. We have seen just such instances as that related by our correspondent, and doubtless like phenomena have come under the observation of others.]

C.B.A., "Do Dogs Dream?" *Forest and Stream* 19, no. 6 (September 7, 1882): 112.

The Working Airedale in Colorado (1910)

B. F. SIMONDS

The Airedale terrier has become in a comparatively short time of all breeds the best big game hunter. The term "big game" applying to such animals as bears, cougars, wild-cats, lynx, 'coons, coyotes, etc. A great many hunters are and were very partial to the game little fox terrier, but wherever the Airedale is given a chance to show his superior strength, endurance, speed and scenting powers in practical hunting he makes good. He is built for the racket and can stand it. In a letter from Frank Onstott, a big game hunter living at La Jara, Colo., is the following:

"I landed in the Buckskin mountains in Arizona, June 20, last, and there I met the game warden and we were off for a lion hunt. In a few days we had some fine chases. The first one was a large one, and my Airedale puppies went right to work at once and ran with the lead dogs all the time until the lion was treed. They worked on the trail just like the hounds, and their scenting power seems just as good. I never saw their equal for their age. They have never yet seen anything that they were afraid of. When we roped the lion and snatched him out of the tree, I had to catch my puppies and hold them. They were going in on the lion and I was afraid they would get hurt as they had no show with a lion. I have had the puppies in several other races and they will run anything that makes a track and have no fear of anything. The little devils tracked a fawn and killed it, and after that they started in to run calves!"

These puppies were only 7 months old at the time Mr. Onstott procured them, and kennel raised. Their sire and dam were not trained hunting dogs and had never scented game, so it seems to be natural for them to hunt.

In another letter Mr. Onstott tells me how his puppies found a wild-cat track and "treed" the cat in a crevice in the rocks. All of the cat that could be seen was his front part, but the puppies were going in on him just the same, and would surely have been cut up pretty badly if their owner hadn't arrived in time to kill the cat.

Mr. Onstott trained his Airedales with a trained hound, and says that after the first chase they knew as much about it as the hound.

J. W. Fry, of Glenwood Springs, Colo., who has used Airedales for the past four years says they have no equal as big game hunters and prefers to use them without hounds. He says they are faster on the trail and will tree anything that wears fur.

Frank Marsh, of Colorado Springs, Colo., has a large ranch and sent one (!) Airedale out there to keep the coyotes from doing so much mischief. One day while in the foot hills he was eating his lunch when he heard a noise and upon looking up saw a coyote coming toward him accelerated by the Airedale. He jumped up and shouted and the coyote turned about—and ran right into the Airedale! "And of all the mix-ups!" You couldn't tell coyote from dog, says Mr. Marsh, but the finish came soon, and it didn't seem as though there was a bone in the coyote's body that wasn't broken.

This Airedale is, of course, not fast enough to catch a coyote. Nevertheless, to quote his owner, he "sure keeps them out of the country."

I received a picture the other day from my friend L. O. Hoeard, of Globe, Ariz. He did not send a letter, but just wrote on the back of the picture: "The results of a three days' hunt in the Magollon mountains, all due to the Airedale." In this case the bag was wild turkeys, and, I have no doubt the dog really was useful in getting them.

The Airedale is, of course, far from being the wonderful dog some attempt to make him out to be. We read of them being used for everything from hunting quail to trailing criminals. To give the dog his just credit, however, he is all right and for certain uses manifestly the best breed. For an all 'round dog, with intelligence and affection enough to commend him to anyone, with a nose for a fair trail and first-class grit and fighting ability, he stacks up as a pretty good deal of a dog.

B. F. Simonds, "The Working Airedale in Colorado." *Recreation* 32 (July 1910): 41–42.

"A prize pointer." Thomas W. Knox. *Dog Stories and Dog Lore.* New York: Cassell and Company, 1887. Image courtesy of Special Collections and Archives, James B. Duke Library, Furman University.

About a Setter Dog (1902)

B.L.S.

Editor *Rural World:* The Countess Nell was a good one and she has gone to the Happy Hunting Grounds, where all the good ones go.

I brought her home one day from the kennel of a friend in one of my coat pockets when she was a little roly-poly thing about the size of your fist.

She showed a lively interest in birds even when quite young, and later, before domestic cares made my trips afield with her impracticable, many a pretty bunch of quail she and I have bagged together. Since then she has taken the garden under her especial care, and, owing to her watchfulness, it has been a success when other gardens about us have suffered greatly or been entirely ruined by the chickens or inconsiderate neighbors.

It was a great show to see her get a chicken out of the garden. She would lie in her kennel, apparently fast asleep, when a chicken would wander across the line, headed for the tomato or melon patch, and then the Countess would be awake in a second and after that chicken as if she had been shot out of a catapult. It had been very forcibly impressed upon her mind early in life that a chicken was something which must not be hurt, but when she found she was permitted to chase them out of the garden, she would take apparent delight in catching up with them and giving a chicken a toss with her nose—sometimes high in the air, and, although, as a rule, a chicken never learns much by experience, they never seemed in a hurry to wander over the line again after one experience with the Countess.

I have strongly impressed upon my memory one of the most sensational "points" I have ever seen a dog make, which occurred on one of our trips after quail in Nebraska. She was quite a fast ranger and was racing down a steep incline at her characteristic pace, almost with the wind, and the combination brought her very close to a bevy of quail, which lay in close cover a little to the side of her course, before she caught the scent. In her frantic attempt to stop instantly and make the point, the ground gave way from beneath her feet and the Countess came to a sudden stop flat on her side and there she lay, stiffened out, with her head bent up and backward toward the hidden bevy, and she would not get up or move until I had scrambled down the bank, flushed the birds and done my part with the gun. That was a pretty picture, indeed; and when the old hunter had retrieved the dead birds she sat up in front of me, looking into my face with a most perfect expression of mirth imaginable, and I am sure she felt the comic part of it as much as I.

But the Countess has gone. Never again will that joyous bark ring out at the sight of gun and hunting coat, when "the frost is on the pumpkin" and the quail are lying 'long the course of the creek by the half sunken rails of that old crooked fence, and the well sheltered nooks where the cover is dense, when the soft glinting rays which the sun has first shed make the carpet of grasses a gem-studded bed for our feet to traverse; and the crisp morning air gives promise most cheering that bob whites are there. Oh that we could to the fields hie away and beat out the bush ere the oncoming day has scattered the dewdrops the sky has just sent to enable you, Nell, to follow the scent of those little "brown beauties." But stop, perchance you are ranging, with spirits congenial, the moors and the meadows of far distant fields, where dogs and their allies have joys that are regal and pleasures far greater than this other sphere yields.

B.L.S.

B.L.S., "About a Setter Dog." *Colman's Rural World* 55, no. 39 (September 24, 1902): 5.

PART 3

Poetry about Dogs

. . . without the intervention of the dog at the precise moment at which he appeared, I should have never become aware of the death's head, and so never the possessor of the treasure.

Edgar Allan Poe, "The Gold Bug," 1843

Most cultures have long and storied traditions of poetry about dogs and doggish things. A large proportion of dog poems, including many in this section, take the form of an elegy for a departed companion. These elegies often tell us as much about their authors' passionate devotion to their dogs as the stellar and noteworthy qualities and exploits of the dogs that are being memorialized. The actions and inherent qualities of good and not-so-good dogs are frequently used in poetry as extended metaphors for human behavior. Dogs often become anthropomorphized stand-ins for people, and their actions and behavior allow poets to criticize those qualities and attributes that we often cannot directly assign to our fellow humans. And still other poems address dogs directly, asking them to consider human ideas and concepts that we wish to share with them, using them as sounding boards or attentive audiences, either in attempts to bridge our mutual worlds, or as a way of holding a mirror up to our world and attempting to see it through the only partially understood world of the dog.

The poems in this section vary widely in intent and audience. F. C. McCarthy, an American soldier, published a short piece of "doggerel" in an early issue of *The Stars and Stripes* about the companionship he found in a dog he met in the trenches of France during World War I. Knowing that George Moses Horton (1798–1884) was enslaved in North Carolina when he wrote and published "The Fate of an Innocent Dog" in 1845 gives the many possible interpretations of this wonderful poem a much deeper resonance. Emily Dickinson's Newfoundland dog companion Carlo appears in several of her poems as a subject of interest and attention, and occasionally as a confidant, such as in the one included here. The cowboy poet Henry Herbert Knibbs has two poems in this volume, one a touching elegy for a favorite dog, and the other a fanciful glimpse of a dog and his owner in heaven, at the cusp of entering the pearly gates, and where the owner was unwilling to pass forward without the presence of his loyal canine companion. "Tumbler's Epitaph," a vernacular elegy, was printed as a broadsheet sometime in the 1840s and exists in only two known copies. One can only speculate on the deep feelings and sense of mission Tumbler's owner had to have gone to such lengths to memorialize his companion and share this work within Tumbler's circle of acquaintances. By contrast, this section concludes with the finely constructed, imagistic work of Louise Imogen Guiney's "To a Dog's Memory."

Epitaph on a Dog (1773)

Reader, if thou can'st read at all, thou'st find
Here lies the fairest of the speechless Kind;
Descended from an ancient noble Race,
Of Ladies' Lapdogs, in their Ladies' Grace.
Miss Abigail (for that's the Lady's Name)
From Nature's Hand received a comely frame;
Long Hair, bright Eyes, a short and dimpled Nose
With all that Nature on a Dog bestows.
Her acting Principle (think what you please on)
At least was next to, if it was not, Reason;
Whether her Soul belonged to Man or Beast,
Let others, with Pythagoras, contest.
Thus I'll affirm, were all dumb Brutes like her,
To most that talk the Silent I'd prefer.
Was she, because she never spoke, a Brute;
How many would appear less such, if mute.
Brute as she was, her Manners yet were such
As to most Men would be a warm Reproach;
No Trust she ever betrayed, no friend forgot,
Nor fawned on Persons if she liked them not.
Chance made her Life twelve Moons, twice told, a Maid;
Obedience made her Change that State, and wed.
Then, Phenix like, she yield'd her latest Breath,
To make Way for her second Self by Death.
Who would not weep the Fate of Abigail,
Who, for her Species' Sake, thus greatly tell.

"Epitaph on a Dog." *Virginia Gazette* (Williamsburg), April 8, 1773, 4.

A Dog (1934)

EDGAR A. GUEST

'Tis pity not to have a dog,
For at the long day's end
The man or boy will know the joy
Of welcome from a friend.
And whether he be rich or poor
Or much or little bring,
The dog will mark his step and bark
As if he were a king.

Though gossips whisper now and then
Of faults they plainly see,
And some may sneer, from year to year
My dog stays true to me.
He's glad to follow where I go,
And though I win or fail
His love for me he'll let me see
By wagging of his tail.

Now if I were to list the friends
Of mine in smiles and tears
Who through and through are staunch
and true
And constant down the years,
In spite of all my many faults
Which critics catalog
Deserving blame, I'd have to name
My ever-faithful dog.

'Tis pity not to have a dog,
Whatever be his breed,
For dogs possess a faithfulness
Which humans sadly need.
And whether skies be blue or gray,

Good luck or ill attend
Man's toil by day, a dog will stay
His ever-constant friend.

Edgar A. Guest, "A Dog." In *The Collected Verse of Edgar A. Guest*. Chicago: Reilly and Lee, 1934, 715–16.

Dan (1921)

CARL SANDBURG

Early May, after cold rain the sun
    baffling cold wind.
Irish setter pup finds a corner
    near the cellar door, all sun and no wind,
Cuddling there he crosses forepaws
    and lays his skull
Sideways on this pillow, dozing in
    a half-sleep,
Browns of hazel nut, mahogany, rosewood,
    played off
             against each other on his paws
             and head.

Carl Sandburg, "Dan." In *Smoke and Steel*. New York: Harcourt, Brace, 1921, 254.

The Fate of an Innocent Dog (1845)

GEORGE MOSES HORTON

When Tiger left his native yard,
He did not many ills regard,
A fleet and harmless cur;
Indeed, he was a trusty dog,
And did not through the pastures prog;
The grazing flocks to stir, poor dog,
The grazing flocks to stir.

He through a field by chance was led,
In quest of game not far ahead,
And made one active leap;
When all at once, alarm'd, he spied,
A creature welt'ring on its side,
A deadly wounded sheep, alas!
A deadly wounded sheep.

He there was fill'd with sudden fear,
Apprized of lurking danger near,
And there he left his trail;
Indeed, he was afraid to yelp,
Nor could he grant the creature help,
But wheel'd and drop'd his tail, poor dog,
But wheel'd and drop'd his tail.

It was his pass-time, pride and fun,
At morn the nimble hare to run,
When frost was on the grass;
Returning home who should he meet?
The weather's owner, coming fleet,
Who scorn'd to let him pass, alas!
Who scorn'd to let him pass.

Tiger could but his bristles raise,
A surly compliment he pays,
Insulted shows his wrath;
Returns a just defensive growl,
And does not turn aside to prowl,
But onward keeps the path, poor dog,
But onward keeps the path.

The raging owner found the brute,
But could afford it no recruit,
Nor raise it up to stand;
'Twas mangled by some other dogs,
A set of detrimental rogues,
Raised up at no command, alas!
Raised up at no command.

Sagacious Tiger left his bogs,
But bore the blame of other dogs,

With powder, fire and ball;
They kill'd the poor, unlawful game,
And then came back and eat the same;
But Tiger paid for all, poor dog,
But Tiger paid for all.

Let ev'ry harmless dog beware
Lest he be taken in the snare,
And scorn such fields to roam;
A creature may be fraught with grace,
And suffer for the vile and base,
By straggling off from home, alas!
By straggling off from home.

The blood of creatures oft is spilt,
Who die without a shade of guilt;
Look out, or cease to roam;
Whilst up and down the world he plays
For pleasure, man in danger strays
Without a friend from home, alas!
Without a friend from home.

George Moses Horton, "The Fate of an Innocent Dog." In *The Poetical Works of George M. Horton, the Colored Bard of North-Carolina, to Which Is Prefixed, the Life of the Author, Written by Himself.* Hillsborough, N.C.: D. Heartt, 1845: 52–54.

What shall I do – it whimpers so (ca. 1861)

EMILY DICKINSON

What shall I do – it whimpers so –
This little Hound within the Heart
All day and night with bark and start –
And yet, it will not go –
Would you *untie* it, were you me –
Would it stop whining – if to Thee –
I sent it – even now?

It should not teaze you –
By your chair – or, on the mat –

Or if it dare – to climb your dizzy knee –
Or – sometimes at your side to run –
When you were willing –
Shall it come?
Tell Carlo –
He'll tell *me!*

Elegy on the Death of Fidelio, a Dog Who Possessed More Merits Than the Poet Has Deigned to Ascribe to Him (1795)

"ZEDA"

When worth belov'd yields to the Tyrant's sway,
   And Friendship—ever faithful—ever dear—
   O'er the sad scene drops many a tender tear,
And from Remembrance never lifts to stay;
   Say then, shall not some grateful Muse,
     Fir'd by Inspiration's lay,
     To the theme a tribute pay,
   And in the wound a balm infuse?
Yes—yes—the willing maid with haste replies,
And humbly thus her feeble art she tries:—

'Tis not the loss of *human form* I sing—
A *theme* as *grateful* claims the sounding string;
Yes, sweet *Fidelio*, 'tis thy memory dear,
Thy gen'rous virtues that demand a tear.
True to thy mistress—ever on thy guard,
Nor age or sex, nor time nor place was spar'd;
   But each insulting hand soon felt
    The power by which thou couldst engage,

And roundly to the foe was dealt
   A copious stream of vengeful rage.

But ah! thou'rt flown—Death's unrelenting hand
   Hath robb'd thy mistress of thy watchful care,
Hath laid thee 'mongst th' inanimated band
   Who draw no more the breath of vital air.

"Farewell, *Fidell*—farewell my faithful slave,
   "Farewell to all the joys by thee inspir'd;
   "The gen'rous ardour which thy bosom fir'd
"No more to guard thy mistress ere shall crave."

'Tis thus, *Fidell,* FELICIA mourns thy fate,
   While each remembrance of thy merry freaks
   Starts the big tear to lave her glowing cheeks,
And deepening sighs thy faithful deeds relate.

Ah! cease, FELICIA—dry that tearful eye,
   No more thy tender heart let anguish rend:
In the dark grave *Fidelio's* ashes lie—
   There let them rest 'till day and night shall end.

Perhaps e'en then his gentle form shall rise—
   Perhaps in realms of bliss he'll on thee wait;
And mounted far above the sapphire skies,
   For thee he'll joy to gambol in an endless state.

Zeda. "Elegy on the Death of Fidelio, A Dog who possessed more Merits than the Poet has deigned to ascribe to him." *New York Magazine, or Literary Repository* 6, no. 10 (October 1795): 632.

Tumbler's Epitaph (ca. 1840)

Here, beneath this plot of grass,
Lies a "Tumbler" not made of glass;
Now in the grave, we lay his remains,
Bound in death's cold clammy chains.

He left no enemies to triumph o'er his death,
But kind sympathizing friends watched his last breath;

Each and every one a prayer, sent to him above,
Fill'd with reverence, esteem and love.

A faithful Dog and sincere friend he was,
A kick from John's old Mare his death did cause;
Although dead, his virtues shine no less,
And he lies on the land of old Jess.

Thus parted this life a noble Dog,
Who oft had been the terror of many a hog;
Whose spirit dwells above with all divine,
Nevermore to haunt the beastly swine.

Although here he lies so low,
To Hell his spirit will never go;
For meaned mortals on this earth doth dwell,
More than enough to people Hell.

A day to be remembered, when Tumbler we did bury,
And to his peace, at old Burley's we'll drink the Tom and Jerry.

"Tumbler's Epitaph." Broadsheet. United States: s.n., 1840s.

[Dog Posing for Portrait in Photographer's Studio Chair].
New York: Rufus Anson, ca. 1855. Image courtesy of the Metropolitan
Museum of Art, accession 2004.219.

An Untitled Poem about Sailor (1845)

J. S. SKINNER

You who wander hither,
Pass not unheeded
This spot, where poor Sailor
Is deposited.
He was born of Newfoundland parent;
His vigilance during many years
Was the safeguard of Cedar Point.
His talents and manners were long
The amusement and delight
Of those who resorted to it.

Of his unshaken fidelity,
Of his cordial attachment
To his master and his family,
A just conception cannot
Be conveyed by language,
Or formed but by those
Who intimately knew him.

J. S. Skinner, "An Untitled Poem about Sailor." In *The Dog and the Sportsman*. Philadelphia: Lea and Blanchard, 1845, 35–36.

The Dog Star Pup (1920)

HENRY HERBERT KNIBBS

On the silver edge of a vacant star near the trembling Pleiades,
A Hobo, lately arrived from earth sat rubbing his rusty chin,
All unaware, as he waited there with his elbows on his knees,
That an angel stood at the Golden Gate, impatient to let him in.

The Hobo, peering across the space on a million worlds below,
Started up as he heard a voice: "Mortal, why ye wait there?"

He scratched his head as he turned and said, "I reckon I got to go,
And mebby the goin' is just as good in Heaven, as anywhere."

A little while and the Hobo stood at the thrice-barred Golden Gate:
"Enter!" the stately angel cried. "You came to a worthy end,
Though the sad arrears of your wasted years have occasioned a brisk debate,
You gave your life in a noble cause—you perished to save a friend."

"Only me dog." And the Hobo smiled, but the startled angel frowned
At that rack of rags that was standing there adorning the right-of-way:
"Him and me we was pardners, see! down there where the world goes round,
And I was waitin' for him to come—but mebby he stopped to play."

"You are late," said the angel, "one year late!" The Hobo turned his head.
"Then who was holdin' the watch on me when I saved me pal? Was you?
Just figure it out, if me dog cashed in a-savin' me life, instead,
Now wouldn't he wait for his missin' mate till he seen I was comin' too?"

Sadly the angel shook his head and lifted the portal bar:
"One minute more and the Scribe will strike your name from the Roll Sublime."
When up from below came a yellow dog a-hopping from star to star,
And wagging his tail as he sniffed the trail that his master had to climb.

Then something slipped in the scheme of things: a comet came frisking by,
A kind of a loco Dog-star pup just out for a little chase;
The yellow pup got his dander up and started across the sky,
As the flickering comet tucked his tail—and never was such a race!

Round the Heavens and back again flew comet and his dog, unchecked;
The Great Bear growled and the Sun Dogs barked. Astronomers had begun
To rub their eyes in a wild surmise that their records were incorrect,
When the puppy, crossing his master's trace, stopped short, and the race
      was done.

Singed and sorry and out of breath he mounted the starry trail,
And trotted to where his master stood by the gate to the Promised Land:
"'T was a flamin' run that you gave him, son, and you made him tuck his tail,"
And the Hobo patted the puppy's head with a soiled but forgiving hand.

When, slowly the Gates dissolved in air and the twain were left along,
On a road that would through fields and flowers, past many a shady tree;
"Now this is like we'd 'a' made it, tike, an' I reckon it's all our own,
And nothin' to do but go," he said, "which is Heaven for you and for me."

Heaven—save that the Hobo felt a kind of uneasy pride
As he pushed his halo a bit aslant and gazed at his garments strange;
But the pup knew naught of these changes wrought since crossing the
  Great Divide
For the heart of a dog—and the love of a man—may never forget or change.

Henry Herbert Knibbs, "The Dog Star Pup." In *Songs of the Trail*. New York: Houghton
  Mifflin, 1920, 59–62.

My Dog (1918)

SGT. F. C. MCCARTHY, AERO SQUADRON

I found him in a shell hole,
  With a gash across his head,
Crouching down beside his master,
  Who he must have known was dead.

Hell was popping all about us,
  So we stayed there through the fight,
Got to sort o' like each other
  Through the mis'ry of that night.

He has fleas; I have cooties;
  He speaks French; I "no compree";
So the rule fifty-fifty goes
  Between my dog and me.

You wouldn't say he's handsome,
  He's been wounded many times;
But when we boys go over,
  Over with us Frenchie climbs.

And when the Boche is gassing,
  And we want to test the air,
We try it on my dog first,
  But he doesn't seem to care.

He gets no *blessé* medals,
  No Distinguished Service bar,

But just our admiration,
    Doubled by each honored scar.

And when the war is over,
    And to our homes we go,
My dog is going back with me—
    What's mine is his, you know.

F. C. McCarthy, "My Dog." *Stars and Stripes,* May 3, 1918, 5.

To My Dog, "Quien Sabe"
(In the Happy Hunting Grounds) (1920)

HENRY HERBERT KNIBBS

Did the phantom hills seem strange, Quien,
When you left the light for the ghostly land?
Do you dream of the open range, Quien,
The tang of sage and the sun-warmed sand?

Does your great heart yearn for the sweep of space,
The desert dawn and the sunset glow,
When we had no care, nor a dwelling-place,
In the lonely land we used to know?

Do you dream of those outland days, Quien,
The fierce, white noon and the pinion shade?
The luck we shared on the ways, Quien,
Young and lusty and unafraid?

Comrade, keen for the hunt and kill;
Comrade, patient and strong and wise,
The firelight flares—and I see you still,
Calling me with your wistful eyes.

You cannot know that I cannot come—
My work is here for a while—and then . . .
My heart cries out, though my lips are dumb,
And my hands are chained to the wheel, Quien.

Yet I am glad that your soul is free
To run the trails of our old delight:
Only—I ask that you wait for me,
And you will know, be it day or night,

Know, and leap at my call, Quien,
And forever pace with pony's stride,
And never a start shall fall, Quien,
And never again our trails divide.

Henry Herbert Knibbs, "To My Dog, 'Quien Sabe' (In the Happy Hunting Grounds)."
In *Songs of the Trail*. New York: Houghton Mifflin, 1920, 20–21.

Sonnet for My Dog (ca. 1939)

THOMAS CURTIS CLARK

In distant lands the statesmen scheme and plot.
A war is in the making. Terror grips
The people and their masters. But you, Spot,
Are undisturbed by guns and battleships.
For you the thrills of life, without a care!
Long months of play in lush green grass await.
The world is good, for you; all days are fair—
You are no citizen of any state!
Rejoice, in your dog-kingdom happy, blest,
And woo us from the bitterness of life.
We, lordly men, with terrors are oppressed;
Our greed for gold and power brings us hate and strife.
Wise little dog, be happy while you can;
Ignore the brutal idiot called man!

Thomas Curtis Clark, "Sonnet for My Dog." In *The Linebook*. Chicago: Chicago Tribune
Co., ca. 1939.

My Dog (1897)

CLARENCE HAWKES

Come in, my dog, nor linger at the door,
Come in, old Gip, and lie upon the floor,
And rest your faithful head upon my knee,
And deem it joy to be alone with me;
My dear old dog, unto creation's end
Of all the world thou art my dearest friend.

Thou dost not ask me to be good to thee,
It is enough that thou dost care for me,
And if this hand could beat thee from my door,
Thou wouldst come back again and whine once more,
And lick the hand that made thy body smart
And love me still deep in your doggish heart.

Thou dost not ask for dainty bread and meat
But lovest best the food I cannot eat,
And sweet the bit, if looks I understand,
That thou canst take from out thy master's hand,
And while wise men in thankfulness may fail
Old Gip says thank you with his wagging tail.

And when my dog is sleeping in the hall
I have no fear that danger will befall,
For thieves would find that passage doubly barred,
A truer soldier never mounted guard.
And lasting is a dog's fidelity,
To those he loves, as man's can ever be.

What love is beaming in those two brown eyes,
When hidden, too, what sorrow in them lies,
And how they follow me from place to place
As though they tried to read his master's face,
And how he springs and barks when I am glad,
How soon his tail will droop when I am sad.

And when I die, if friends forget to pine,
I know there'll be one faithful dog to whine,
To bark impatient at my bedroom door,
To hunt the meadow and the woodland o'er,
And watch and whine for master who is late,
And die at last, still watching at the gate.

*The author of these lines is blind.

Clarence Hawkes, "My Dog." *Outing* 29, no. 5 (February 1897): 487.

The Good, True Dog (1913)

C. A. FONERDEN

Thou noble, honest canine brute, with countenance benign,
How good art thou, Telemachus, what virtues great are thine!
No dog, whate'er his pedigree, can take from thee thy right;
Few are the dogs comparable to thee when thou wouldst fight.

Oh, handsome dog, Telemachus, I love to sit and see
Thy thankful tail atwinkle when thy nose is on my knee—
Not utterance of oral kind can make true love avail,
More potently than thou canst do in wagging of thy tail.

Thy wistful eyes gleam up to mine with twinkling gratitude,
While thine uplifted, swaying paw bespeaks thy loving mood;
And love like thine, my faithful friend, shall never be forgot,
And love like mine, Telemachus, for thee shall falter not.

A friend have I, while thou shalt live, in whom I may confide;
I prize so true a heart as thine, though it shall thus abide
In my old dog Telemachus, for it were hard to find
A heart so faithful and so true of any human kind.

I sorrow that a good dog's life should be so short a span,
While life of three score years and ten allotted is to man;
For dogs like thee, Telemachus, are moral teachers true,
And men would nobler be did they only what good dogs do.

How I shall grieve when thou art gone, my good and faithful friend;
No more to have thy twinkling tail its fellowship extend,

No more to see thy loving eyes agleam with pure delight
When I caress thy pretty face, with countenance so bright.

But let me not forestall that day of evil unto me;
Let nothing mar my present days of happiness with thee,
And while together on this earth in union we remain
Let love and friendship, as with us, good dogs and men retain.

Thy gentle tongue hath licked my hand like word was never spoken,
Nor in the love thou gavest me was thy faith ever broken;
And I will monument thy grave with tender tears of rue,
Sighing, here lies my faithful friend, Telemachus the true!

C. A. Fonerden, "The Good, True Dog." In *Dog Tales and Cat Tales*. New Market, Va.:
Henkel, 1913, 3–4.

To a Dog's Memory (1889)

LOUISE IMOGEN GUINEY

The gusty morns are here,
When all the reeds ride low with level spear;
And on such nights as lured us far of yore,
The Hound-star and the pagan Hunter shine
Down rocky alleys yet, and through the pine:
But I and thou, ah, field-fellow of mine,
Together roam no more!

The world, all grass and air,
Somehow hath lost thee; and the roadsides wear
A heavy silence since thy welcomes fail
Bonfire, and fiddles, and the van we knew
Gleaming with gypsies, and the bear that drew
Thy kindled eye, the sulky dancer through
Our leafy Auburndale.

Soft showers go laden now
With odors of the sappy orchard bough,
And brooks, bewitched, begin a madder march;
The late frost smokes from hollow sedges high;
The finch is come, the flame-blue dragon-fly,

The cowslip's outcast gold that children spy,
  The plume upon the larch.

  There is a music fills
The oaks of Belmont and the Wayland hills
Southward to Dewing's little bubbly stream—
The heavenly weather's call! O, who alive
Hastes not to start, delays not to arrive,
Having free feet that never felt a gyve
  Weigh, even in a dream?

  But thou, instead, hast found
The sunless April uplands underground;
And still, wherever thou art, I must be.
My beautiful! arise in might and mirth,
(For we were tameless travellers from our birth)—
Arise against thy narrow door of earth,
  And keep the watch for me!

Louise Imogen Guiney, "To a Dog's Memory." *Century Magazine* 38, no. 12 (October 1889): 947.

PART 4

Companion Dogs

They [the Huron] believe that souls are immortal, and that when they leave the body they go at once to dance and rejoice in the presence of Yoscha and his grandmother Ataensiq, taking the route and the way of stars, which they call *Atiskein andahatey,* the path of souls, which we call the Milky Way or the Starry Scarf, and simple folk the Road of St. James. They say that the souls of dogs go there also by way of certain stars which are near neighbours of the soul's path, and which they call *Gagnenon anhahatey,* that is to say, the path of the dogs.

Father Gabriel Sagard, *The Long Journey to the Country of the Hurons,* 1632

In America today rare indeed is the person who has not had some type of memorable relationship with one or another of the many popular breeds of dogs—either his or her own or that of a neighbor, family member, or friend. However, excepting those canine noses belonging to dogs who are owned and used for hunting or other kinds of useful work, the noses belonging to most dogs are either employed in sniffing the familiar fabric of their masters' homes and yards or the intoxicating smells of the many treats that are lavished on them. And while many specially trained dogs serve our civilian and military organizations in capacities from drug sniffers to rescuers of lost children to therapy dogs for injured or elderly persons, the vast majority of dogs today fill the roles of cherished and beloved companions.

Having largely transcended their earlier, mostly pragmatic duties and identities, most American dogs, unlike American horses, remain vital parts of the landscape of both rural and urban communities. The following question in the minds of those who do not love and appreciate dogs would seem unintelligible to those of us who do: "If a dog is not needed for some utilitarian function, why incur the expense and trouble of keeping a dog in the first place?" To answer that question, one has only to read the following selections. However, we shall try in part to answer it here.

Perhaps the first part of our answer is best couched in terms of the dog's inherited pack instinct. Dogs are pack animals in much the same way as the wolves from whom they were descended. Moreover they need to feel that the pack leaders are competent and fully able to insure the pack's survival through their leadership and their ability to enforce the necessary discipline. In the domestic world, that pack leadership falls on the dog's master, and to him a dog's loyalty is unswerving and absolute. Dogs therefore not only form bonds of affection for their masters, but their instincts strengthen those bonds with their inherited need to survive. As a result the pack leader becomes the center of every dog's life, even if that master is less than attentive to this intense attachment. At any moment dogs are ready to lay down their lives for their master, for their pack's and their own survival.

The unquestioning love and devotion that stems from these instinctual bonds for their pack leaders form a large part of a dog's perception of the world in which they live. Like any other intelligent, well-organized, and sentient being, dogs respond to acts of kindness that intensify these bonds and help them to have confidence in their masters as necessary adjuncts to their lives. While their attachment to their masters is absolute, so too is the absolute nature of a dog's perception of everything else. This occasionally interrupts the seamless tranquility of the human-canine relationship. It is no exaggeration to say that a dog lives in the realm of the absolute, the apotheosis, the ideal, and the immediate. In fact one of the major elements in the charm of the canine character is that they are so intently serious about everything they do. Dogs are continually being surprised by their world, and they respond to it instinctively and with an immediacy that often surprises and sometimes frustrates their masters. Dedicated professionals who train dogs for a living would agree unanimously with famous handler Kenneth Roebuck that if correction is needed, it must be administered at one and the same moment the infraction occurs, for it is only in this way that the dog is able to associate the correction with the deed.*

This combination of unquestioned, enduring fidelity and immediate, instinctual responses to fascinating stimuli results in human-canine relationships where both the master and the dog are continually surprising each other. While a dog may turn on his master's canine antagonists like the faithful hunting dog in the "Testimony of James Smith," and while he may become a faithful and beloved companion whose courage and selflessness result in his own undoing as in H. A. Freeman's "A Dog's Story," he may just as quickly abandon his mistress and surrender to his instinctual urge to pursue and kill game, as in Anna Lea Merritt's tale "My Dog (A Hamlet in Old Hampshire)." The canine heroes of the stories and anecdotes that follow struggle with the duality of their natures as portrayed when their devotion to their human pack leaders comes into conflict with their

---

*Kenneth C. Roebuck, *Gun Dog Training: Pointing Dogs* (Harrisburg, Penn.: Stackpole Books, 1983), 48–52.

instinctive drives for food and fun and freedom. That very conflict and tension is what gives these stories their plausibility and their unmistakable charm. What makes them essential to our understanding of the canine persona is the heart-warming ways that, despite their frequent outbursts of immoral opportunism, the dogs portrayed here remain treasured and steadfast members of their human pack.

The Animal Mind (1913)

JOHN BURROUGHS

Considering the gulf that separates man from the lower orders, I often wonder how, for instance, we can have such a sense of companionship with a dog. What is it in the dog that so appeals to us? It is probably his quick responsiveness to our attention. He meets us half way. He gives caress for caress. Then he is that light-hearted, irresponsible vagabond that so many of us half-consciously long to be if we could and dared. To a dog, a walk is the best of good fortunes; he sniffs adventure at every turn, is sure something thrilling will happen the next bend in the path. How much he gets out of it that escapes me!—the excitement of all the different odors that my sense is too dull to take it. The ground to him is written over with the scent of game of some sort, the air is full of the lure of wild adventure. How human he is at such times! He is out on a lark. In his spirit of hilarity, he will chase hens, pigs, sheep, cows, which ordinarily he would give no heed to, just as boys abroad in the fields and woods will commit depredations that they would be ashamed of at home.

When I go to my neighbor's house his dog of many strains, and a great crony of mine, becomes riotous with delight. He whines with joy, hops upon my lap, caresses me, then springs to the door, and with wagging tail and speaking looks and actions says, "Come on, let's off!" I open the door and say, "Go if you want to." He leaps back upon my lap and says, "No, no, not without you." Then to the door again with his eloquent pantomime, till I finally follow him forth into the street. Then he tears up the road to the woods, saying so plainly, "Better one hour of Slabsides than a week of humdrum at home." At such times, if we chance to meet his master or his mistress on the road, he heeds them not, and is deaf to their calls.

Well, I do not suppose the dog is in our line of descent, but his stem-form must join ours not very far back. He is our brother at not very many removes, and he has been so modified and humanized by his long intercourse with our kind, stretching no doubt through hundreds of thousands of years, that we are near to him and he is near to us. I do not suppose, if this affectionate intercourse were to continue any number of ages or cycles longer, the dog would ever be any more developed on his intellectual side; he can never share our thoughts any more than he does now. He has not, nor have any of the lower orders, that which Ray Lankester aptly calls educability—that which distinguishes man from all other creatures. We can train animals to do wonderful things, but we cannot develop in them, or graft upon them, this capacity for intellectual improvement,—to grasp and wield and store up ideas. Man's effect upon trained animals is like the effect of a magnet upon a piece of steel: for the moment he imparts some of his own powers to them, and holds them up to the ideal plane, but they are not permanently intellectualized; no new power is developed in them; and they soon fall back to their natural state. What they seem to acquire is not free intelligence that they can apply to other problems. We have not enlarged their minds, but have shaped their impulses to a new pattern. They are no wiser, but they are more apt. They do a human "stunt," but they do not think human thoughts.

John Burroughs, "The Animal Mind." In *The Summit of the Years*. New York: Houghton
    Mifflin, 1913, 131–33.

From *The History of New England*
from 1630 to 1649 (1644)

JOHN WINTHROP

1644

One Dalkin and his wife dwelling near Meadford [Medford] coming from Cambridge, where they had spent their Sabbath, and being to pass over the river at a ford, the tide not being fallen enough, the husband adventured over, and finding it too deep, persuaded his wife to stay a while, but raining very sore, she would needs adventure over, and was carried away with the stream past her depth. Her husband not daring to go help her, cried out, and thereupon his dog, being at his house near by, came forth, and seeing something in the water, swam to her, and she caught hold on the dog's tail, so he drew her to the shore and saved her life.

John Winthrop, *The History of New England from 1630 to 1649*. Volume 2. Boston: Thomas
    B. Wait and Son, 1826, 161–62.

From the Journals of the
Lewis and Clark Expedition (1805)

MERIWETHER LEWIS

Wednesday May 29th 1805.

Last night we were all allarmed by a large buffaloe Bull, which swam over from the opposite shore and coming along side of the white perouge, climbed over it to land, he then allarmed ran up the bank in full speed directly towards the fires, and was within 18 inches of the heads of some of the men who lay sleeping before the centinel could allarm him or make him change his course, still more allarmed, he now took his direction immediately towards our lodge, passing between 4 fires and within a few inches of the heads of one range of the men as they yet lay sleeping, when he came near the tent, my dog saved us by causing him to change his course a second time, which he did by turning a little to the right, and was quickly out of sight, leaving us by this time all in an uproar with our guns in o[u]r hands, enquiring of each other the ca[u]se of the alarm, which after a few moments was explained by the centinel: we were happy to find no one hirt. The next morning we found that the buffaloe in passing the perouge had trodden on a rifle, which belonged to Capt. Clark's black man, who had negligently left her in the perouge, the rifle was mich bent, he had also broken the spindle; pivit, and shattered the stock of one of the blunderbusses on board, with this damage I felt well content, happy indeed, that we had sustained no further injury.

Original Journals of the Lewis and Clark Expedition, 1804–1806. Ed. Reuben Gold Thwaites. Volume 2, part 1. New York: Dodd, Mead, 1904, 91.

Stickeen (1909)

JOHN MUIR

In the summer of 1880 I set out from Fort Wrangell in a canoe to continue the exploration of the icy region of southeastern Alaska, begun in the fall of 1879. After the necessary provisions, blankcts, etc., had been collected and stowed away, and my Indian crew were in their places ready to start, while a crowd of their relatives and friends on the wharf were bidding them good-by and good-luck, my companion, the Rev. S. H. Young, for whom we were waiting, at last came aboard, followed by a little black dog, that immediately made himself at home by curling up in a hollow among the baggage. I like dogs, but this one seemed so small and worthless that I objected to his going, and asked the missionary why he was taking him.

"Such a little helpless creature will only be in the way," I said; "you had better pass him up to the Indian boys on the wharf, to be taken home to play with the children. This trip is not likely to be good for toy-dogs. The poor silly thing will be in rain and snow for weeks or months, and will require care like a baby." But his master assured me that he would be no trouble at all; that he was a perfect wonder of a dog, could endure cold and hunger like a bear, swim like a seal, and was wondrous wise and cunning, etc., making out a list of virtues to show he might be the most interesting member of the party.

Nobody could hope to unravel the lines of his ancestry. In all the wonderfully mixed and varied dog-tribe I never saw any creature very much like him, though in some of his sly, soft, gliding motions and gestures he brought the fox to mind. He was short-legged and bunch-bodied, and his hair, though smooth, was long and silky and slightly waved, so that when the wind was at his back it ruffled, making him look shaggy. At first sight his only noticeable feature was his fine tail, which was about as airy and shady as a squirrel's, and was carried curling forward almost to his nose. On closer inspection you might notice his thin sensitive ears, and sharp eyes with cunning tan-spots above them. Mr. Young told me that when the little fellow was a pup about the size of a woodrat he was presented to his wife by an Irish prospector at Sitka, and that on his arrival at Fort Wrangell he was adopted with enthusiasm by the Stickeen Indians as a sort of new good-luck totem, was named "Stickeen" for the tribe, and became a universal favorite; petted, protected, and admired wherever he went, and regarded as a mysterious fountain of wisdom.

On our trip he soon proved himself a queer character—odd, concealed, independent, keeping invincibly quiet, and doing many little puzzling things that piqued my curiosity. As we sailed week after week through the long intricate channels and inlets among the innumerable islands and mountains of the coast, he spent most of the dull days in sluggish ease, motionless, and apparently as unobserving as if in deep sleep. But I discovered that somehow he always knew what was going on. When the Indians were about to shoot at ducks or seals, or when anything along the shore was exciting our attention, he would rest his chin on the edge of the canoe and calmly look out like a dreamy-eyed tourist. And when he heard us talking about making a landing, he immediately roused himself to see what sort of a place we were coming to, and made ready to jump overboard and swim ashore as soon as the canoe neared the beach. Then, with a vigorous shake to get rid of the brine in his hair, he ran into the woods to hunt small game. But though always the first out of the canoe, he was always the last to get into it. When we were ready to start he could never be found, and refused to come to our call. We soon found out, however, that though we could not see him at such times, he saw us, and from the cover of the briers and huckleberry bushes in the fringe of the woods was watching the canoe with wary eye. For as soon as we were fairly off he came trotting down the beach, plunged into the surf, and swam after us, knowing well that we would cease rowing and take him in. When the contrary little vagabond came alongside, he was lifted by the neck, held at arm's length a moment to drip, and dropped aboard. We tried to cure him of this trick by compelling him to swim a long way, as if we had a mind to abandon him; but this did no good; the longer the swim the better he seemed to like it.

Though capable of great idleness, he never failed to be ready for all sorts of adventures and excursions. One pitch-dark rainy night we landed about ten o'clock at the mouth of a salmon stream when the water was phosphorescent. The salmon were running, and the myriad fins of the onrushing multitude were churning all the stream into a silvery glow, wonderfully beautiful and impressive in the ebon darkness. To get a good view of the show I set out with one of the Indians and sailed up through the midst of it to the foot of a rapid about half a mile from camp, where the swift current dashing over rocks made the luminous glow most glorious. Happening to look back down the stream, while the Indian was catching a few of the struggling fish, I saw a long spreading fan of light like the tail of a comet, which we thought must be made by some big strange animal that was pursuing us. On it came with its magnificent train, until we imagined we could see the monster's head and eyes; but it was only Stickeen, who, finding I had left the camp, came swimming after me to see what was up.

When we camped early, the best hunter of the crew usually went to the woods for a deer, and Stickeen was sure to be at his heels, provided I had not gone out. For, strange to say, though I never carried a gun, he always followed me, forsaking the hunter and even his master to share my wonderings. The days that were too stormy for sailing I spent in the woods, or on the adjacent mountains, wherever my studies called me; and Stickeen always insisted on going with me, however wild the weather, gliding like a fox through dripping huckleberry bushes and thorny tangles of panax and rubus, scarce stirring their rain-laden leaves; wading and wallowing through snow, swimming icy streams, skipping over logs and rocks and the crevasses of glaciers with the patience and endurance of a determined mountaineer, never tiring or getting discouraged. Once he followed me over a glacier the surface of which was so crusty and rough that it cut his feet until every step was marked with blood; but he trotted on with Indian fortitude until I noticed his red track, and, taking pity on him, made him a set of moccasins out of a handkerchief. However great his troubles he never asked help or made any complaint, as if, like a philosopher, he had learned that without hard work and suffering there could be no pleasure worth having.

Yet none of us was able to make out what Stickeen was really good for. He seemed to meet danger and hardships without anything like reason, insisted on having his own way, never obeyed an order, and the hunter could never set him on anything, or make him fetch the birds he shot. His equanimity was so steady it seemed due to want of feeling; ordinary storms were pleasures to him, and as for mere rain, he flourished in it like a vegetable. No matter what advances you might make, scarce a glance or a tail-wag would you get for your pains. But though he was apparently as cold as a glacier and about as impervious to fun, I tried hard to make his acquaintance, guessing there must be something worthwhile hidden beneath so much courage, endurance, and love of wild-weathery adventure. No superannuated mastiff or bulldog grown old in office surpassed this fluffy midget in stoic dignity. He sometimes reminded me of a small, squat, unshakable desert cactus. For he never displayed a single trace of the merry, tricksy, elfish fun of the terriers and collies that we all know, nor of their touching affection and devotion. Like children, most small dogs beg to be loved and allowed to love; but Stickeen seemed a very Diogenes, asking only to be let alone: a true child of the wilderness, holding the even tenor of his hidden life with the silence and serenity of nature. His strength of character lay in his eyes. They looked as old as the hills, and as young, and as wild. I never tired of looking into them: it was like looking into a landscape; but they were small and rather deep-set, and had no explaining lines around them to give out particulars. I was accustomed to look into the faces of plants and animals, and I watched the little sphinx more and more keenly as an interesting study. But there is no estimating the wit and wisdom concealed and latent in our lower fellow mortals until made manifest by profound experiences; for it is through suffering that dogs as well as saints are developed and made perfect.

After exploring the Sum Dum and Tahkoo fiords and their glaciers, we sailed through Stephen's Passage into Lynn Canal and thence through Icy Strait into Cross Sound, searching for unexplored inlets leading toward the great fountain ice-fields of the Fairweather Range. Here, while the tide was in our favor, we were accompanied by a fleet of icebergs drifting out to the ocean from Glacier Bay. Slowly we paddled around Vancouver's Point, Wimbledon, our frail canoe tossed like a feather on the massive heaving swells coming in past Cape Spenser.

For miles the sound is bounded by precipitous mural cliffs, which, lashed with wave-spray and their heads hidden in clouds, looked terribly threatening and stern. Had our canoe been crushed or upset we could have made no landing here, for the cliffs, as high as those of Yosemite, sink sheer into deep water. Eagerly we scanned the wall on the north side for the first sign of an opening fiord or harbor, all of us anxious except Stickeen, who dozed in peace or gazed dreamily at the tremendous precipices when he heard us talking about them. At length we made the joyful discovery of the mouth of the inlet now called "Taylor Bay," and about five o'clock reached the head of it and encamped in a Spruce grove near the front of a large glacier.

While camp was being made, Joe the hunter climbed the mountain wall on the east side of the fiord in pursuit of wild goats, while Mr. Young and I went to the glacier. We found that it is separated from the waters of the inlet by a tide-washed moraine, and extends, an abrupt barrier, all the way across from wall to wall of the inlet, a distance of about three miles. But our most interesting discovery was that it had recently advanced, though again slightly receding. A portion of the terminal moraine had been plowed up and shoved forward, uprooting and overwhelming the woods on the east side. Many of the trees were down and buried, or nearly so, others were leaning away from the ice-cliffs, ready to fall, and some stood erect, with the bottom of the ice plow still beneath their roots and its lofty crystal spires towering huge above their tops. The spectacle presented by these century-old trees standing close beside a spiry wall of ice, with their branches almost touching it, was most novel and striking. And when I climbed around the front, and a little way up the west side of the glacier, I found that it had swelled and increased in height and width in accordance with its advance, and carried away the outer ranks of trees on its bank.

On our way back to camp after these first observations I planned a far-and-wide excursion for the morrow. I awoke early, called not only by the glacier, which had been on my mind all night, but by a grand flood-storm. The wind was blowing a gale from the north and the rain was flying with the clouds in a wide passionate horizontal flood, as if it were all passing over the country instead of falling on it. The main perennial streams were booming high above their banks, and hundreds of new ones, roaring like the sea, almost covered the lofty gray walls of the inlet with white cascades and falls. I had intended making a cup of coffee and getting something like a breakfast before starting, but when I heard the storm and looked out I made haste to join it; for many of Nature's finest lessons are to be found in her storms, and if careful to keep in right relations with them, we may go safely abroad with them, rejoicing in the grandeur and beauty of their works and ways, and chanting with the old Norsemen, "The blast of the tempest aids our oars, the hurricane is our servant and drives us whither we wish to go." So, omitting breakfast, I put a piece of bread in my pocket and hurried away.

Mr. Young and the Indian were asleep, and so, I hoped, was Stickeen; but I had not gone a dozen rods before he left his bed in the tent and came boring through the blast after me. That a man should welcome storms for their exhilarating music and motion, and go forth to see God making landscapes, is reasonable enough; but what fascination could there be in such tremendous weather for a dog? Surely nothing akin to human enthusiasm for scenery or geology. Anyhow, on he came, breakfastless, through the choking blast. I stopped and did my best to turn him back. "Now don't," I said, shouting to make myself heard in the storm. "Now don't, Stickeen. What has got into your queer noddle now? You must be daft. This wild day has nothing for you. There is no game abroad, nothing but weather. Go back to camp and keep warm, get a good breakfast with your master, and be sensible for once. I can't carry you all day or feed you, and this storm will kill you."

But Nature, it seems, was at the bottom of the affair, and she gains her ends with dogs as well as with men, making us do as she likes, shoving and pulling us along her ways, however rough, all but killing us at times in getting her lessons driven hard home. After I had stopped again and again, shouting good warning advice, I saw that he was not to be shaken off; as well might the earth try to shake off the moon. I had once led his master into trouble, when he fell on one of the topmost jags of a mountain and dislocated his arm; now the turn of his humble companion was coming. The pitiful wanderer just stood there in the wind, drenched and blinking, saying doggedly, "Where thou goest I will go." So at last I told him to come on if he must, and gave him a piece of the bread I had in my pocket; then we struggled on together, and thus began the most memorable of all my wild days.

The level flood, driving hard in our faces, thrashed and washed us wildly until we got into the shelter of a grove on the east side of the glacier near the front, where we stopped awhile for breath and to listen and look out. The exploration of the glacier was my main object, but the wind was too high to allow excursions over its open surface, where one might be dangerously shoved while balancing for a jump on the brink of a crevasse. In the mean time the storm was a fine study. There the end of the glacier, descending an abrupt swell of resisting rock about five hundred feet high, leans forward and falls in ice-cascades. And as the storm came down the glacier from the north, Stickeen and I were beneath the main current of the blast, while favorably located to see and hear it. What a psalm the storm was singing, and how fresh the smell of the washed earth and leaves, and how sweet the still small voices of the storm! Detached wafts and swirls were coming through the woods, with music from the leaves and branches and furrowed boles, and even from the splintered rocks and ice-crags overhead, many of the tones soft and low and flute-like, as if each leaf and tree, crag and spire were a tuned reed. A broad torrent, draining the side of the glacier, now swollen by scores of new streams from the mountains, was rolling boulders along its rocky channel, with thudding, bumping, muffled sounds, rushing toward the bay with tremendous energy, as if in haste to get out of the mountains; the winters above and beneath calling to each other, and all to the ocean, their home.

Looking southward from our shelter, we had this great torrent and the forested mountain wall above it on our left, the spiry ice-crags on our right, and smooth gray gloom ahead. I tried to draw the marvelous scene in my note-book, but the rain blurred the page in spite of all my pains to shelter it, and the sketch was almost worthless. When the wind began to abate, I traced the east side of the glacier. All the trees standing on the edge of the woods were barked and bruised, showing high-ice mark in a very telling way, while tens of thousands of those that had stood for centuries on the bank of the glacier farther out lay crushed and being crushed. In many places I could see down fifty feet or so beneath the margin of the glacier-mill, where trunks from one to two feet in diameter here being ground to pulp against outstanding rock-ribs and bosses of the bank.

About three miles above the front of the glacier I climbed to the surface of it by means of axe-steps made easy for Stickeen. As far as the eye could reach, the level, or nearly level, glacier stretched away indefinitely beneath the gray sky, a seemingly boundless prairie of ice. The rain continued, and grew colder, which I did not mind, but a dim snowy look in the drooping clouds made me hesitate about venturing far from land. No trace of the west shore was visible, and in case the clouds would settle and give snow, or the wind again become violent. I feared getting caught in a tangle of crevasses. Snow-crystals, the flowers of the mountain clouds, are frail, beautiful things, but terrible then flying on storm-winds in darkening, benumbing swarms or when welded together into glaciers full of deadly crevasses. Watching the weather, I sauntered about on the crystal sea. For a mile or so out I found the ice remarkably safe. The marginal crevasses mere mostly narrow, while the few wider ones were easily avoided by passing around them, and the clouds began to open here and there.

Thus encouraged, I at last pushed out for the other side; for Nature can make us do anything she likes. At first we made rapid progress, and the sky was not very threatening, while I took bearings occasionally with a pocket compass to enable me to find my way back more surely in case the storm should become blinding; but the structure lines of the glacier were my main guide. Toward the west side we came to a closely crevassed section in which we had to make long, narrow tacks and doublings, tracing the edges of tremendous traverse and longitudinal crevasses, many of which were from twenty to thirty feet wide, and perhaps a thousand feet deep—beautiful and awful. In working a way through them I was severely cautious, but Stickeen came on as unhesitating as the flying clouds. The widest crevasse that I could jump he would leap without so much as halting to take a look at it. The weather was now making quick changes, scattering bits of dazzling brightness through the wintry gloom at rare intervals, when the sun broke forth wholly free, the glacier was seen from shore to shore with a bright array of encompassing mountains partly revealed, wearing the clouds as garments, while the prairie bloomed and sparkled with irised light from myriads of washed crystals. Then suddenly all the glorious show would be darkened and blotted out.

Stickeen seemed to care for none of these things, bright or dark, nor for the crevasses, wells, moulins, or swift flashing streams into which he might fall. The little adventurer was only about two years old, yet nothing seemed novel to him. Nothing daunted him. He showed neither caution nor curiosity, wonder nor fear, but bravely trotted on as if glaciers were playgrounds. His stout, muffled body seemed all one skipping muscle, and it was truly wonderful to see how swiftly and to all appearance heedlessly he flashed across nerve-trying chasms six or eight feet wide. His courage was so unwavering that it seemed to be due to dullness of perception, as if he were only blindly bold; and I kept warning him to be careful. For we had been close companions on so many wilderness trips that I had formed the habit of talking to him as if he were a boy and understood every word.

We gained the west shore in about three hours; the width of the glacier here being about seven miles. Then I pushed northward in order to see as far back as possible into the fountains of the Fairweather Mountains, in case the clouds should rise. The walking was easy along the margin of the forest, which, of course, like that on the other side, had been invaded and crushed by the swollen, overflowing glacier. In an hour or so, after passing a massive headland, we came suddenly on a branch of the glacier, which, in the form of a magnificent ice-cascade two miles wide, was pouring over the rim of the main basin in a westerly direction, its surface broken into wave-shaped blades and shattered blocks, suggesting the wildest updashing, heaving, plunging motion of a great river cataract. Tracing it down three or four miles, I found that it discharged into a lake, filling it with icebergs.

I would gladly have followed the lake outlet to tide-water, but the day was already far spent, and the threatening sky called for haste on the return trip to get off the ice before dark. I decided therefore to go no farther and, after taking a general view of the wonderful region, turned back, hoping to see it again under more favorable auspices. We made good speed up the cañon of the great ice-torrent, and out on the main glacier until we had left the west shore about two miles behind us. Here we got into a difficult network of crevasses, the gathering clouds began to drop misty fringes, and soon the dreaded snow came flying thick and fast. I now began to feel anxious about finding a way in the blurring storm. Stickeen showed no trace of fear. He was still the same silent, able little hero. I noticed, however, that after the storm-darkness came on he kept close up behind me. The snow urged us to make still greater haste, but at the same time hid our way. I pushed on as best I could, jumping innumerable crevasses, and for every hundred rods or so of direct advance traveling a mile in doubling up and down in the turmoil of chasms and dislocated ice-blocks. After an hour or two of this work we came to a series of longitudinal crevasses of appalling width, and almost straight and regular in trend, like immense furrows. These I traced with firm nerve, excited and strengthened by the danger, making wide jumps, poising cautiously on their dizzy edges after cutting hollows for my feet before making the spring, to avoid possible slipping or any uncertainty on the farther sides, where only one trial is granted—exercise at once frightful and inspiring. Stickeen followed seemingly without effort.

Many a mile we thus traveled, mostly up and down, making but little real headway in crossing, running instead of walking most of the time as the danger of being compelled to spend the night on the glacier became threatening. Stickeen seemed able for anything. Doubtless we could have weathered the storm for one night, dancing on a flat spot to keep from freezing, and I faced the threat without feeling anything like despair; but we were hungry and wet, and the wind from the mountains was still thick with snow and bitterly cold, so of course that night would have seemed a very long one. I could not see far enough through the blurring snow to judge in which general direction the least dangerous route lay, while the few dim, momentary glimpses I caught of mountains through rifts in the flying clouds were far from encouraging either as weather signs or as guides. I had simply to grope my way from crevasse to crevasse, holding a general direction by the ice-structure, which was not to be seen everywhere, and partly by the wind. Again and again I was put to my mettle, but Stickeen followed easily, his nerve apparently growing more unflinching as the danger increased. So it always is with mountaineers when hard beset. Running hard and jumping, holding every minute of the remaining daylight, poor as it was, precious, we doggedly persevered and tried to hope that every difficult crevasse we overcame would prove to be the last of its kind. But on the contrary, as we advanced they became more deadly trying.

At length our way was barred by a very wide and straight crevasse, which I traced rapidly northward a mile or so without finding a crossing or hope of one; then down the glacier about as far, to where it united with another uncrossable crevasse. In all this distance of perhaps two miles there was only one place where I could possibly jump it, but the width of this jump was the utmost I dared attempt, while the danger of slipping on the farther side was so great that I was loath to try it. Furthermore, the side I was on was about a foot higher than the other, and even with this advantage the crevasse seemed dangerously wide. One is liable to underestimate the width of crevasses where the magnitudes in general are great. I therefore stared at this one mighty keenly, estimating its width and the shape of the edge on the farther side, until I thought that I could jump it if necessary, but that in case I should be compelled to jump back from the lower side I might fail. Now, a cautious mountaineer seldom takes a step on unknown ground which seems at all dangerous that he cannot retrace in case he should be stopped by unseen obstacles ahead. This is the rule of mountaineers who live long, and, though in haste, I compelled myself to sit down and calmly deliberate before I broke it.

Retracing my devious path in imagination as if it were drawn on a chart, I saw that I was recrossing the glacier a mile or two farther up stream than the course pursued in the morning, and that I was now entangled in a section I had not before seen. Should I risk this dangerous jump, or try to regain the woods on the west shore, make a fire, and have only hunger to endure while waiting for a new day! I had already crossed so broad a stretch of dangerous ice that I saw it would be difficult to get back to the woods through the storm, before dark, and the attempt would most likely result in a dismal night-dance on the glacier; while just beyond the present barrier the surface seemed more promising, and the east shore was now perhaps about as near as the west. I was therefore eager to go on. But this wide jump was a dreadful obstacle.

At length, because of the dangers already behind me, I determined to venture against those that might be ahead, jumped and landed well, but with so little to spare that I more than ever dreaded being compelled to take that jump back from the lower side. Stickeen followed, making nothing of it, and we ran eagerly forward, hoping we were leaving all our troubles behind. But within the distance of a few hundred yards we were stopped by the widest crevasse yet encountered. Of course I made haste to explore it, hoping all might yet be remedied by finding a bridge or a way around either end. About three fourths of a mile up stream I found that it united with the one we had just crossed, as I feared it would. Then, tracing it down, I found it joined the same crevasse at the lower end also, maintaining throughout its whole course a width of forty to fifty feet. Thus to my dismay I discovered that we were on a narrow island about two miles long, with two barely possible ways to escape: one back by the way we came, the other ahead by an almost inaccessible sliver-bridge that crossed the great crevasse from near the middle of it!

After this nerve-trying discovery I ran back to the sliver-bridge and cautiously examined it. Crevasses, caused by strains from variations in the rate of motion of different parts of the glacier and convexities in the channel, are mere cracks when they first open, so narrow as hardly to admit the blade of a pocket-knife, and gradually widen according to the extent of the strain and the depth of the glacier. Now some of these cracks are interrupted, like the cracks in wood, and in the opening the strip of ice between overlapping ends is dragged out, and may maintain a continuous connection between the side, just as the two sides of a slivered crack in wood that is being split are connected. Some crevasses remain open for months or even years, and by the melting of their sides continue to increase in width long after the opening strain has ceased; while the sliver-bridges, level on top at first and perfectly safe, are at length melted to thin, vertical, knife-edged blades, the upper portion being most exposed to the weather; and since the exposure is greatest in the middle. They at length curve downward like the cables of suspension bridges. This one was evidently very old, for it had been weathered and wasted until it was the most dangerous and inaccessible that ever lay in my way. The width of the crevasse was here about fifty feet, and the sliver crossing diagonally was about seventy feet long; its thin knife-edge near the middle was depressed twenty-five or thirty feet below the level of the glacier, and the up-curving ends were attached to the sides eight or ten feet below the brink. Getting down the nearly vertical wall to the end of the sliver and up the other side were the main difficulties, and they seemed all but insurmountable. Of the many perils encountered in my years of wandering on mountains and glaciers none seemed so plain and stern and merciless as this. And it was presented when we were wet to the skin and hungry, the sky dark with quick driving snow, and the night near. But we were forced to face it. It was a tremendous necessity.

Beginning, not immediately above the sunken end of the bridge, but a little to one side, I cut a deep hollow on the brink for my knees to rest in. Then, leaning over, with my short-handled axe I cut a step sixteen or eighteen inches below, which on account of the sheerness of the wall was necessarily shallow. That step, however, was well made; its floor sloped slightly inward and formed a good hold for my heels. Then, slipping cautiously upon it, and crouching as low as possible, with my left side toward the wall, I steadied myself against the wind with my left hand in a slight notch, while with the right I cut other similar steps and notches in succession, guarding against losing balance by glinting of the axe, or by wind-gusts, for life and death were in every stroke and in the niceness of finish of every foothold.

After the end of the bridge was reached I chipped it down until I had made a level platform six or eight inches wide, and it was a trying thing to poise on this little slippery platform while bending over to get safely astride of the sliver. Crossing was then comparatively easy by chipping off the sharp edge with short, careful strokes, and hitching forward an inch or two at a time, keeping my balance with my knees pressed against the sides. The tremendous abyss on either hand I studiously ignored. To me the edge of that blue sliver was then all the world. But the most trying part of the adventure, after working my way across inch by inch and chipping another small platform, was to rise from the safe position astride and to cut a step-ladder in the nearly vertical face of the wall,—chipping, climbing, holding on with feet and fingers in mere notches. At such times one's whole body is eye, and common skill and fortitude are replaced by power beyond our call or knowledge. Never before had I been so long under deadly strain. How I got up that cliff I never could tell. The thing seemed to have been done by somebody else. I never have held death in contempt, though in the course of my explorations I have oftentimes felt that to meet one's fate on a noble mountain, or in the heart of a glacier, would be blessed as compared with death from disease, or from some shabby lowland accident. But the best death, quick and crystal-pure, set so glaringly open before us, is hard enough to face, even though we feel gratefully sure that we have already had happiness enough for a dozen lives.

But poor Stickeen, the wee, hairy, sleekit beastie, think of him! When I had decided to dare the bridge, and while I was on my knees chipping a hollow on the rounded brow above it, he came behind me, pushed his head past my shoulder, looked down and across, scanned the sliver and its approaches with his mysterious eyes, then looked me in the face with a startled air of surprise and concern, and began to mutter and whine; saying as plainly as if speaking with words, "Surely, you are not going into that awful place." This was the first time I had seen him gaze deliberately into a crevasse, or into my face with an eager, speaking, troubled look. That he should have recognized and appreciated the danger at the first glance showed wonderful sagacity. Never before had the daring midget seemed to know that ice was slippery or that there was any such thing as danger anywhere. His looks and tones of voice when he began to complain and speak his fears were so human that I unconsciously talked to him in sympathy as I would to a frightened boy, and in trying to calm his fears perhaps in some measure moderated my own. "Hush your fears, my boy," I said, "we will get across safe, though it is not going to be easy. No right way is easy in this rough world. We must risk our lives to save them. At the worst we can only slip, and then how grand a grave we will have, and by and by our nice bones will do good in the terminal moraine."

But my sermon was far from reassuring him: he began to cry, and after taking another piercing look at the tremendous gulf, ran away in desperate excitement, seeking some other crossing. By the time he got back, baffled of course, I had made a step or two. I dared not look back, but he made himself heard; and when he saw that I was certainly bent on crossing he cried aloud in despair. The danger was enough to haunt anybody, but it seems wonderful that he should have been able to weight and appreciate it so justly. No mountaineer could have seen it more quickly or judged it more wisely, discriminating between real and apparent peril.

When I gained the other side, he screamed louder than ever, and after running back and forth in vain search for a way of escape, he would return to the brink of the crevasse above the bridge, moaning and wailing as if in the bitterness of death. Could this be the silent, philosophic Stickeen? I shouted encouragement, telling him the bridge was not so bad as it looked, that I had left it flat and safe for his feet, and he could walk it easily. But he was afraid to try. Strange so small an animal should be capable of such big, wise fears. I called again and again in a reassuring tone to come on and fear nothing; that he could come if he would only try. He would hush for a moment, look down again at the bridge, and shout his unshakable conviction that he could never, never come that way; then lie back in despair, as if howling, "O-o-oh! what a place! No-o-o, I can never go o o down there!" His natural composure and courage had vanished utterly in a tumultuous storm of fear. Had the danger been less, his distress would have seemed ridiculous. But in this dismal, merciless abyss lay the shadow of death, and his heart-rending cries might well have called Heaven to his help. Perhaps they did. So hidden before, he was now transparent, and one could see the workings of his heart and mind like the movements of a clock out of its case. His voice and gestures, hopes and fears, were so perfectly human that none could mistake them; while he seemed to understand every word of mine. I was troubled at the thought of having to leave him out all night, and of the danger of not finding him in the morning. It seemed impossible to get him to venture. To compel him to try through fear of being abandoned, I started off as if leaving him to his fate, and disappeared back of a hummock; but this did no good; he only lay down and moaned ill utter hopeless misery. So, after hiding a few minutes, I went back to the brink of the crevasse and in a severe tone of voice shouted across to him that now I must certainly leave him, I could wait no longer, and that, if he would not come, all I could promise was that I would return to seek him next day. I warned him that if he went back to the woods the wolves would kill him, and finished by urging him once more by words and gestures to come on, come on.

He knew very well what I meant, and at last, with the courage of despair, hushed and breathless, he crouched down on the brink in the hollow I had made for my knees, pressed his body against the ice as if trying to get the advantage of the friction of every hair, gazed into the first step, put his little feet together and slid them slowly, slowly over the edge and down into it, bunching all four in it and almost standing on his head. Then, without lifting his feet, as well as I could see through the snow, he slowly worked them over the edge of the step and down into the next and the next in succession in the same way, and gained the end of the bridge. Then, lifting his feet with the regularity and slowness of the vibrations of a seconds pendulum, as if counting and measuring one-two-three, holding himself steady against the gusty wind, and giving separate attention to each little step, he gained the foot of the cliff, while I was on my knees leaning over to give him a lift should he succeed in getting within reach of my arm. Here he halted in dead silence, and it was here I feared he might fail, for dogs are poor climbers. I had no cord. If I had had one, I would have dropped a noose over his head and hauled him up. But while I was thinking whether an available cord might be made out of clothing, he was looking keenly into the series of notched steps and finger-holds I had made, as if counting them, and fixing the position of each one of them in his mind. Then suddenly up he came in a springy rush, hooking his paws into the steps and notches so quickly that I could not see how it was done, and whizzed past my head, safe at last!

And now came a scene! "Well done, well done, little boy! Brave boy!" I cried, trying to catch and caress him; but he would not be caught. Never before or since have I seen anything like so passionate a revulsion from the depths of despair to exultant, triumphant, uncontrollable joy. He flashed and darted hither and thither as if fairly demented, screaming and shouting, swirling round and round in giddy loops and circles like a leaf in a whirlwind, lying down, and rolling over and over, sidewise and heels over head, and pouring forth a tumultuous flood of hysterical cries and sobs and gasping mutterings. When I ran up to him to shake him, fearing he might die of joy, he flashed off two or three hundred yards, his feet in a mist of motion; then, turning suddenly, came back in a wild rush and launched himself at my face, almost knocking me down, all the while screeching and screaming and shouting as if saying, "Saved! saved! saved!" Then away again, dropping suddenly at times with his feet in the air, trembling and fairly sobbing. Such passionate emotion was enough to kill him. Moses' stately song of triumph after escaping the Egyptians and the Red Sea was nothing to it. Who could have guessed the capacity of the dull, enduring little fellow for all that most stirs this mortal frame? Nobody could have helped crying with him!

But there is nothing like work for toning down excessive fear or joy. So I ran ahead, calling him in as gruff a voice as I could command to come on and stop his nonsense, for we had far to go and it would soon be dark. Neither of us feared another trial like this. Heaven would surely count one enough for a lifetime. The ice ahead was gashed by thousands of crevasses, but they were common ones. The joy of deliverance burned in us like fire, and we ran without fatigue, every muscle with immense rebound glorying in its strength. Stickeen flew across everything in his way, and not till dark did he settle into his normal fox-like trot. At last the cloudy mountains came in sight, and we soon felt the solid rock beneath our feet, and were safe. Then came weakness. Danger had vanished, and so had our strength. We tottered down the lateral moraine in the dark, over boulders and tree trunks, through the bushes and devil-club thickets of the grove where we had sheltered ourselves in the morning, and across the level mudslope of the terminal moraine. We reached camp about ten o'clock, and found a big fire and a big supper. A party of Hoona Indians had visited Mr. Young, bringing a gift of porpoise meat and wild strawberries, and Hunter Joe had brought in a wild goat. But we lay down, too tired to eat much, and soon fell into a troubled sleep. The man who said, "The harder the toil, the sweeter the rest," never was profoundly tired. Stickeen kept springing up and muttering in his sleep, no doubt dreaming that he was still on the brink of the crevasse; and so did I, that night and many others long afterward, when I was over-tired.

Thereafter Stickeen was a changed dog. During the rest of the trip, instead of holding aloof, he always lay by my side, tried to keep me constantly in sight, and would hardly accept a morsel of food, however tempting, from any hand but mine. At night, when all was quiet about the camp-fire, he would come to me and rest his head on my knee with a look of devotion as if I were his god. And often as he caught my eye he seemed to be trying to say, "Wasn't that an awful time we had together on the glacier?"

Nothing in after years has dimmed that Alaska storm-day. As I write it all comes rushing and roaring to mind as if I were again in the heart of it. Again I see the gray flying clouds with their rain-floods and snow, the ice-cliffs towering above the shrinking forest, the majestic ice-cascade, the vast glacier outspread before its white mountain-fountains, and in the heart of it the tremendous crevasse,—emblem of the valley of the shadow of death,—low clouds trailing over it, the snow falling into it; and on its brink I see little Stickeen, and I hear his cries for help and his shouts of joy. I have known many dogs, and many a story

I could tell of their wisdom and devotion; but to none do I owe so much as to Stickeen. At first the least promising and least known of my dog-friends, he suddenly became the best known of them all. Our storm-battle for life brought him to light, and through him as through a window I have ever since been looking with deeper sympathy into all my fellow mortals.

None of Stickeen's friends knows what finally became of him. After my work for the season was done I departed for California, and I never saw the dear little fellow again. In reply to anxious inquiries his master wrote me that in the summer of 1883 he was stolen by a tourist at Fort Wrangell and taken away on a steamer. His fate is wrapped in mystery. Doubtless he has left this world—crossed the last crevasse—and gone to another. But he will not be forgotten. To me Stickeen is immortal.

John Muir, *Stickeen.* 1909. Boston: Houghton Mifflin, 1913.

Testimony of James Smith, Field Hand, Enslaved in Virginia and Georgia. Interviewed by Henry Bibb (1852)

James Smith, a refugee from slavery, has met with the unspeakable joy of finding his wife in Canada, after an absence of 17 years.

He gives the following interesting sketch of his experience, escape, &c. . . . Mr. Smith who is a clergyman of the Baptist faith and order, it will be remembered was held and worked for many years in the state of Virginia, by a member of the same denomination, who separated him from his wife and little ones and sold him to a slave trader in Georgia. . . . From thence they were driven to Georgia where poor Smith was placed under an overseer and a cruel driver, on a cotton plantation where there were not less than 300 hands.

. . .

[When Smith escaped and returned to his Virginia home looking for his wife he was caught, eds.]

While there he learned from another slave that his wife for whom he had suffered almost death itself, had been sold by her master to a trader, who carried her to the State of Kentucky.

At length his master came after him with the spirit of a demon. After having him stripped and most unmercifully flogged, a hot iron was applied to the quivering flesh on one side of his face and back of his neck, which left stamped, in letters of flesh and blood, the initials of his master's name.

A few days after this punishment, he was sold at public auction to Wm. Graham, with whom he lived about three years, during which time he resolved to run away to Canada, where he had learned from an Irishman, that every colored man who ran away from slavery and went there was made free by the laws of Great Britain.

This secret he communicated to another slave who agreed to come with him to Canada. Their masters worked them both hard, and fed them very scantily, and had it not been for the raccoons, opossums, and other small game which Mr. Smith and his friend used to catch in the woods after night, by the aid of a good hunting dog, they must have suffered many times almost unto starvation; but Smith had taken the precaution to train up a good hunting dog which by the by, will be seen to have proved truer to his master, than his supposed human friend, for on the night that they were to start for this country they had agreed to meet together at a certain place, where Smith did arrive at the appointed hour; but instead of finding his professed friend there he found a company of armed white men, who had been advised of the scheme by Smith's companion for the sum of one dollar in money, and a half gallon of whiskey. When Smith started from his humble cabin, that night, in pursuit of his long subverted rights, his faithful hunting dog moved on prancing before him. Smith tried to drive him back, but this proved to be all in vain; as he drew near the spot where he and his friend were to meet, the dog commenced to growl and bark, and got before his master as though he was trying to prevent him from advancing to the place where these highwaymen were lying concealed to capture the poor man who supposed that the dog was only barking at his professed friend, until his enemies had surrounded and taken him as a criminal condemned for the love of liberty. The struggle was desperate for a while between the white men against the slave and his devoted dog before they were conquered. After Smith was knocked down and completely overcome, his dog, which had bit two of the party in the contest, reluctantly fled away, or followed at a great distance; doubtless fearing that he should be killed for the active part which he had taken in defense of his master: but still bore his testimony against them by raising an awful howling when he heard the piteous cries of his master, who was stripped, tied up and flogged by the bloodthirsty party who captured him. Then they took him home and called upon the man who had betrayed him, and who was there made to repeat the whole plot over before Smith. They then and there paid the traitor, a half gallon of whiskey and one dollar in money for his base treachery to Smith. The whole crowd drank whiskey so freely, that night that they became stupid and careless about Smith, after they supposed that they had got him drunk, for they made him drink several times, after which he made them believe that he was almost dead drunk. Several of them said that he was so drunk that he would not be able to stir before the next morning, so they retired and left him lying on the kitchen floor, as they supposed drunk and asleep. About one hour afterwards when he supposed that all were asleep he bid a final adieu to the abodes of slavery and resumed his journey for Canada. He had not proceeded far from the house before he was again greeted by his devoted hunting dog, which seemed to be filled with joy at the release of his master. He endeavored to drive him back, but did not succeed, the dog was determined to follow him. When he had travelled about fifteen miles on his way he discovered the dawn of daylight breaking upon him, which forced him to seek a place of concealment during the day. He crouched by the side of an old mossy log with his dog close by his side. The dog seemed to be quite restless and to be filled with fearful apprehensions, every stick that cracked or leaf that rattled, seemed to arouse his senses to watchful care, so that Smith thought that he had better kill him, lest someone should be passing through the woods and the dog bark at them which would betray his whereabouts; having with him the rope with which the drunken party had left him tied the night before: he fastened it about the dog's neck and led him to a small tree where the poor fellow was to be executed. The dog looked up at his master while he was tying the rope, with all the intelligence of a human being and the devotion of an undaunted friend, making no resistance whatever but appeared to be willing to lay down his life for the liberation of his master. This singular conduct on the part of the dog, led him to pause and ask himself the question, whether it would be right in the sight of God for him to take the life of that dog, which had proved so true to him in the hour of danger? Just as he was reflecting over the matter he heard the yelling of a pack of blood hounds coming on his trail, so he immediately released his dog and started on a run, but did not proceed far before they were overtaken by the dogs.

To be finished in our next if the writer is not necessarily called away.

In No. 4 Smith, and his hunting dog, surrounded and kept at bay for a short time, by the blood hounds; but there being only three of them in number, they were soon killed or compelled to retreat. Smith had prepared himself with a heavy club for self-defense, and at the approach of the blood-hounds, his dog seized one of them by the neck and held him fast, which resulted in bringing the dogs all into a bloody fight, during which engagement Smith succeeded in killing two of the blood-hounds with his club, and the other was glad to escape with his life, which was in great danger. This victorious struggle, by the aid of the faithful hunting dog, endeared him to his master stronger than ever; for without his aid Smith must have been taken back into slavery. From thence they proceeded north to the Virginia and Ohio line, which occupied several nights.

They travelled by night and kept concealed by day, until they reached the above river with no other guide than the north star. In wandering up and down the stream to find a conveyance to cross he saw a large steamboat passing down the stream, which confirmed him in the belief that this was the Ohio river, having heard much about the steamboats running that river. He at length found a skiff tied to a tree on the shore, in which he ferried himself across, leaving his dog behind, but he had not proceeded far before he discovered that the dog had plunged into the steam and was close behind the boat, and succeeded in crossing even before his master.

The next morning he saw an old gentleman in the woods chopping some poles, to whom he ventured to speak, and in whom he found a friend and an abolitionist. This friend took him and his dog with him home, and after giving them some refreshments sent them on to another friend about thirty miles distance, who gave him employment for five years, and while there his valuable dog died. He was engaged in agricultural pursuits and preached occasionally among the people of color in that vicinity.

From thence he came to Huron Co., Ohio, where he purchased a small farm and lived on it about seven years, having given up all hopes of ever seeing his wife again: but in the fall of 1850, after the enactment of the Fugitive Slave Bill, the news came to him that a warrant was out for him, and that if he did not flee away to Canada, he would be taken as a slave. On the strength of this report, at a very great sacrifice, he sold his property and came to Canada.

"Testimony of James Smith, Field Hand, Enslaved in Virginia and Georgia." *Voice of the Fugitive* (Windsor, Ontario), January 15, February 26, March 11, April 22, and June 3, 1852.

A Yellow Dog

A California Story (1895)

BRET HARTE

I never knew why in the Western States of America a yellow dog should be proverbially considered the acme of canine degradation and incompetency, nor why the possession of one should seriously affect the social standing of its possessor.

But the fact being established, I think we accepted it at Rattlers Ridge without question. The matter of ownership was more difficult to settle; and although the dog I have in my mind at the present writing attached himself impartially and equally to everyone in camp, no one ventured to exclusively claim him; while, after the perpetration of any canine atrocity, everybody repudiated him with indecent haste.

"Well, I can swear he hasn't been near our shanty for weeks," or the retort, "He was last seen comin' out of YOUR cabin," expressed the eagerness with which Rattlers Ridge washed its hands of any responsibility. Yet he was by no means a common dog, nor even an unhandsome dog; and it was a singular fact that his severest critics vied with each other in narrating instances of his sagacity, insight, and agility which they themselves had witnessed.

He had been seen crossing the "flume" that spanned Grizzly Canyon at a height of nine hundred feet, on a plank six inches wide. He had tumbled down the "shoot" to the South Fork, a thousand feet below, and was found sitting on the riverbank "without a scratch, 'cept that he was lazily givin' himself with his off hind paw." He had been forgotten in a snowdrift on a Sierran shelf, and had come home in the early spring with the conceited complacency of an Alpine traveler and a plumpness alleged to have been the result of an exclusive diet of buried mail bags and their contents. He was generally believed to read the advance election posters, and disappear a day or two before the candidates and the brass band—which he hated—came to the Ridge. He was suspected of having overlooked Colonel Johnson's hand at poker, and of having conveyed to the Colonel's adversary, by a succession of barks, the danger of betting against four kings. While these statements were supplied by wholly unsupported witnesses, it was a very human weakness of Rattlers Ridge that the responsibility of corroboration was passed to the dog himself, and *he* was looked upon as a consummate liar.

"Snoopin' round yere, and CALLIN' yourself a poker sharp, are ye! Scoot, you yaller pizin!" was a common adjuration whenever the unfortunate animal intruded upon a card party. "Ef thar was a spark, an ATOM of truth in THAT DOG, I'd believe my own eyes that I saw him sittin' up and trying to magnetize a jay bird off a tree. But wot are ye goin' to do with a yaller equivocator like that?"

I have said that he was yellow—or, to use the ordinary expression, "yaller." Indeed, I am inclined to believe that much of the ignominy attached to the epithet lay in this favorite pronunciation. Men who habitually spoke of a "YELLOW bird," a "YELLOW-hammer," a "YELLOW leaf," always alluded to him as a "YALLER dog."

He certainly WAS yellow. After a bath—usually compulsory—he presented a decided gamboge streak down his back, from the top of his forehead to the stump of his tail, fading in his sides and flank to a delicate straw color. His breast, legs, and feet—when not reddened by "slumgullion," in which he was fond of wading—were white. A few attempts at ornamental decoration from the India-ink pot of the storekeeper failed, partly through the yellow dog's excessive agility, which would never give the paint time to dry on him, and partly through his success in transferring his markings to the trousers and blankets of the camp.

The size and shape of his tail—which had been cut off before his introduction to Rattlers Ridge—were favorite sources of speculation to the miners, as determining both his breed and his moral responsibility in coming into camp in that defective condition. There was a general opinion that he couldn't have looked worse with a tail, and its removal was therefore a gratuitous effrontery.

His best feature was his eyes, which were a lustrous Vandyke brown, and sparkling with intelligence; but here again he suffered from evolution through environment, and their original trustful openness was marred by the experience of watching for flying stones, sods, and passing kicks from the rear, so that the pupils were continually reverting to the outer angle of the eyelid.

Nevertheless, none of these characteristics decided the vexed question of his BREED. His speed and scent pointed to a "hound," and it is related that on one occasion he was laid on the trail of a wildcat with such success that he followed it apparently out of the State, returning at the end of two weeks footsore, but blandly contented.

Attaching himself to a prospecting party, he was sent under the same belief, "into the brush" to drive off a bear, who was supposed to be haunting the campfire. He returned in a few minutes WITH the bear, DRIVING IT INTO the unarmed circle and scattering the whole party. After this the theory of his being a hunting dog was abandoned. Yet it was said—on the usual uncorroborated evidence—that he had "put up" a quail; and his qualities as a retriever were for a long time accepted, until, during a shooting expedition for wild ducks, it was discovered that the one he had brought back had never been shot, and the party were obliged to compound damages with an adjacent settler.

His fondness for paddling in the ditches and "slumgullion" at one time suggested a water spaniel. He could swim, and would occasionally bring out of the river sticks and pieces of bark that had been thrown in; but as *he* always had to be thrown in with them, and was a good-sized dog, his aquatic reputation faded also. He remained simply "a yaller dog." What more could be said? His actual name was "Bones"—given to him, no doubt, through the provincial custom of confounding the occupation of the individual with his quality, for which it was pointed out precedent could be found in some old English family names.

But if Bones generally exhibited no preference for any particular individual in camp, he always made an exception in favor of drunkards. Even an ordinary roistering bacchanalian party brought him out from under a tree or a shed in the keenest satisfaction. He would accompany them through the long straggling street of the settlement, barking his delight at every step or misstep of the revelers, and exhibiting none of that mistrust of eye which marked his attendance upon the sane and the respectable. He accepted even their uncouth play without a snarl or a yelp, hypocritically pretending even to like it; and I conscientiously believe would have allowed a tin can to be attached to his tail if the hand that tied it on were only unsteady, and the voice that bade him "lie still" were husky with liquor. He would "see" the party cheerfully into a saloon, wait outside the door—his tongue fairly lolling from his mouth in enjoyment—until they reappeared, permit them even to tumble over him with pleasure, and then gambol away before them, heedless of awkwardly projected stones and epithets. He would afterward accompany them separately home, or lie with them at crossroads until they were assisted to their cabins. Then he would trot rakishly to his own haunt by the saloon stove, with the slightly conscious air of having been a bad dog, yet of having had a good time.

We never could satisfy ourselves whether his enjoyment arose from some merely selfish conviction that he was more *secure* with the physically and mentally incompetent, from some active sympathy with active wickedness, or from a grim sense of his own mental superiority at such moments. But the general belief leant toward his kindred sympathy as a "yaller dog" with all that was disreputable. And this was supported by another very singular canine manifestation—the "sincere flattery" of simulation or imitation.

"Uncle Billy" Riley for a short time enjoyed the position of being the camp drunkard, and at once became an object of Bones' greatest solicitude. He not only accompanied him everywhere, curled at his feet or head according to Uncle Billy's attitude at the moment, but, it was noticed, began presently to undergo a singular alteration in his own habits and appearance. From being an active, tireless scout and forager, a bold and unovertakable marauder, he became lazy and apathetic; allowed gophers to burrow under him without endeavoring to undermine the settlement in his frantic endeavors to dig them out, permitted squirrels to flash their tails at him a hundred yards away, forgot his usual caches, and left his favorite bones unburied and bleaching in the sun. His eyes grew dull, his coat lusterless, in proportion as his companion became blear-eyed and ragged; in running, his usual arrowlike directness began to deviate, and it was not unusual to meet the pair together, zigzagging up the hill. Indeed, Uncle Billy's condition could be predetermined by Bones' appearance at times when his temporary master was invisible. "The old man must have an awful jag on today," was casually remarked when an extra fluffiness and imbecility was noticeable in the passing Bones. At first it was believed that he drank also, but when careful investigation proved this hypothesis untenable, he was freely called a "derned time-servin', yaller hypocrite." Not a few advanced the opinion that if Bones did not actually lead Uncle Billy astray, he at least "slavered him over and coddled him until the old man got conceited in his wickedness." This undoubtedly led to a compulsory divorce between them, and Uncle Billy was happily dispatched to a neighboring town and a doctor.

Bones seemed to miss him greatly, ran away for two days, and was supposed to have visited him, to have been shocked at his convalescence, and to have been "cut" by Uncle Billy in his reformed character; and he returned to his old active life again, and buried his past with his forgotten bones. It was said that he was afterward detected in trying to lead an intoxicated tramp into camp after the methods employed by a blind man's dog, but was discovered in time by the—of course—uncorroborated narrator.

I should be tempted to leave him thus in his original and picturesque sin, but the same veracity which compelled me to transcribe his faults and iniquities obliges me to describe his ultimate and somewhat monotonous reformation, which came from no fault of his own.

It was a joyous day at Rattlers Ridge that was equally the advent of his change of heart and the first stagecoach that had been induced to diverge from the high road and stop regularly at our settlement. Flags were flying from the post office and Polka saloon, and Bones was flying before the brass band that he detested, when the sweetest girl in the county—Pinkey Preston—daughter of the county judge and hopelessly beloved by all Rattlers Ridge, stepped from the coach which she had glorified by occupying as an invited guest.

"What makes him run away?" she asked quickly, opening her lovely eyes in a possibly innocent wonder that anything could be found to run away from her.

"He don't like the brass band," we explained eagerly.

"How funny," murmured the girl; "is it as out of tune as all that?"

This irresistible witticism alone would have been enough to satisfy us—we did nothing but repeat it to each other all the next day—but we were positively transported when we saw her suddenly gather her dainty skirts in one hand and trip off through the red dust toward Bones, who, with his eyes over his yellow shoulder, had halted in the road, and half-turned in mingled disgust and rage at the spectacle of the descending trombone. We held our breath as she approached him. Would Bones evade her as he did us at such moments, or would he save our reputation, and consent, for the moment, to accept her as a new kind of inebriate? She came nearer; he saw her; he began to slowly quiver with excitement—his stump of a tail vibrating with such rapidity that the loss of the missing portion was scarcely noticeable. Suddenly she stopped before him, took his yellow head between her little hands, lifted it, and looked down in his handsome brown eyes with her two lovely blue ones. What passed between them in that magnetic glance no one ever knew. She returned with him; said to him casually: "We're not afraid of brass bands, are we?" to which he apparently acquiesced, at least stifling his disgust of them while he was near her—which was nearly all the time.

During the speechmaking her gloved hand and his yellow head were always near together, and at the crowning ceremony—her public checking of Yuba Bill's "waybill" on behalf of the township, with a gold pencil presented to her by the Stage Company—Bones' joy, far from knowing no bounds, seemed to know nothing but them, and he witnessed it apparently in the air. No one dared to interfere. For the first time a local pride in Bones sprang up in our hearts—and we lied to each other in his praises openly and shamelessly.

Then the time came for parting. We were standing by the door of the coach, hats in hand, as Miss Pinkey was about to step into it; Bones was waiting by her side, confidently looking into the interior, and apparently selecting his own seat on the lap of Judge Preston in the corner, when Miss Pinkey held up the sweetest of admonitory fingers. Then, taking his head between her two hands, she again looked into his brimming eyes, and said, simply, "GOOD dog," with the gentlest of emphasis on the adjective, and popped into the coach.

The six bay horses started as one, the gorgeous green and gold vehicle bounded forward, the red dust rose behind, and the yellow dog danced in and out of it to the very outskirts of the settlement. And then he soberly returned.

A day or two later he was missed—but the fact was afterward known that he was at Spring Valley, the county town where Miss Preston lived, and he was forgiven. A week afterward he was missed again, but this time for a longer period, and then a pathetic letter arrived from Sacramento for the storekeeper's wife.

"Would you mind," wrote Miss Pinkey Preston, "asking some of your boys to come over here to Sacramento and bring back Bones? I don't mind having the dear dog walk out with me at Spring Valley, where everyone knows me; but here he DOES make one so noticeable, on account of HIS COLOR. I've got scarcely a frock that he agrees with. He don't go with my pink muslin, and that lovely buff tint he makes three shades lighter. You know yellow is so trying."

A consultation was quickly held by the whole settlement, and a deputation sent to Sacramento to relieve the unfortunate girl. We were all quite indignant with Bones—but, oddly enough, I think it was greatly tempered with our new pride in him. While he was with us alone, his peculiarities had been scarcely appreciated, but the recurrent phrase "that yellow dog that they keep at the Rattlers" gave us a mysterious importance along the countryside, as if we had secured a "mascot" in some zoological curiosity.

This was further indicated by a singular occurrence. A new church had been built at the crossroads, and an eminent divine had come from San Francisco to preach the opening sermon. After a careful examination of the camp's wardrobe, and some felicitous exchange of apparel, a few of us were deputed to represent "Rattlers" at the Sunday service. In our white ducks, straw hats, and flannel blouses, we were sufficiently picturesque and distinctive as "honest miners" to be shown off in one of the front pews.

Seated near the prettiest girls, who offered us their hymn books—in the cleanly odor of fresh pine shavings, and ironed muslin, and blown over by the spices of our own woods through the open windows, a deep sense of the abiding peace of Christian communion settled upon us. At this supreme moment someone murmured in an awe-stricken whisper:

"WILL you look at Bones?"

We looked. Bones had entered the church and gone up in the gallery through a pardonable ignorance and modesty; but, perceiving his mistake, was now calmly walking along the gallery rail before the astounded worshipers. Reaching the end, he paused for a moment, and carelessly looked down. It was about fifteen feet to the floor below—the simplest jump in the world for the mountain-bred Bones. Daintily, gingerly, lazily, and yet with a conceited airiness of manner, as if, humanly speaking, he had one leg in his pocket and were doing it on three, he cleared the distance, dropping just in front of the chancel, without a sound, turned himself around three times, and then lay comfortably down.

Three deacons were instantly in the aisle, coming up before the eminent divine, who, we fancied, wore a restrained smile. We heard the hurried whispers: "Belongs to them." "Quite a local institution here, you know." "Don't like to offend sensibilities;" and the minister's prompt "By no means," as he went on with his service.

A short month ago we would have repudiated Bones; today we sat there in slightly supercilious attitudes, as if to indicate that any affront offered to Bones would be an insult to ourselves, and followed by our instantaneous withdrawal in a body.

All went well, however, until the minister, lifting the large Bible from the communion table and holding it in both hands before him, walked toward a reading stand by the altar rails. Bones uttered a distinct growl. The minister stopped.

We, and we alone, comprehended in a flash the whole situation. The Bible was nearly the size and shape of one of those soft clods of sod which we were in the playful habit of launching at Bones when he lay half-asleep in the sun, in order to see him cleverly evade it.

We held our breath. What was to be done? But the opportunity belonged to our leader, Jeff Briggs—a confoundedly good-looking fellow, with the golden mustache of a northern viking and the curls of an Apollo. Secure in his beauty and bland in his self-conceit, he rose from the pew, and stepped before the chancel rails.

"I would wait a moment, if I were you, sir," he said, respectfully, "and you will see that he will go out quietly."

"What is wrong?" whispered the minister in some concern.

"He thinks you are going to heave that book at him, sir, without giving him a fair show, as we do."

The minister looked perplexed, but remained motionless, with the book in his hands. Bones arose, walked halfway down the aisle, and vanished like a yellow flash!

With this justification of his reputation, Bones disappeared for a week. At the end of that time we received a polite note from Judge Preston, saying that the dog had become quite domiciled in their house, and begged that the camp, without yielding up their valuable PROPERTY in him, would allow him to remain at Spring Valley for an indefinite time; that both the judge and his daughter—with whom Bones was already an old friend—would be glad if the members of the camp would visit their old favorite whenever they desired, to assure themselves that he was well cared for.

I am afraid that the bait thus ingenuously thrown out had a good deal to do with our ultimate yielding. However, the reports of those who visited Bones were wonderful and marvelous. He was residing there in state, lying on rugs in the drawing-room, coiled up under the judicial desk in the judge's study, sleeping regularly on the mat outside Miss Pinkey's bedroom door, or lazily snapping at flies on the judge's lawn.

"He's as yaller as ever," said one of our informants, "but it don't somehow seem to be the same back that we used to break clods over in the old time, just to see him scoot out of the dust."

And now I must record a fact which I am aware all lovers of dogs will indignantly deny, and which will be furiously bayed at by every faithful hound since the days of Ulysses. Bones not only FORGOT but absolutely CUT US! Those who called upon the judge in "store clothes" he would perhaps casually notice, but he would sniff at them as if detecting and resenting them under their superficial exterior. The rest he simply paid no attention to. The more familiar term of "Bonesy"—formerly applied to him, as in our rare moments of endearment—produced no response. This pained, I think, some of the more youthful of us; but, through some strange human weakness, it also increased the camp's respect for him. Nevertheless, we spoke of him familiarly to strangers at the very moment he ignored us. I am afraid that we also took some pains to point out that he was getting fat and unwieldy, and losing his elasticity, implying covertly that his choice was a mistake and his life a failure.

A year after, he died, in the odor of sanctity and respectability, being found one morning coiled up and stiff on the mat outside Miss Pinkey's door. When the news was conveyed to us, we asked permission, the camp being in a prosperous condition, to erect a stone over his grave. But when it came to the inscription we could only think of the two words murmured to him by Miss Pinkey, which we always believe effected his conversion:

"GOOD Dog!"

Bret Harte, "A Yellow Dog: A California Story" *McClure's Magazine* 5, no. 3 (August 1895): 235–39.

"A somewhat nonplussed terrier." Thomas W. Knox. *Dog Stories and Dog Lore.*
New York: Cassell and Company, 1887. Image courtesy of Special Collections and
Archives, James B. Duke Library, Furman University.

A Dog's Ghost

A Story from the Tobique River, New Brunswick (1892)

"GEOFF"

Snow! Snow! Snow! For the last three days the air had been full of it; and yet, as I stood gazing out of the window, those eternal flakes came whirling in myriads, each one as if in gleeful pursuit of its predecessor. Not a sound broke the stillness outside, and here was I, landed at a small hotel, the only one in the little village of Andover, on the Tobique River, New Brunswick.

My employers had sent me up from St. John, with instructions to go back sixty-five miles from this place to the shanties of a "jobber," who was getting out logs for us, and report.

"Well, mister," said a voice behind me, which I recognized as that of mine host, "there ain't much chance of further progress. Seems to me we're agoing to have a fall like that of '54, when the snow was thirteen feet deep on the level. A terrible place for blizzards this 'ere."

And off he went, muttering away to himself and trying to get a puff or two of smoke from a black, played-out, old brier-pipe, which certainly for the last three days, as far as my knowledge went, had never left his lips, except at meal-times, and then only for a short interval.

Thoroughly disgusted at my delay, I turned away from the window and sought consolation, after my host's lead, in the soothing effects of tobacco-smoke.

After dinner, things looked a bit brighter. The snow had nearly ceased falling, and far away in the northwest a patch of blue sky had made its appearance. The wind had sprung up and was momentarily increasing. The night turned out bitterly cold, with a bright moon, and the wind fell almost as quickly as it had risen.

The next morning I woke up with the sun streaming into my bedroom, and the temperature of the apartment about that of a refrigerator. I was soon undergoing the process of thawing out before the large dining-room stove, enjoying its cheerful influence, as the fire roared and crackled, and shed a ruddy glow from the many cracks in its ancient sides.

"Well," said I to my host, "how am I to get on now?"

"Must wait till the roads are broken," he replied.

"Can't!" I cried. But he only shrugged his shoulders.

Ten o'clock found me all ready for a start. After walking all day long, just stopping at a farm-house for a meal, I was pushing forward, thoroughly fagged out by such unusual exertion and exercise, and as far as I could judge from the description given me of the road, I judged that I was about three miles from my destination for the night. It was about eight o'clock, and the moon pierced through the shade of spruce trees that lined each side of the road, filling the path before me with shadows varied and grotesque. The wind, which had sprung up into a gentle breeze, sighed sadly through the trees, coming and going in a fitful manner. No sound but this broke the stillness; indeed so still was it that the creaking and soft "whish" of my snowshoes, slowly dragged along by wearied feet, seemed to be the echo of following footsteps, and, involuntarily, with suspicious eye, I would look over my shoulder, expecting to see, I knew not what. Only those who have experienced it can know the utter loneliness of being by one's self in a Canadian forest on a winter's night.

I tried whistling to throw off my nervousness, but to no effect. The whistle, through want of breath from exertion, ended in a nearly soundless gasp. And this sound again, although I knew it was caused by myself, seemed to come from a distance, and brought with it a suggestion of wolves.

Suddenly there came the short, sharp bark of a dog.

In an instant all my fears vanished, and with renewed energy I pushed forward. Ahead was a clearing, and one of those quaint and very old stone houses— probably built by some of the first settlers.

The house stood back from the road, in an open space of some few acres, backed by the dark, dismal wood and a snake-fence.

Ahead of me on the road I distinguished clearly the figure of a dog, evidently the author of the bark I had heard. His long, white hair gleamed in the moonbeams like silver. I can yet see in my imagination the bright, phosphorescent-like light of his eyes as they turned towards me.

There was no light from the house, and, as I approached, the dog retreated over the snake-fence, taking up his stand on the cottage doorstep.

As I came nearer my spirits once more dropped to zero. The place was falling to pieces and evidently devoid of occupants. The dog stood in the doorway. I whistled to him and used all the usual terms of endearment to attract him to my side, but he made no advances, only standing there monotonously wagging his bushy tail, and every now and then giving tongue to another of those short, sharp barks which had at first attracted my attention. I left him, disgusted at his want of manners towards strangers, and pushed on discouraged. I looked back over my shoulder once or twice to see if he was following, but there was no evidence of his appearance.

At last lights gleamed out of the darkness ahead, and I emerged from the gloom of the woods into a large clearing. There stood a farm-house, hazy in the moonlight, with its long array of barns, stables, etc., the smoke lazily curling up from its chimney into the cold, clear sky, and the ruddy light from its window speaking of warmth and comfort within. It was not long before I was feasting upon a substantial supper.

My host, a tall man of herculean build, with sandy hair, long beard, and keen blue eyes, showed Scotch extraction in his high cheek-bones and broad accent. He sat over by the stove, contemplatively mending a piece of harness, and puffing away at a short clay pipe.

I found him a most agreeable companion, modest in his opinions, well read, and of an inquiring turn of mind. We discussed the lumbering prospects, the farming resources of that part of the country, etc., etc. Then, at last, our conversation drifted on to the subject of my day's walk, and incidentally I mentioned the old, ruined house, and the meeting with that unfriendly Pomeranian dog.

I noticed his face grew more serious, and his answers to my inquiries haphazard and hardly to the point.

"That was no dog you saw," he said.

"What!" said I, "no dog? Why, man, you must be mistaken. I saw him as distinctly as I now see you!"

He only shook his head slowly.

"It was a dog once," he said, "ten years ago, but it's the ghost of a dog now."

Could anything be more preposterous—the ghost of a dog! Who ever heard of such a thing, thought I; and yet, in a moment flashed across my mind's eye the appearance of that animal, as he stood there on the dismantled-doorstep of that lonely building, the moon pouring its rays down upon his long, white coat, and then, those uncanny phosphorescent, piercing eyes staring through his tangled mane.

"Yes," my host continued, "that was a dog ten years ago, but he died then, and he's a ghost now. Ah, there is a queer story in connection with that ghost dog, and if you'd like to hear it I'll tell it to you. Mind, I don't expect you to believe it; few do, but I know it to be true. S'pose you don't believe in ghosts? After hearing my story you shall judge for yourself whether that was a ghost dog or not."

* * * * *

After this introduction he related the following:

Some fifteen years ago—I am thirty-five now—an aunt of mine who owned this property, died, leaving it to me. I then came up here for the first time to look over the place, and although it had been much neglected, it had the making of a snug little property, the land being first-rate. I determined to locate, and with a younger brother of mine came up here to live. In those days the ruined house you passed tonight was owned and inhabited by an old man named James Meikle.

He had been there since the earliest remembrances of any one living on the Tobique, and had owned a considerable amount of property round and about. This property by degrees he sold, but what became of the money gotten by these sales no one knew; he never seemed to go down to Andover, our nearest village, the only places from which he could send a deposit down to the bank, and he got the reputation of having fabulous wealth hidden away in that old house.

Certainly he could not spend much on himself, for he was always in rags, picking up any old thrown-off scraps of clothing he could find, and patching these into garments for himself as best he could. Then, as for food, old Meikle grew a few vegetables on that small patch of ground in front of his house, and these, together with what he could beg, borrow or steal from his neighbors, formed his subsistence.

I soon got to know the old chap, but could never get any conversation out of him more than a good-morning, so that I remained as much in ignorance about the man and his position as anyone else. No one, to my knowledge, had ever been in his cottage; he always scrupulously barred the door against all visitors. In those days he owned that white dog you saw tonight, a surly sort of animal enough, always ready to sneak up behind you, when you were passing and not on the lookout, grabbing the unwary by the leg, after the manner of such curs.

Ten years back the dog died; whether he was killed or not on account of these little civilities and habits of snapping, I can't say, but certain it is that the old man took the loss of his beast very much to heart. I saw him myself, happening to pass at the time, burying the poor remains beneath that spruce tree on the right of the house, with many tears and lamentations.

After this old Meikle kept more to himself than ever. Sometimes a month at a time would elapse between the intervals of my meeting him, though I used to pass his house almost every day.

So two years rolled by, the old man still keeping his seclusion, but in other respects, as an occasional glimpse of him told me, not materially changing in appearance. A dirtier old "coon" I never saw in my life. His face, covered for the most part by a grizzled and matted beard, was almost as black as an Indian's and his whole appearance utterly neglected and forlorn.

One night, about eight years ago, I was returning from Andover, having been down to sell some hay. It was winter, and the roads in perfect condition. The moon shone bright, and not a breath of air stirred the frosty atmosphere. The horses, knowing they were near home, got along at a splendid pace, and the sleigh, lightened of its morning's load, simply flew over the road's frozen surface. I was all alone, heartily tired and hungry after my long drive. I consoled myself with the thoughts of the cozy supper awaiting me beside a warm stove. Mary— that's my wife's name,—and I had only been married two months. Just as we came out of the woods into Meikle's clearance, and were passing his old house, what was my surprise to see a white Pomeranian dog bound over the snake-fence and rush to the heads of my team, jumping up and barking furiously, as if in an attempt to stop them. The dog was an exact double of that formerly owned by Meikle, which as I told you had been killed two years before. I thought it very strange at the moment, but considered that the old man must have got another of the same breed.

The horses kept on trotting as fast as ever, being accustomed to dogs, and pawing at this one with their front hoofs as they stepped out.

At last, seeing, I suppose, that it was hopeless to try and stop us in this way, the animal came around to the side of the sleigh, leaping up and still continuing to bark, looking into my face with flashing, intelligent eyes, and saying as plainly as a dog could say, that he had some news to impart.

I thought it singular and pulled up for a moment. As soon as the horses came to a stand he ceased barking, trotted a few yards back down the road, wagging his tail, then stopping, looking around as if expecting me to follow him. I have always had a great belief in the sagacity of animals, dogs in particular, and this chap showed so plainly that he wanted me to return the way I had come, I determined to indulge him out of mere curiosity to see what he was up to. So, turning the horses, I drove down towards old Meikle's place. The dog trotting on ahead seemed perfectly satisfied now, wagging his tail vigorously, and looking around every now and again as if to make certain that we were following.

When once more in the clearance and not more than fifteen yards from the cottage, my canine guide turned sharp to right, bounded over the snake-fence before the house and—completely disappeared.

I pulled up sharply, looking around in vain for the animal; he was nowhere to be seen. How he could so mysteriously have vanished from sight was altogether beyond my comprehension. I got down and carefully examined the snow all around the place, but not a track could I discover on its light surface.

It was certainly very curious, and I must confess that I felt more than startled, if not actually afraid. The night, as I said, was perfectly calm, the only sound that disturbed its stillness was the panting of my tired horses and the throbbing of my own heart. Try as I might I could not stop its fast beating, nor conceal from myself the fact that I was at least very much startled. No light shone out from the cottage, and I concluded old Meikle must be in bed, and yet, another strange thing that struck me was that no smoke curled up from the rickety old chimney.

Could Meikle be away? I certainly had not seen him for over a month, but as I said just now, that was nothing unusual.

I shouted his name at the top of my voice. No response, only the sound of my own re-echoed through the woods and died away softly in the distance. Determining to return next day and find out both as to the old man and dog, I got into the sleigh and turned my horses' heads towards home. Hardly had they turned when the most anguished howl I ever heard in my life arose from the cottage, and echoing through the woods gradually died away in the distance, ending in a wail of abject misery.

The horses heard it too, and, terrified out of their lives, plunged forward and bolted, never stopping until they had reached the door of their stables.

Never, as long as I live, shall I forget that furious gallop through the shadows of the woods. Thoroughly unnerved I attended to the wants of the horses, putting them into their stable and rubbing them down, endeavoring to the best of my ability to re-assure them. Then, having given the beasts their supper, and seen that all was snug for the night, I barred the door and went into the house. My wife noticed my pale face and disturbed manner, but I thought it better not to tell her what had occurred till I had to some extent cleared up the mystery of the night.

Next morning the snow was falling gently in large flakes, covering as it were with a veil the landscape around.

My brother was still living with us then, but I had not seen him the night before. He laughed at the whole thing, saying that my nerves were a bit unstrung by the fatigues of the day, and that no doubt old Meikle had a new dog which I had not seen before, and as for the howl, the animal was just begging to be let into the cottage, naturally not wanting to be left out in the cold all night, and the loneliness of the place, together with my nervousness, had made me imagine that this brute's howl was unlike any other dog's. Finally, as to there being no response to my call, old Meikle was in the first place deaf and probably never heard, it, and in the second place was of such a kind as totally to disregard it if he had. Then the horses got tired of waiting, bolted—and I imagined the rest.

So my brother Andrew explained it away. But I myself thought otherwise, and at length persuaded him to agree to accompany me to Meikle's place. After breakfast we started on foot, the snow still falling, though lightly, and the day warm with a probability of brighter weather later on, betokened by the broken state of the clouds. A southerly wind blew gently through the woods, murmuring among the branches, the foliage was covered with a soft coating of the clinging snow, and every now and then a bird or a squirrel with sharp little "chirp" in striking against the boughs would send down a shower as of white feathers, leaving the branch trembling and dripping green in the soft light. Andrew chatted away gayly, laughing at what he called my "vain imaginings" of the night before; but I remained silent, foreboding I knew not what.

At last we arrived, and saw the walls of the building standing out through the snow. We climbed the fence in front, and knee-deep in snow made our way up to the door. Here we knocked loudly, but no answer greeted us from within. We waited, then again and again hammered a summons on the wooden panel, but no one responded.

We tried the latch, but the door was locked. I climbed up to the window-sill and attempted to look in, but a piece of sacking hung on the inside obscured the view, the same with the window on the other side of the door.

At last we gave up our attempts on the front of the house and went around to the back, fully determined to run the risk of forcing an entrance. At the back there was one solitary window, open, and the sacking which covered this moved slowly backwards and forwards, swayed by the light wind. On examination we discovered one pane of glass broken in its frame, and to the jarred fragments still remaining in the putty a small piece of cloth adhered.

Here, then, was our chance of gaining an entrance. I noticed that Andrew rather hung back, and I certainly did not like going in first. For aught we could tell, Meikle inside might take us for robbers, and use his old flint-lock musket. I had sometimes seen him shooting birds around his garden in summer-time.

We listened—not a sound within. At last curiosity overcame prudence, and I drew aside the sacking and looked in. The room was small, faintly lighted, and apparently without the least bit of furniture. Here and there the rough boarding of the floor was pulled up, and a door opposite to the window, closed, evidently led into another apartment. Slowly and cautiously, followed by Andrew, I crept in. Cautiously we picked our way over the gaps in the flooring to the door on the opposite side, and here again paused and listened, but, re-assured by the stillness of the farther room, I opened it. At first nothing could be made out, owing to the darkness, but after a time I could see what might be a bed, a table and a chair. Slowly moving to the window, my foot slipped on something soft and I fell on my hands and knees.

At this moment Andrew tore down the sacking which covered the casement.

A cold, dim light stole in—and I see him now, in my mind's eye, standing there with staring eyes, gazing down at something just behind me. Good God! as I looked around what a sight met my eye. Lying there on the floor at my back was a human form, both arms thrown behind its head, surrounded by a dark pool of blood. Terrified, I rose to my feet, and there I saw the figure once more of that white dog standing in the doorway, as if to cut off our retreat. His eyes, ablaze with that unearthly fire, seemed to pierce my very soul.

Still looking at him, fascinated by those luminous orbs, his form gradually, very gradually, died away from sight, and a blast as of a piercing wind chilled me through and through. Spasmodically I turned my gaze again towards the face of that form on the floor, and recognized the features of old Meikle. A dark stain marked the side of his cheek from the forehead downwards, and now I could distinguish the gleaming blade of an axe, with its long handle upraised, embedded in the skull.

The fingers of his hands were entangled in his blood-matted hair, in a last death agony.

Andrew stood at the window like a statue, his features frozen into an expression of horror. Then with uncertain footsteps I moved towards the door leading out to the road, and finding the key in the lock turned it and threw it open. The familiar sound of my voice seemed once more to awaken my brother to his senses, and with one bound he was by my side, out in the daylight and 'neath the still falling snow.

Both of us were overcome by this awful scene. Certainly a murder had been committed, and we concluded that the best thing to do would be to go straight down to Andover and there report the affair to the authorities. Of course, as we would have to be gone all night, the facts must be concealed from my wife, as she and the servant girl would be alone and terribly frightened at the idea of their close proximity to that scene of blood with its attendant dog spirit. Having so arranged for our future course of action, we were about to start for home, both equally determined not to enter that cottage again on any account, when once more the quietude was broken by that awful howl I had heard the night before. In an instant I was over the fence and by Andrew's side.

The match dropped from his hands, and the pipe from his lips, his feet hardly seemed to touch the ground, as he disappeared up the road into the woods in rapid flight. I can assure you, sir, I was not long after him.

The air was full of that terrible cry; and for months afterwards I would wake at night, sit up in bed and listen, imagining that I heard those anguished wails coming again through the stillness.

The rest of my story is soon told. The same day Andrew and myself drove down to Andover, going by a back road five miles out of our way to avoid that cottage, for neither of us would face the possibilities we might encounter in passing it.

The Andover people sent up a couple of constables, and a detective soon put in an appearance from St. John.

They discovered, beyond all question, that the poor old man was murdered—a thing Andrew and I could have told them from the first; but you know what the police are. The whole place had been ransacked, the flooring torn up, hearthstone lifted, and in fact everything turned upside down, in a search for his supposed hidden treasure. The body was buried by the side of the Pomeranian dog, under the spruce tree, and although by means of that piece of cloth which I told you we noticed on the jagged edge of the window-sill, and which the police would never have seen had not Andrew pointed it out to them, a man was traced to Woodstock, yet there all clew was lost, and the perpetrator of this awful deed has never yet been discovered. Nor was there any store of wealth found in the cottage, which was carefully searched, so that if there really had been any, the murderer must have come upon it, and carried off his ill-gotten gains with him.

Thus my host ended his story. "But," said I, "did none of the people engaged on the inquiry and around the cottage see anything of that dog?"

"Ah," he replied hastily, "I forgot to tell you. When we were burying poor old Meikle's remains, and had lowered the coffin into the grave, filled up the hole with earth and turned away, the burial service being over, it was evening, and six of us were doing the work, suddenly Mr. Sturder, the parson from Andover, happening to look back, said, 'Who owns that dog over there?'

"We all turned around, and there sure enough was the white Pomeranian, standing on the freshly turned sods and looking towards us. Those phosphorescent, glowing orbs that I so well remember fixed upon our little party—there is no earthly fire with which you can compare that light. And as our gaze was still riveted, dimmer and dimmer grew the brightness of those eyes, and more and more shadowy that white figure till it had totally disappeared. With a shiver we turned aside, and as our little party wound its way through the darkening woods to my house, you may be sure we kept very close together and repeatedly cast anxious glances behind us as I narrated to them the story of my experiences with the dog, hitherto concealed by Andrew and myself, for fear of the ridicule of our hearers. Since then never again, although the dog is often seen by strangers like yourself, and frequently by those living around here, has that agonized howl been heard.

"For my part, I think that the faithful animal, true even after death to its master, having succeeded in bringing to light that awful crime, now rests more content. If the perpetrator of the dark deed shall once again pass by, who can say what may happen?"

And as my host ceased speaking, a silence fell upon us, the old clock still ticked on with its monotonous stroke, and the sleeping infant's regular breathing came soft and hushed to our ears. The red glow from the coals shone out brightly through the stove door, and the lamp after one or two spasmodic flickers of light left us nearly in darkness. We relighted our pipes for a last whiff ere going to bed, our minds too full of that story to speak.

Geoff. "A Dog's Ghost: A Story from the Tobique River, New Brunswick." *Outing* 21 (March 1892): 481–86.

Memoirs of a Yellow Dog (1906)

O. HENRY

I don't suppose it will knock any of you people off your perch to read a contribution from an animal. Mr. Kipling and a good many others have demonstrated the fact that animals can express themselves in remunerative English, and no magazine goes to press nowadays without an animal story in it, except the old-style monthlies that are still running pictures of Bryan and the Mont Pelee horror.

But you needn't look for any stuck-up literature in my piece, such as Bearoo, the bear, and Snakoo, the snake, and Tammanoo, the tiger, talk in the jungle books. A yellow dog that's spent most of his life in a cheap New York flat, sleeping in a corner on an old sateen underskirt (the one she spilled port wine on at the Lady Longshoremen's banquet), mustn't be expected to perform any tricks with the art of speech.

I was born a yellow pup; date, locality, pedigree and weight unknown. The first thing I can recollect, an old woman had me in a basket at Broadway and Twenty-third trying to sell me to a fat lady. Old Mother Hubbard was boosting me to beat the band as a genuine Pomeranian-Hambletonian-Red-Irish-Cochin-China-Stoke-Pogis fox terrier. The fat lady chased a V around among the samples of gros grain flannelette in her shopping bag till she cornered it, and gave up. From that moment I was a pet—a mamma's own wootsey squidlums. Say, gentle reader, did you ever have a 200-pound woman breathing a flavour of Camembert cheese and Peau d'Espagne pick you up and wallop her nose all over you, remarking all the time in an Emma Eames tone of voice: "Oh, oo's um oodlum, doodlum, woodlum, toodlum, bitsy-witsy skoodlums?"

From a pedigreed yellow pup I grew up to be an anonymous yellow cur looking like a cross between an Angora cat and a box of lemons. But my mistress never tumbled. She thought that the two primeval pups that Noah chased into the ark were but a collateral branch of my ancestors. It took two policemen to keep her from entering me at the Madison Square Garden for the Siberian bloodhound prize.

I'll tell you about that flat. The house was the ordinary thing in New York, paved with Parian marble in the entrance hall and cobblestones above the first floor. Our flat was three—well, not flights—climbs up. My mistress rented it unfurnished, and put in the regular things—1903 antique upholstered parlor set, oil chromo of geishas in a Harlem tea house, rubber plant and husband.

By Sirius! there was a biped I felt sorry for. He was a little man with sandy hair and whiskers a good deal like mine. Henpecked?—well, toucans and flamingoes and pelicans all had their bills in him. He wiped the dishes and listened to my mistress tell about the cheap, ragged things the lady with the squirrel-skin coat on the second floor hung out on her line to dry. And every evening while she was getting supper she made him take me out on the end of a string for a walk.

If men knew how women pass the time when they are alone they'd never marry. Laura Lean Jibbey, peanut brittle, a little almond cream on the neck muscles, dishes unwashed, half an hour's talk with the iceman, reading a package of old letters, a couple of pickles and two bottles of malt extract, one hour peeking through a hole in the window shade into the flat across the air-shaft—that's about all there is to it. Twenty minutes before time for him to come home from work she straightens up the house, fixes her rat so it won't show, and gets out a lot of sewing for a ten-minute bluff.

I led a dog's life in that flat. 'Most all day I lay there in my corner watching that fat woman kill time. I slept sometimes and had pipe dreams about being out chasing cats into basements and growling at old ladies with black mittens, as a dog was intended to do. Then she would pounce upon me with a lot of that drivelling poodle palaver and kiss me on the nose—but what could I do? A dog can't chew cloves.

I began to feel sorry for Hubby, dog my cats if I didn't. We looked so much alike that people noticed it when we went out; so we shook the streets that Morgan's cab drives down, and took to climbing the piles of last December's snow on the streets where cheap people live.

One evening when we were thus promenading, and I was trying to look like a prize St. Bernard, and the old man was trying to look like he wouldn't have murdered the first organ-grinder he heard play Mendelssohn's wedding-march, I looked up at him and said, in my way: "What are you looking so sour about, you oakum trimmed lobster? She don't kiss you. You don't have to sit on her lap and listen to talk that would make the book of a musical comedy sound like the maxims of Epictetus. You ought to be thankful you're not a dog. Brace up, Benedick, and bid the blues begone."

The matrimonial mishap looked down at me with almost canine intelligence in his face.

"Why, doggie," says he, "good doggie. You almost look like you could speak. What is it, doggie—Cats?"

Cats! Could speak!

But, of course, he couldn't understand. Humans were denied the speech of animals. The only common ground of communication upon which dogs and men can get together is in fiction.

In the flat across the hall from us lived a lady with a black-and-tan terrier. Her husband strung it and took it out every evening, but he always came home cheerful and whistling. One day I touched noses with the black-and-tan in the hall, and I struck him for an elucidation.

"See, here, Wiggle-and-Skip," I says, "you know that it ain't the nature of a real man to play dry nurse to a dog in public. I never saw one leashed to a bow-wow yet that didn't look like he'd like to lick every other man that looked at him. But your boss comes in every day as perky and set up as an amateur prestidigitator doing the egg trick. How does he do it? Don't tell me he likes it."

"Him?" says the black-and-tan. "Why, he uses Nature's Own Remedy. He gets spifflicated. At first when we go out he's as shy as the man on the steamer who would rather play pedro when they make 'em all jackpots. By the time we've been in eight saloons he don't care whether the thing on the end of his line is a dog or a catfish. I've lost two inches of my tail trying to sidestep those swinging doors."

The pointer I got from that terrier—vaudeville please copy—set me to thinking.

One evening about 6 o'clock my mistress ordered him to get busy and do the ozone act for Lovey. I have concealed it until now, but that is what she called me. The black-and-tan was called "Tweetness." I consider that I have the bulge on him as far as you could chase a rabbit. Still "Lovey" is something of a nomenclatural tin can on the tail of one's self respect.

At a quiet place on a safe street I tightened the line of my custodian in front of an attractive, refined saloon. I made a dead-ahead scramble for the doors, whining like a dog in the press despatches that lets the family know that little Alice is bogged while gathering lilies in the brook.

"Why, darn my eyes," says the old man, with a grin; "darn my eyes if the saffron-coloured son of a seltzer lemonade ain't asking me in to take a drink. Lemme see—how long's it been since I saved shoe leather by keeping one foot on the foot-rest? I believe I'll—"

I knew I had him. Hot Scotches he took, sitting at a table. For an hour he kept the Campbells coming. I sat by his side rapping for the waiter with my tail, and eating free lunch such as mamma in her flat never equalled with her homemade truck bought at a delicatessen store eight minutes before papa comes home.

When the products of Scotland were all exhausted except the rye bread the old man unwound me from the table leg and played me outside like a fisherman plays a salmon. Out there he took off my collar and threw it into the street.

"Poor doggie," says he; "good doggie. She shan't kiss you any more. 'S a darned shame. Good doggie, go away and get run over by a street car and be happy."

I refused to leave. I leaped and frisked around the old man's legs happy as a pug on a rug.

"You old flea-headed woodchuck-chaser," I said to him—"you moon-baying, rabbit-pointing, eggstealing old beagle, can't you see that I don't want to leave you? Can't you see that we're both Pups in the Wood and the missis is the cruel uncle after you with the dish towel and me with the flea liniment and a pink bow to tie on my tail. Why not cut that all out and be pards forever more?"

Maybe you'll say he didn't understand—maybe he didn't. But he kind of got a grip on the Hot Scotches, and stood still for a minute, thinking.

"Doggie," says he, finally, "we don't live more than a dozen lives on this earth, and very few of us live to be more than 300. If I ever see that flat any more I'm a flat, and if you do you're flatter; and that's no flattery. I'm offering 60 to 1 that Westward Ho wins out by the length of a dachshund."

There was no string, but I frolicked along with my master to the Twenty-third street ferry. And the cats on the route saw reason to give thanks that prehensile claws had been given them.

On the Jersey side my master said to a stranger who stood eating a currant bun: "Me and my doggie, we are bound for the Rocky Mountains."

But what pleased me most was when my old man pulled both of my ears until I howled, and said: "You common, monkey-headed, rat-tailed, sulphur-coloured son of a door mat, do you know what I'm going to call you?"

I thought of "Lovey," and I whined dolefully.

"I'm going to call you 'Pete,'" says my master; and if I'd had five tails I couldn't have done enough wagging to do justice to the occasion.

O. Henry, "Memoirs of a Yellow Dog." 1906. In *The Four Million*. New York: Doubleday, Page, 1915, 110–18.

"Illustration to accompany a pattern for a crochet jacket for a greyhound."
Godey's Lady's Book and Magazine 86 (May 1873). Image courtesy of Special
Collections and Archives, James B. Duke Library, Furman University.

A Dog's Story (1898)

H. A. FREEMAN

This is the story the dog told. How I was able to understand him and put it in words is my own affair. The dog told it for truth; and it is true—every word.— THE WRITER.

It was an ugly day; one of those b-r-r-r-r days when the wet wind blows a chill right into the hollow places in a body's bones. It was too cold for rain and too wet to be sleeting.

Sometimes dogs are lucky enough to have free range of a warm kitchen or a comfortable bar-room on such days. I had my choice of both, fortunately for my master, as you shall see.

He was not a kind or happy man, but he was good to me, and I gave up my life for him and his.

What more could anyone do?—and I'm only a dog.

I never was a very bright dog. I have always been rather serious and what men call psychic, having been born on a mountain top where both men and animals live close to nature. I have deeper instincts and can see farther into things than can these frisky, fly-about dogs that care only for a romp or something to bark at. And when I come within any man's aura—that invisible emanation of good or evil thought that every man gives off insensibly—I know instantly more about his disposition than his closest friends can discover in a lifetime.

Men cannot sense these sure tell-tales, but serious dogs can, and it speaks well for a dog's fidelity when he sticks faithfully to a man immeasurably beneath him—as are most dogs' masters.

That is why I liked my master though men did not, and why I disliked his false friend though he stood high in reputation among men. I let him stroke and pat me and I ate whatever he offered me though I distrusted him. Sycophantic, you think? Well, I'm only a dog.

Besides, Lackwill was not very much to blame for his vicious thoughts and desires, any more than my master was for his moroseness and fits of melancholy. Let me tell you something. Dogs see things that men know little about. Did you know that the space about you is thickly peopled with invisibles? Did you know that the ether which envelops the earth is alive with vampires, and spooks, and deevs, and elementals or part-souls, the enemies of mortal man? Well, it is; and every dog knows it and senses them; and so do horses and deer and elephants. People say that dogs bark at the moon. That's a foolish fancy. The moon is innocent enough. It's only a dull mass of cold deadness. But the things that make it their home would cause your flesh to creep if you could see them as we dogs do.

We do not fear them, for we have only animal souls and they cannot harm us, but we hate them for the evil they work upon mankind. I have seen them swarm about the head of a "sensitive"—a medium, men called him—and fill him full of fiendish thoughts and evil impulses. Many a good man have they hunted to death or worse, and many a man has been hanged or sent to prison who should have been protected from them before his crime rather than punished afterward.

The day I speak of was just suited for the air-dwellers or evil elementals. On dull and gloomy days when the sun is powerless to dispel them, they can reach a sensitive as easily as at night, and on this day they drove Clowder, my master, nearly to desperation.

They had controlled him for years, had these imps of madness, and a weary life they gave him. His doctors said he was morbid, which is only a word and doesn't mean anything; and they gave him pills for a sluggish liver. Pills to cure the attacks of invisible air-demons!

What do doctors know, anyway? I went whimpering with toothache to one once and he drove me away lest I should give him hydrophobia. Just as if anything could make him hate water worse than he already did. But what's the use of talking? They are men and think they know—and I'm only a dog.

On that day Clowder had been unusually unhappy and Lackwill more than ordinarily attentive to pretty Mrs. Clowder, my master's young wife.

He had even gone so far as to call her Fanny once or twice, as if by accident, in the course of conversation. But these slips occurred only when my master was absent from the room, and Mrs. Clowder didn't seem to notice them.

Four doors around the corner from our home was Kelley's Café, a saloon and club-house with a faro game upstairs. It was a grand place and I went there often with my master. Kelley was a big, round-faced man, jolly and generous. But I didn't like him, although he often fed me dainties from the lunch counter. I didn't like his aura. He thought he was a good fellow, but he wasn't. He did much harm because his place was so attractive and respectable.

And his faro tables were ruining my master.

I used to curl down back of the big, handsome gas stove that heated the barroom and there I would lie safe from the danger of being trampled upon and watch the thoughts come out of the people who stood before the bar.

Oh, the foulness of some of those emanations and the blackness of those evil thoughts!

After Clowder had left the house that afternoon, and left Lackwill to call Mrs. Clowder "Fanny" to his heart's content, I followed him over to Kelley's. I was very sorry for him that day, and much concerned. I knew he was in danger, but I had not yet been able to sense wherein the danger lay. Dogs have premonitions of evil but are not very clairvoyant. I suppose that is because they are only dogs and have only animal souls. I did not fear any influence Lackwill might exert over my mistress. Her thoughts were always as clear and pure as crystal.

When the black imps were at their worst, my master used to open the way for them with brandy. There is nothing that puts a man more into their power than alcohol, not even opium.

Clowder went directly to the bar and the attendant knew intuitively what to put before him. Skillful barkeepers often have this gift. It is the only resemblance to a good dog that they can boast.

Kelley came forward and shook hands with my master. "Ugly day, Mr. Clowder," he said heartily. "Have this drink with me. Will you step upstairs? Dan's up there with the boys and there's a hot game. Two hundred dollar limit and a hundred to case-cards. We are over four thousand loser to-day already. Better go upstairs and sit in. This may be your lucky day."

I never saw Kelley look handsomer than he did when he opened a hospitable door for my master to court Fortune and I never saw him look less sincere. His thoughts looked like rotting muck. They were not black and horrible like murder thoughts, nor reddish-purple like Lackwill's when he was talking with Fannie Clowder, but they were treacherous—a dirty, muddy green, very different from the bright-green thoughts of an honest, hopeful man.

I determined to go and keep an eye on Dan the dealer and see that no harm came to my master. I lay down near the roulette table, for both of the faro tables were crowded and a solitary player sat before the roulette game keeping it going by playing a chip or two every turn of the wheel. I could see by his thoughts that he belonged in the place, a capper for the game. I heard what he said to Tony the roulette dealer and what Tony said to him, and I read their thoughts.

"There comes old Clowder with his cross dog," said Tony. "He's a high roller and Dan is laying for him to-day. Dan won't do a thing to him but get his bank roll. He's dealing from his two-card box this afternoon."

The capper glanced lazily over toward the faro tables where my master was just putting down his bets.

"Clowder's getting the worst of it for fair these days," he responded, "with the brace game he's up against here and the brace game Ed Lackwill's giving his wife."

"How's Ed progressing, do you reckon?" queried Tony.

"Oh, I dunno. He gave us a great game of talk last night. He offered to bet Kelley fifty cases that he'd get her to throw the old guy over within a week."

I couldn't quite understand this, but it troubled me. I moved over to where my master was playing. The game appeared to be approaching a crisis. I could see that he was under a severe strain. He had all his betting massed in two great risks. I glanced at the dealer, who sat coldly impassive waiting to make the last turn out of the box. I saw by his emanations that he knew he was safe to win. He was dealing out of his two-card box. I looked at my master, and saw that if he lost, his next move would be to shoot himself. I saw Dan's finger stir to make the turn. I could no longer restrain myself. I started up and growled. My suddenness startled the dealer and he forgot to slip two cards instead of one. He made the turn honestly, instead of fraudulently, as he had intended. My master looked at the turn as the cards appeared and I knew he had won heavily.

"What's the matter with that infernal dog of yours, Clowder?" snarled Dan viciously. "He nearly made me drop the box." And, oh! how black his thoughts streamed from him! I knew he would kill me if ever he got a chance.

"Oh, he's all right. He was dreaming, I guess," said my master. "Lie down, sir!"

But I didn't care; I had saved my master, and I was ready to die for him if necessary. Dogs are that way.

I lay and watched the game proceed. As the deal progressed, I could see that my master was winning. He was very exultant, and played to the limit allowed by the rules of the gambling house. Presently I saw that the dealer had found another opportunity to sweep the board by a false play; that is, by pushing out of his silver box two cards instead of one and thus getting rid of a card that would make the house lose and the heaviest betters win. I saw the exultant flash of his thought radiate from his impassive face. My master placed his bets and sat expectant; the other players were following his play as gamblers do when a heavy better is winning. With a snarl of rage I flew at Dan's throat and shook him like the vile rat he was.

My master caught me by the neck and beat and choked me, and when I let go of the man who was robbing him he kicked me here—here where my side is crushed in. He kicked me hard and savagely, and I am not very strong. I am only a dog.

But the turn had been made. The house lost heavily, and I had done for Dan for that night at least.

I slipped downstairs behind my master and got away, for there was black murder in his mind and I knew I was doomed.

I crawled home and got into the house and hid in my mistress' room, hoping her gentle entreaty might save my life.

In the next room I heard her voice and that of Lackwill. He was urging her to leave her sullen, morose brute of a husband and go with him. He had known and pitied her so long, he said.

He recalled the slights and snubs that she had daily to endure, and painted glowingly the lifelong happiness that she had only to accept from him. I could hear her sobbing, and begging him to leave her alone to her misery. I felt that she was in need of me. But what could I do, with my ribs crushed and my strength gone? I crawled to the doorway and saw him grasp her arm. I saw his vile thoughts pouring out of him and fouling the air with their reddish-purple tinge. And as he argued and implored and at last struggled with her, I watched them turn darker and darker until suddenly they became a murderous black, and then I knew I must act speedily if ever. I forgot my hurts and my weakness and thought only of saving my mistress. I tore him and sank my sharp teeth deep into his wicked, lying throat. And then I heard my master's step.

***

Weeks have passed since I fled to escape my master's wrath, and I have starved by day and frozen by night and am near to death. A dog always knows when death draws nigh. I wonder if he has forgotten me. I should like him to know that I died to save him from treachery and ruin. It seems a pity that what I have learned should die with me and what I have done should not count for me in some way. When men die for loyalty they are gratefully remembered. But I am only a dog.

H. A. Freeman, "A Dog's Story." *Cosmopolitan Magazine* 24, no. 5 (March 1898): 550–52.

From "Our Dogs" (1867)

HARRIET BEECHER STOWE

I

We who live in Cunopolis are a dog-loving family. We have a warm side towards everything that goes upon four paws, and the consequence has been that, taking things first and last, we have been always kept in confusion and under the paw, so to speak, of some honest four-footed tyrant, who would go beyond his privilege and overrun the whole house. Years ago this begun, when our household consisted of a papa, a mamma, and three or four noisy boys and girls, and a kind Miss Anna who acted as a second mamma to the whole. There was also one more of our number, the youngest, dear little bright-eyed Charley, who was king over us all, and rode in a wicker wagon for a chariot, and had a nice little nurse devoted to him; and it was through him that our first dog came.

One day Charley's nurse took him quite a way to a neighbor's house to spend the afternoon; and, he being well amused, they stayed till after nightfall. The kind old lady of the mansion was concerned that the little prince in his little coach, with his little maid, had to travel so far in the twilight shadows, and so she called a big dog named Carlo, and gave the establishment into his charge.

Carlo was a great, tawny-yellow mastiff, as big as a calf, with great, clear, honest eyes, and stiff, wiry hair; and the good lady called him to the side of the little wagon, and said, "Now, Carlo, you must take good care of Charley, and you mustn't let anything hurt him."

Carlo wagged his tail in promise of protection, and away he trotted, home with the wicker wagon; and when he arrived, he was received with so much applause by four little folks, who dearly loved the very sight of a dog, he was so stroked and petted and caressed, that he concluded that he liked the place better than the home he came from, where were only very grave elderly people. He tarried all night, and slept at the foot of the boys' bed, who could hardly go to sleep for the things they found to say to him, and who were awake ever so early in the morning, stroking his rough, tawny back, and hugging him.

At his own home Carlo had a kennel all to himself, where he was expected to live quite alone, and do duty by watching and guarding the place. Nobody petted him, or stroked his rough hide, or said, "Poor dog!" to him, and so it appears he had a feeling that he was not appreciated, and liked our warm-hearted little folks, who told him stories, gave him half of their own supper, and took him to bed with them sociably. Carlo was a dog that had a mind of his own, though he couldn't say much about it, and in his dog fashion proclaimed his likes and dislikes quite as strongly as if he could speak. When the time came for taking him home, he growled and showed his teeth dangerously at the man who was sent for him, and it was necessary to drag him back by force, and tie him into his kennel. However, he soon settled that matter by gnawing the rope in two and padding down again and appearing among his little friends, quite to their delight. Two or three times was he taken back and tied or chained; but he howled so dismally, and snapped at people in such a misanthropic manner, that finally the kind old lady thought it better to have no dog at all than a dog soured by blighted affection. So she loosed his rope, and said, "There, Carlo, go and stay where you like;" and so Carlo came to us, and a joy and delight was he to all in the house. He loved one and all; but he declared himself as more than all the slave and property of our Prince Charley. He would lie on the floor as still as a door-mat, and let him pull his hair, and roll over him, and examine his eyes with his little fat fingers; and Carlo submitted to all these personal freedoms with as good an understanding as papa himself. When Charley slept, Carlo stretched himself along under the crib; rising now and then, and standing with his broad breast on a level with the slats of the crib, he would look down upon him with an air of grave protection. He also took a great fancy to papa, and would some-times pat with tiptoe care into his study, and sit quietly down by him when he was busy over his Greek or Latin books, waiting for a word or two of praise or encouragement. If none came, he would lay his rough horny paw on his knee, and look in his face with such an honest, imploring expression, that the professor was forced to break off to say, "Why, Carlo, you poor, good, honest fellow,—did he want to be talked to?—so he did. Well, he shall be talked to;—he's a nice, good dog;"—and during all these praises Carlo's transports and the thumps of his rough tail are not to be described.

He had great, honest, yellowish-brown eyes,—not remarkable for their beauty, but which used to look as if he longed to speak, and he seemed to have a yearning for praise and love and caresses that even all our attentions could scarcely satisfy. His master would say to him sometimes, "Carlo, you poor, good, homely dog,—how loving you are!"

Carlo was a full-blooded mastiff, and his beauty, if he had any, consisted in his having all the good points of his race. He was a dog of blood, come of real old mastiff lineage, his stiff, wiry hair, his big, rough paws, and great brawny chest, were all made for strength rather than beauty; but for all that he was a dog of tender sentiments. Yet, if any one intruded on his rights and dignities, Carlo showed that he had hot blood in him; his lips would go back, and show a glisten-ing row of ivories that one would not like to encounter, and if any intruded on his privileges, he would give a deep warning growl,—as much as to say, "I am your slave for love, but you must treat me well, or I shall be dangerous." A blow he would not bear from any one: the fire would flash from his great yellow eyes, and he would snap like a rifle;—yet he would let his own Prince Charley pound on his ribs with both baby fists, and pull his tail till he yelped, without even a show of resistance.

At last came a time when the merry voice of little Charley was heard no more, and his little feet no more pattered through the halls; he lay pale and silent in his little crib, with his dear life ebbing away, and no one knew how to stop its going. Poor old Carlo lay under the crib when they would let him, sometimes rising up to look in with an earnest, sorrowful face; and sometimes he would stretch himself out in the entry before the door of little Charley's room, watching with his great open eyes lest the thief should come in the night to steal away our treasure.

But one morning when the children woke, one little soul had gone in the night,—gone upward to the angels; and then the cold, pale little form that used to be the life of the house was laid away tenderly in the yard of a neighboring church.

Poor old Carlo would pit-pat silently about the house in those days of grief, looking first into one face and then another, but no one could tell him where his gay little master had gone. The other children had hid the baby-wagon away in the lumber-room lest their mamma should see it, and so passed a week or two, and Carlo saw no trace of Charley about the house. But then a lady in the neighborhood, who had a sick baby, sent to borrow the wicker wagon, and it was taken from its hiding-place to go to her. Carlo came to the door just as it was being drawn out of the gate into the street. Immediately he sprung, cleared the fence with a great bound, and ran after it. He overtook it, and poked his nose between the curtains, there was no one there. Immediately he turned away, and padded dejectedly home. What words could have spoken plainer of love and memory than this one action?

Carlo lived with us a year after this, when a time came for the whole family hive to be taken up and moved away from the flowery banks of the Ohio to the piny shores of Maine. All our household goods were being uprooted, disordered, packed, and sold; and the question daily arose, "What shall we do with Carlo?" There was hard begging on the part of the boys that he might go with them, and one even volunteered to travel all the way in baggage cars to keep Carlo company. But papa said no, and so it was decided to send Carlo up the river to the home of a very genial lady who had visited in our family, and who appreciated his parts, and offered him a home in hers.

The matter was anxiously talked over one day in the family circle while Carlo lay under the table, and it was agreed that papa and Willie should take him to the steamboat landing the next morning. But the next morning Mr. Carlo was nowhere to be found. In vain was he called, from garret to cellar; nor was it till papa and Willie had gone to the city that he came out of his hiding-place. For two or three days it was impossible to catch him, but after a while his suspicions were laid, and we learned not to speak out our plans in his presence, and so the transfer at last was prosperously effected.

We heard from him once in his new home, as being a highly appreciated member of society, and adorning his new situation with all sorts of dog virtues, while we wended our ways to the coast of Maine. But our hearts were sore for want of him; the family circle seemed incomplete, until a new favorite appeared to take his place, of which I shall tell you next month.

II

A neighbor, blessed with an extensive litter of Newfoundland pups, commenced one chapter in our family history by giving us a puppy, brisk, funny, and lively enough, who was received in our house with acclamations of joy, and christened "Rover." An auspicious name we all thought, for his four or five human playfellows were all rovers,—rovers in the woods, rovers by the banks of a neighboring patch of water, where they dashed and splashed, made rafts, inaugurated boats, and lived among the cat-tails and sweet flags as familiarly as so many musk-rats. Rovers also they were, every few days, down to the shores of the great sea, where they caught fish, rowed boats, dug clams,—both girls and boys,—and one sex quite as handily as the other. Rover came into such a lively circle quite as one of them, and from the very first seemed to regard himself as part and parcel of all that was going on, indoors or out. But his exuberant spirits at times brought him into sad scrapes. His vivacity was such as to amount to decided insanity,—and mamma and Miss Anna and papa had many grave looks over his capers. Once he actually tore off the leg of a new pair of trousers that Johnny had just donned, and came racing home with it in his mouth, with its bare-legged little owner behind, screaming threats and maledictions on the robber. What a commotion! The new trousers had just been painfully finished, in those days when sewing was sewing and not a mere jig on a sewing-machine; but Rover, so far from being abashed or ashamed, displayed an impish glee in his performance, bounding and leaping hither and thither with his trophy in his mouth, now growling and mangling it, and shaking it at us in elfish triumph as we chased him hither and thither,—over the wood-pile, into the woodhouse, through the barn, out of the stable door,—vowing all sorts of dreadful punishments when we caught him. But we might well say that, for the little wretch would never be caught; after one of his tricks he always managed to keep himself out of arm's length till the thing was a little blown over, when in he would come, airy as ever, and wagging his little pudgy puppy tail with an air of the most perfect assurance in the world.

There is no saying what youthful errors were pardoned to him. Once he ate a hole in the bed-quilt as his night's employment, when one of the boys had surreptitiously got him into bed with them; he nibbled and variously maltreated sundry sheets; and once actually tore up and chewed off a corner of the bedroom carpet, to stay his stomach during the night season. What he did it for, no mortal knows; certainly it could not be because he was hungry, for there were five little pairs of hands incessantly feeding him from morning till night. Beside which, he had a boundless appetite for shoes, which he mumbled, and shook, and tore, and ruined, greatly to the vexation of their rightful owners,—rushing in and carrying them from the bedsides in the night-watches, racing off with them to any out-of-the-way corner that hit his fancy, and leaving them when he was tired of the fun. So there is no telling of the disgrace into which he brought his little masters and mistresses, and the tears and threats and scoldings which were all wasted on him, as he would stand quite at his ease, lolling out his red, saucy tongue, and never deigning to tell what he had done with his spoils.

Notwithstanding all these sins, Rover grew up to doghood, the pride and pet of the family,—and in truth a very handsome dog he was.

It is quite evident from his looks that his Newfoundland blood had been mingled with that of some other races; for he never attained the full size of that race, and his points in some respects resembled those of a good setter. He was grizzled black and white, and spotted on the sides in little inky drops about the size of a three-cent piece; his hair was long and silky, his ears beautifully fringed, and his tail long and feathery. His eyes were bright, soft, and full of expression, and a jollier, livelier, more loving creature never wore dog-skin. To be sure, his hunting blood sometimes brought us and him into scrapes. A neighbor now and then would call with a bill for ducks, chickens, or young turkeys, which Rover had killed. The last time this occurred it was decided that something must be done; so Rover was shut up a whole day in a cold lumber-room, with the murdered duck tied round his neck. Poor fellow! How dejected and ashamed he looked, and how grateful he was when his little friends would steal in to sit with him, and "poor" him in his disgrace! The punishment so improved his principles that he let poultry alone from that time, except now and then, when he would snap up a young chick or turkey, in pure absence of mind, before he really knew what he was about. We had great dread lest he should take to killing sheep, of which there were many flocks in the neighborhood. A dog which once kills sheep is a doomed beast,—as much as a man who has committed murder; and if our Rover, through the hunting blood that was in him, should once mistake a sheep for a deer, and kill him, we should be obliged to give him up to justice, all his good looks and good qualities could not save him.

What anxieties his training under this head cost us! When we were driving out along the clean, sandy roads, among the piny groves of Maine, it was half our enjoyment to see Rover, with ears and tail wild and flying with excitement and enjoyment, bounding and barking, now on this side the carriage, now on that,—now darting through the woods straight as an arrow, in his leaps after birds or squirrels, and anon returning to trot obediently by the carriage, and, wagging his tail, to ask applause for his performances. But anon a flock of sheep

appeared in a distant field, and away would go Rover in full bow-wow, plunging in among them, scattering them hither and thither in dire confusion. Then
Johnny and Bill and all hands would spring from the carriage in full chase of
the rogue; and all of us shouted vainly in the rear; and finally the rascal would
be dragged back, panting and crestfallen, to be admonished, scolded, and cuffed
with salutary discipline, heartily administered by his best friends for the sake
of saving his life. "Rover, you naughty dog! Don't you know you mustn't chase
the sheep? You'll be killed, some of these days." Admonitions of this kind, well
shaken and thumped in, at last seemed to reform him thoroughly. He grew so
conscientious that, when a flock of sheep appeared on the side of the road, he
would immediately go to the other side of the carriage, and turn away his head,
rolling up his eyes meanwhile to us for praise at his extraordinary good conduct.
"Good dog, Rove! nice dog! good fellow! he doesn't touch the sheep,—no, he
doesn't." Such were the rewards of virtue which sweetened his self-denial; hearing
which, he would plume up his feathery tail, and loll out his tongue, with an air
of virtuous assurance quite edifying to behold.

Another of Rover's dangers was a habit he had of running races and cutting
capers with the railroad engines as they passed near our dwelling.

We lived in plain sight of the track, and three or four times a day the old,
puffing, smoking iron horse thundered by, dragging his trains of cars, and making the very ground shake under him. Rover never could resist the temptation to
run and bark, and race with so lively an antagonist; and, to say the truth, John
and Willy were somewhat of his mind,—so that, though they were directed to
catch and hinder him, they entered so warmly into his own feelings that they
never succeeded in breaking up the habit. Every day when the distant whistle
was heard, away would go Rover, out of the door or through the window—no
matter which,—race down to meet the cars, couch down on the track in front
of them, barking with all his might, as if it were only a fellow-dog, and when
they came so near that escape seemed utterly impossible, he would lie flat down
between the rails and suffer the whole train to pass over him, and then jump up
and bark, full of glee, in the rear. Sometimes he varied this performance more
dangerously by jumping out full tilt between two middle cars when the train
had passed half-way over him. Everybody predicted, of course, that he would be
killed or maimed, and the loss of a paw, or of his fine, saucy tail, was the least
of the dreadful things which were prophesied about him. But Rover lived and
throve in his imprudent courses notwithstanding.

The engineers and firemen, who began by throwing sticks of wood and bits
of coal at him, at last were quite subdued by his successful impudence, and

came to consider him as a regular institution of the railroad, and, if any family excursion took him off for a day, they would inquire with interest, "Where's our dog?—what's become of Rover?" As to the female part of our family, we had so often anticipated piteous scenes when poor Rover would be brought home with broken paws or without his pretty tail, that we quite used up our sensibilities, and concluded that some kind angel, such as is appointed to watch over little children's pets, must take special care of our Rover.

Rover had very tender domestic affections. His attachment to his little play-fellows was most intense; and one time, when all of them were taken off together on a week's excursion, and Rover left alone at home, his low spirits were really pitiful. He refused entirely to eat for the first day, and finally could only be coaxed to take nourishment, with many strokings and caresses, by being fed out of Miss Anna's own hand. What perfectly boisterous joy he showed when the children came back!—careering round and round, picking up chips and bits of sticks, and coming and offering them to one another, in the fullness of his doggish heart, to show how much he wanted to give them something.

This mode of signifying his love by bringing something in his mouth was one of his most characteristic tricks. At one time he followed the carriage from Brunswick to Bath, and in the streets of the city somehow lost his way, so that he was gone all night. Many a little heart went to bed anxious and sorrowful for the loss of its shaggy playfellow that night, and Rover doubtless was remembered in many little prayers; what, therefore, was the joy of being awakened by a joyful barking under the window the next morning, when his little friends rushed in their nightgowns to behold Rover back again, fresh and frisky, bearing in his mouth a branch of a tree about six feet long, as his offering of joy.

When the family removed to Zion Hill, Rover went with them, the trusty and established family friend. Age had somewhat matured his early friskiness. Perhaps the grave neighborhood of a theological seminary and the responsibility of being a professor's dog might have something to do with it, but Rover gained an established character as a dog of respectable habits, and used to march to the post-office at the heels of his master twice a day as regularly as any theological student.

Little Charley the second—the youngest of the brood, who took the place of our lost little Prince Charley—was yet padding about in short robes, and seemed to regard Rover in the light of a discreet older brother, and Rover's manners to him were of most protecting gentleness. Charley seemed to consider Rover in all things as such a model, that he overlooked the difference between a dog and a boy, and wearied himself with fruitless attempts to scratch his ear with his foot as Rover did, and one day was brought in dripping from a neighboring swamp, where he had been lying down in the water, because Rover did.

Once in a while a wild oat or two from Rover's old sack would seem to entangle him. Sometimes, when we were driving out, he would, in his race after the carriage, make a flying leap into a farmer's yard, and, if he lighted in a flock of chickens or turkeys, gobble one off-hand, and be off again and a mile ahead before the mother hen had recovered from her astonishment. Sometimes, too, he would have a race with the steam-engine just for old acquaintance' sake. But these were comparatively transient follies; in general, no members of the grave institutions around him behaved with more dignity and decorum than Rover. He tried to listen to his master's theological lectures, and to attend chapel on Sundays; but the prejudices of society were against him, and so he meekly submitted to be shut out, and waited outside the door on these occasions.

He formed a part of every domestic scene. At family prayers, stretched out beside his master, he looked up reflectively with his great soft eyes, and seemed to join in the serious feeling of the hour. When all were gay, when singing, or frolicking, or games were going on, Rover barked and frisked in higher glee than any. At night it was his joy to stretch his furry length by our bedside, where he slept with one ear on cock for any noise which it might be his business to watch and attend to. It was a comfort to hear the tinkle of his big collar when he moved in the night, or to be wakened by his cold nose pushed against one's hand if one slept late in the morning. And then he was always so glad when we woke; and when any member of the family circle was gone for a few days, Rover's warm delight and welcome were not the least of the pleasures of return.

And what became of him? Alas! the fashion came up of poisoning dogs, and this poor, good, fond, faithful creature was enticed into swallowing poisoned meat. One day he came in suddenly, ill and frightened, and ran to the friends who always had protected him,—but in vain. In a few moments he was in convulsions, and all the tears and sobs of his playfellows could not help him; he closed his bright, loving eyes, and died in their arms.

If those who throw poison to dogs could only see the real grief it brings into a family to lose the friend and playfellow who has grown up with the children, and shared their plays, and been for years in every family scene,—if they could know how sorrowful it is to see the poor dumb friend suffer agonies which they cannot relieve,—if they could see all this, we have faith to believe they never would do so more.

Our poor Rover was buried with decent care near the house, and a mound of petunias over him kept his memory ever bright; but it will be long before his friends will get another as true.

V

Well, after the departure of Madame Florence there was a long cessation of the dog mania in our family. We concluded that we would have no more pets; for they made too much anxiety, and care, and trouble, and broke all our hearts by death or desertion.

At last, however, some neighbors of ours took unto themselves, to enliven their dwelling, a little saucy Scotch terrier, whose bright eyes and wicked tricks so wrought upon the heart of one of our juvenile branches, that there was no rest in the camp without this addition to it. Nothing was so pretty, so bright, so knowing and cunning, as a "Scotch terrier," and a Scotch terrier we must have,—so said Miss Jenny, our youngest.

And so a bargain was struck by one of Jenny's friends with some of the knowing ones in Boston, and home she came, the happy possessor of a genuine article,—as wide awake, impertinent, frisky, and wicked a little elf as ever was covered with a shock of rough tan-colored hair.

His mistress no sooner gazed on him, than she was inspired to give him a name suited to his peculiar character;—so he frisked into the front door announced as Wix, and soon made himself perfectly at home in the family circle, which he took, after his own fashion, by storm. He entered the house like a small whirlwind, dashed, the first thing, into the Professor's study, seized a slipper which was dangling rather uncertainly on one of his studious feet, and, wresting it off, raced triumphantly with it around the hall, barking distractedly every minute that he was not shaking and worrying his prize.

Great was the sensation. Grandma tottered with trembling steps to the door, and asked, with hesitating tones, what sort of a creature that might be; and being saluted with the jubilant proclamation, "Why, Grandma, it's my dog—a real genuine Scotch terrier; he'll never grow any larger, and he's a perfect beauty! don't you think so?"—Grandma could only tremblingly reply, "Oh, there is not any danger of his going mad, is there? Is he generally so playful? "

Playful was certainly a mild term for the tempest of excitement in which master Wix flew round and round in giddy circles, springing over ottomans, diving under sofas, barking from beneath chairs, and resisting every effort to recapture the slipper with bristling hair and blazing eyes, as if the whole of his dog-life consisted in keeping his prize; till at length he caught a glimpse of pussy's tail,—at which, dropping the slipper, he precipitated himself after the flying meteor, tumbling, rolling, and scratching down the kitchen stairs, standing on his hind-legs barking distractedly at poor Tom, who had taken refuge in the sink, and sat with his tail magnified to the size of a small bolster.

This cat, the most reputable and steady individual of his species, the darling of the most respectable of cooks, had received the name of Thomas Henry, by which somewhat lengthy appellation he was generally designated in the family circle, as a mark of the respect which his serious and contemplative manner commonly excited. Thomas had but one trick of popularity. With much painstaking and care the cook had taught him the act of performing a somerset over our hands when held at a decent height from the floor; and for this one elegant accomplishment, added to great success in his calling of rat-catching, he was held in great consideration in the family, and had meandered his decorous way about the house, slept in the sun, and otherwise conducted himself with the innocent and tranquil freedom which became a family cat of correct habits and a good conscience.

The irruption of Wix into our establishment was like the bursting of a bomb at the feet of some respectable citizen going tranquilly to market. Thomas was a cat of courage, and rats of the largest size shrunk appalled at the very sight of his whiskers; but now he sat in the sink quite cowed, consulting with great, anxious, yellow eyes the throng of faces that followed Wix down the stairs, and watching anxiously the efforts Miss Jenny was making to subdue and quiet him.

"Wix, you naughty little rascal, you mustn't bark at Thomas Henry; be still!" Whereat Wix, understanding himself to be blamed, brought forth his trump card of accomplishments, which he always offered by way of pacification whenever he was scolded. He reared himself up on his hind-legs, hung his head languishingly on one side, lolled out his tongue, and made a series of supplicatory gestures with his fore-paws,—a trick which never failed to bring down the house in a storm of applause, and carry him out of any scrape with flying colors.

Poor Thomas Henry, from his desolate sink, saw his terrible rival carried off in Miss Jenny's arms amid the applauses of the whole circle, and had abundance of time to reflect on the unsubstantial nature of popularity. After that he grow dejected and misanthropic,—a real Cardinal Wolsey in furs,—for Wix was possessed with a perfect cat-hunting mania, and, when he was not employed in other mischief, was always ready for a bout with Thomas Henry.

It is true, he sometimes came back from these encounters with a scratched and bloody nose, for Thomas Henry was a cat of no mean claw, and would turn to bay at times; but generally he felt the exertion too much for his advanced years and quiet habits, and so for safety he passed much of his time in the sink, over the battlements of which he would leisurely survey the efforts of the enemy to get at him. The cook hinted strongly of the danger of rheumatism to her favorite from these damp quarters, but Wix at present was the reigning favorite, and it was vain to dispute his sway.

Next to Thomas Henry, Wix directed his principal efforts to teasing Grand-mamma. Something or other about her black dress and quiet movements seemed to suggest to him suspicions. He viewed her as something to be narrowly watched; he would lie down under some chair or table, and watch her motions with his head on his forepaws as if he were watching at a rat-hole. She evidently was not a rat, he seemed to say to himself, but who knows what she may be; and he would wink at her with his great bright eyes, and, if she began to get up, would spring from his ambush and bark at her feet with frantic energy,—by which means he nearly threw her over two or three times.

His young mistress kept a rod, and put him through a severe course of discipline for these offenses; after which he grew more careful,—but still the unaccountable fascination seemed to continue; still he would lie in ambush, and, though forbidden to bark, would dart stealthily forward when he saw her preparing to rise, and be under her dress smelling in a suspicious manner at her heels. He would spring from his place at the fire, and rush to the staircase when he heard her leisurely step descending the stairs, and once or twice nearly overset her by being under her heels, bringing on himself a chastisement which he in vain sought to avert by the most vigorous deprecatory pawing.

Grandmamma's favorite evening employment was to sit sleeping in her chair, gradually bobbing her head lower and lower,—all which movements Wix would watch, giving a short snap, or a suppressed growl, at every bow. What he would have done, if, as John Bunyan says, he had been allowed to have his "doggish way" with her, it is impossible to say. Once he succeeded in seizing the slipper from her foot as she set napping, and a glorious race he had with it,—out at the front door, up the path to the Theological Seminary, and round and round the halls consecrated to better things, with all the glee of an imp. At another time he made a dart into her apartment, and seized a turkey-wing which the good old lady had used for a duster, and made such a regular forenoon's work of worrying, shaking, and teasing it, that every feather in it was utterly demolished.

In fact, there was about Wix something so elfish and impish, that there began to be shrewd suspicions that he must be somehow or other a descendant of the celebrated poodle of Faust, and that one need not be surprised some day to have him suddenly looming up into some uncanny shape, or entering into conversation, and uttering all sorts of improprieties unbefitting a theological professor's family.

He had persistence in wicked ways that resisted the most energetic nurture and admonition of his young mistress. His combativeness was such, that a peace-able walk down the fashionable street of Zion Hill in his company became im-possible; all was race and scurry, cackle and flutter, wherever he appeared,—hens and poultry flying, frightened cats mounting trees with magnified tails, dogs yelping and snarling, and children and cows running in every direction. No modest young lady could possibly walk out in company with such a son of confusion. Beside this, Wix had his own private inexplicable personal piques against different visitors in the family, and in the most unexpected moment would give a snap or a nip to the most unoffending person. His friends in the family circle dropped off. His ways were pronounced too bad, his conduct perfectly indefensible; his young mistress alone clung to him, and declared that her vigorous system of education would at last reform his eccentricities, and turn him out a tip-top dog. But when he would slyly leave home, and, after rolling and steeping himself in the ill-smelling deposits of the stable or drain, come home and spring with impudent ease into her lap, or put himself to sleep on her little white bed, the magic cords of affection gave out, and disgust began to succeed. It began to be remarked that this was a stable-dog, educated for the coach-boy and stable, and to be doubted whether it was worthwhile to endeavor to raise him to a lady's boudoir; and so at last, when the family removed from Zion Hill, he was taken back and disposed of at a somewhat reduced price.

Since then, as we are informed, he has risen to fame and honor. His name has even appeared in sporting gazettes as the most celebrated "ratter" in little Boston, and his mistress was solemnly assured by his present possessor that for "cat work" he was unequaled, and that he would not take fifty dollars for him. From all which it appears that a dog which is only a torment and a nuisance in one sphere may be an eminent character in another.

Harriet Beecher Stowe, "Our Dogs." In *Queer Little People*. Boston: Ticknor and Fields, 1867, 91–140.

My Dog (A Hamlet in Old Hampshire) (1901)

ANNA LEA MERRITT

This chapter is devoted to my dog. It is a sad chapter, for this dog proved faithful and human beyond words, and its mistress but a faithless cur. It is the only friendship which I have ever deserted, and even now the bond may be renewed if the dear creature will forgive.

It began with a tramp—a big, bold, burly tramp who knocked at the kitchen door and demanded broken china to rivet. Now, the maid who then served me was that sort of maid who runs very fast when carrying a tray, looking backward meanwhile, thus causing many things of brittle nature to fly off and break. If she carried a chair from one room to the next she would hold it horizontally, so that either legs or back could not get through the door, and as her impetus did not allow her to stop, legs or back usually fell off. Therefore was she glad to find a tramp ready to repair, and she handed him a vegetable-dish with a division-piece in the middle that her strong hand had disconnected. Later on, the bold, bad tramp reappeared at the front door and demanded two shillings and sixpence for putting in a rivet. This he had done by drilling a hole through the bottom of the dish, which would consequently leak, and the condition thereof be worse than before. I explained that sixpence was the usual price of a rivet. He returned the message that that rivet was of an extraordinary kind; which indeed it was, for with thumb and finger I straightway picked it out and returned it. Whereupon he became furious. I sent word that he could have one shilling—no more. His fury became a hurricane, and he deposited the rivet on a window-sill, demanding half a crown, and threatening his permanent company. I drew my bolts, and despatched the nimble maid over the fields back of the cottage in search of the policeman, while I retired to the upper floor, keeping watch over the excited man and feeling like the solitary defender of a fortress. From behind my thin curtains I could look calmly down upon the enemy, who grew with every breath redder and louder. From above I announced that the shilling was ready for him, but a witness would be required to the payment. It was the hour when men should return from the fields and pass my door, but never had they seemed so slow; and meanwhile the foe announced that he adhered to the demand for two shillings and sixpence, and that he was prepared to use bad language if refused. No doubt he had a grand vocabulary in this kind of language, for his words came faster and fiercer; but what did it profit him? It is a fine thing to have command of language. It is a fine thing to fling winged words upon the stillness of a summer afternoon, but if they are words that no one understands, of what use? Study language, by all means; but if you speak German to a Chinese or Arabic to an American, or bad language to a lady, it is really a waste of feeling to resent what she cannot understand. Some of his words, such as "bloody" and "d——," I had known about. They are sometimes seen in print in "Punch," and a big, big D—— even played an important part in a celebrated operetta. These I knew, but the next of his remarks was of no meaning. His face grew so red in this effort that I feared an attack of apoplexy, and calmly and gently looked out of my window and softly begged him not to tire himself, which only made him the more furious.

A full half-hour had passed and still no policeman; no swift maid to herald his coming. The village women had hurried away from the terrible roar of the tramp and left me to my solitary defiance. I hoped they would tell the nearest farmer, but hoped in vain. When the laborers were passing from the fields the tramp bellowed out for his half-crown. When there was no one to witness, he would signify his willingness to accept a shilling, but I knew he would afterward demand more. It is curious what a sense of superiority is found in a mind *sibi conscia recti.*

I felt quite unruffled and only anxious for his health and escape from fits, while he continued to bellow the louder, to the great injury of his health.

At last, what was that? A little skirmish of petticoats bringing news of relief. Some village women, not venturing too near, called out that the policeman was coming, and the steady, unhurrying steps of the well-shod man of the law rang out down the flinty road. "Chuck it out! Chuck it out!" roared the tramp; so, having witnesses to my payment, out of the window I "chucked" the shilling, wrapped in white paper to mark its flight. The man snatched it up quickly, and scuttled up the hill at a good pace, saving his breath for the steep climb.

A holy silence fell on the hot July evening, and a languor of fatigue possessed my wearied ears. The wretch well out of sight, a number of defenders and sympathizers appeared who had been unaccountably invisible through the brunt of the fray, and I could only feel thankful that bad language had not been included in my early studies, as, for once, want of knowledge proved a safe thing. There must be a dog, said the farmers; certainly a lone woman must have a dog. But while waiting for them to hear of a desirable canine protector, I proceeded to a shop, bought the largest pair of hobnailed shoes on the premises, put in old laces, and dragged them in mud. Made properly crusty and worn-looking, they stood for many a day just outside the kitchen door waiting to be cleaned—and striking terror into all travelers.

A few days after, a dog was announced. A beautiful creature, my friendly farmer said. It would lie quiet and never disturb me at my painting—and I could have it for half a guinea. Its master was parting with it because it was of no use with cows. It had only one fault: it was a female. "Dear me!" I thought, "here too, even in the animal world, are women-folks at a discount. Poor dear! Let her come to me. I quite sympathize with her views of cows feminine." So she came, Lady by name, fine lady by character. Of course she would not herd cows—a creature of greyhound and deerhound breed! Believe me, the mixed race enhanced her charms of character and intelligence. Her beautiful large eyes had the deepest gaze, and how pretty were her little velvet ears! Her mouth could open almost as wide as a crocodile's, displaying a set of terrible teeth—alarming indeed to those who knew her not. So tall was she that she was able to stand with a paw on my shoulder and lick my cheek. Dear Lady, how often she took this engaging familiarity, gazing at me eye to eye, transferring her thoughts to mine, and entreating compliance! All day we worked together in the studio, I

standing, Lady stretched at length on a soft rug, with eyes fixed upon me, waiting. I stand at my easel; but sometimes, and that rarely, sit down for a minute,
not so much for rest as for reflection. On these occasions Lady quickly would
have her elbows on my lap and her face close to mine, with a lick too affectionate to be altogether forbidden, and saying in her gaze-language, "How much
longer is this stupid painting going to continue?" At four o'clock we had our tea
together on the lawn. Lady had a large cup just like mine and bread and butter,
her favorite meal. This consumed, painting was intolerable to her. The beautiful
hour was approaching, the breeze from the hill bore the fragrance of the down,
and perhaps some sniff of rabbits and hares in their pleasant upland pastures.
Lady would not let me go back to studio painting. At full height on end, with
paws on my shoulders, she would bar the way to the studio, and her dark eyes
meant: "Come away up the hill, away to the common or the woods! Come away!
come away!" and I promised. Then she watched at the door while I prepared my
light sketching-materials, and off we went.

Never was there such an ill-assorted couple—a little elderly lady decidedly
thick for her height, fat, and scant of breath, laden with paint-box and brushes,
and perhaps a pole-easel and umbrella, somewhat tired, too, with having stood
already seven hours at the easel, accompanied by a hound built for the extreme
of swiftness, every muscle perfect to its use, bounding and joyous after long
idleness, with a pure joy to leap the gate backward and forward, circling around
me as a gull on the wing around a panting steamship. On like an arrow, then
back again to encourage me, she ran, with a flying caper to lick off my eye-glass,
perhaps—a terrible mishap, but forgiven. Many the mile we walked thus together. But the dear dog never realized how many and many a time her poor mistress came home tired out and exhausted with a modest five-mile run, the merest
stroll. A great inducement to the walk was to watch her graceful movement, the
exquisite curve of her bounding form, the flexibility, the ease, the grace. What
a wonderful thing to be so made for speed and beauty! The dear creature com-
miserated my slowness, and often returned, to pace demurely at my side with
affectionate, inquiring eyes uplifted, and obedient to the softest word. At the
approach of people or vehicles she instantly drew beside me and assumed the
air of guardian. No one then seeing her could have guessed that she was thinking chiefly of rabbits. Her real plan in these excursions was to find a nice place
for me to establish the easel, open the umbrella, and take out the paints. While
these preparations were being completed she lay on the velvety turf, basking in
contentment and absorbed in my arrangements; but when the sketch was begun
she gradually changed her position, so as to be behind me and give the flatter-
ing impression that she was watching the progress of the picture. Sometimes she

strayed a little farther, just to take a view from the higher path, but flew back on my lightest call. When at last I became really intent, with both eyes on my work, her little digressions were unnoticed, and then silently on tiptoe, not so much as stirring a dead leaf, and carefully keeping to the noiseless turf, away went Lady. What has possessed that wheat-field? Is it a wind rustling the ripening grain? What a curious ripple it has far down the valley! How swiftly in circles and eddies flows the curious wave, and now, good heavens! there is the bounding Lady in the midst of the whirlpool of rustling wheat, springing entirely above it, just to take an observation, and then diving below. Oh, if only I could whistle! But I can't. To call "Lady! Lady!" at the top of my voice will only carry the news of her delinquency to every farm-house in the valley. In this still air, when the fields are growing and labor is at rest, a whisper can be heard for miles.

"Oh, Lady, Lady, how unkind of you! You little cheat, you dreadful dog, come back, and don't disgrace me! Dear Lady, oh, dear dog, come back!"

A poor flying hare darts out of the hedge, over the road, past me, through another hedge, and Lady after it, deaf now to all entreaty. Could I expect a human being in the hour of success to heed my call? The poor hare doubles again through the briers, and Lady too, and quickly the chase is ended. I hide my eyes while the triumphant dog endeavors dutifully to bring me her present of game. "Foolish person," she thinks, "who cares not for the fine supper provided!" Luckily the postman is just coming up the hill, and a laborer from the opposite direction. They receive the half-dead hare, and quickly end its pain, and will give it to its rightful owner. "But that's a good dog," they say; "a fine dog." And Lady, aware only of a success which few hounds single-handed can achieve, comes to me, radiant for approval. Dear Lady, how can I scold her! She had spent half her young life acquiring this very accomplishment, and she brought her booty faithfully home. Dear dog, don't do it again! So the next time we go afield I must carry a chain, and the only post to fasten it to be my own ankle. It is quite inconvenient to both of us. Lady alternates patience with entreaties. When I am balanced on a very small folding-seat, with a palette in one hand and a brush in the other, and a little upsetting easel in front, it is not a well-chosen moment for a dog of her size to climb upon my lap. As there is no place to put down my brushes and colors, we all upset together, and come out of it considerably variegated from the palette. A general cleaning wastes much more of the beautiful afternoon, and then we begin again, Lady fast to my foot. The farmer who had introduced her rides by, and stops to approve. "If you want a good dog, you must never be separated from it," he tells me.

What, never! My heart does sink a little at the thought that in taking this dear companion for protection against tramps I am really chaining myself to the dog.

Tramping is not at all suited to my physique, and now even my sketches must be made far from any tempting cover. It is a duty, no doubt, when one belongs to an animal, to serve it faithfully. The weak are ever the masters of the strong, is an old saying, and here Lady must be the weaker, for clearly she is the master. She has also a silent contempt for my painting that is really discouraging. For many months together I see no one but Lady, have no other friend at hand, and naturally it is depressing to have my constant companion considered foolish. She certainly does think it foolish, and lies there gazing at me, thinking: "Foolish, foolish mistress! Is it trying to copy God's works you are? Give it up. There's no sunlight in your colors—nothing but petroleum and dirty paint. Throw away this thin image; come into the real fields up the hillside, close to the hedge fragrant with honeysuckle and sweetbrier. I'll show you where partridges are hiding. I'll startle them out of their cover in the growing wheat. Come up to the common, where the last sunlight lingers; the rabbits are venturing out into the dusk to bite the dewy grass. We will rush in among them like a tempest, and scatter them to the winds. Grand fun it is; and one or two I'll catch for our supper."

The entreating eyes said all this, and made me obey in all points save the catching of a rabbit. A little chase I'd sometimes allow when the game was there in hundreds, for on such occasions they always got off. The multitude seemed bewildering, or perhaps the dog only enjoyed scattering them.

In these long walks I realized the troubles and cares of guardian angels, and often thought of them with sympathy and commiseration. It must be weary work for an angel to have a pet human, and be bound to follow him everywhere on foot or in thought—to be always there, saying, "Don't! Don't!" Think what a lot this must be for one of the heavenly choir! A human child, or even man, like the hound, would fain dart away after every wild hare that crosses its path, and perhaps is less obedient than the hound to the voice of the master. Lady would pace by my side, stepping on tiptoes in the softest place to make no sound, quivering from nostril to tip of tail with eagerness to be off, with bunnies on all sides feeding on the grassy lanes, skipping in and out of the copse and bracken; but always she obeyed my voice gently saying, "No, dear dog; not now. No; keep close." She would walk through a warren and touch nothing, if I kept repeating my caution. The position of guardian angel is fatiguing, however, and there were occasions when other thoughts preoccupied me. Not her fault, poor dog, but mine, that she fell into temptation. Do the angels bear the blame of our lapses?

More and more hypnotic influence was acquired by Lady. She dined at my table on gooseberry tart, omelets, and curry. Did you ever taste dog-biscuits? The insipidity of such food is an insult to a canine epicure. In the evening she lay on a small Chippendale settee, and I sat beside her, holding her hand. She had a comfortable bedroom and a proper bed spread with a sheet. My friends, the few that I saw at long intervals, got an impression that my table-talk was all doggerel, and did not hesitate to speak slightingly of my better self. They saw, perhaps, that, like one in a trance, I could not choose but do her will.

There came at last an unavoidable separation. I was obliged to leave England for six months, and a kind friend, who kept a carriage, offered to receive as a guest the personage called my tyrant. We started in the train together. Lady had forebodings, and she pressed close to my side; at last, at the junction, with one sorrowing embrace, I handed her chain to a porter. The tears were on my cheek—and on hers, dear Lady.

There was not a day of my long absence that was not cheered by thoughts of her gentle affection; and yet a certain sense of repose and freedom, quite new, was perceptibly, palpably felt. How pleasant to hold a book without that black little nose immediately shoving it away! It was a comfort to sew occasionally; and as for pictures, a great many ideas came to me, and I could really concentrate attention upon such work.

As months went by and former habits were resumed and the thread of earlier life was taken up, it sometimes seemed a pity that a person of some little attainment and education should be directed by a dog. Still, I longed to see her again; I remembered daily more of her grace and charm, I forgot my fetters. As soon as I reached home, dear Lady was sent for. Glad she was to see me. She ran at once to the grass, where she rolled, as was her wont, to be brushed; for she always had ordered me to spend half an hour of the best morning light brushing and polishing her coat. The old life began again at once, just where we had broken off.

But—here is my humiliation—it was I who failed. It was I, alas! who now called it slavery, and talked in my mind about ambition, pictures—nay, work and livelihood itself, sacrificed to humor a dog. Something within me had changed; fickleness, alas!

When it was known that I wished to part with my Lady, every laborer in the village offered to keep her. She was indeed a valuable helpmate for any one who relished rabbit or hare. But Lady returned to the kind friend with the carriage. It is the carriage and the horse that she loves; she will not step inside the house or make friends with her mistress. Poor dog! No doubt she fears we are all fickle. But I long to see her, and perhaps we might pull together again.

Another dog has come to live here and frighten tramps—a useful little dog, which is always amused and needs no companionship. He plays with other dogs, of the nicer sort, and lives in the kitchen, and in winter days he trots down to the shop where many dogs assemble to discuss affairs and make notes of passers-by. I have nothing to say to him.

Anna Lea Merritt, "My Dog (A Hamlet in Old Hampshire)." *Century Illustrated Magazine* 62, no. 2 (June 1901): 251–55.

Thoughts on Dogs (1793)

BY THE LATE GOVERNOR [WILLIAM] LIVINGSTON

Impastae fugistis aves, rabidamque canum vim.—Statius.*

I have, I must own, no small veneration for the memory of *Argus,* a favourite dog of *Ulysses;* that upon the testimony of Homer, recognised his master after twenty years absence—an affectionate dog, who by wagging his tail, and giving every other token of joy that a dog can give, welcomed the celebrated hero's return to Ithaca, and then instantly expired. But I do not like all dogs; and pray who ever admired the snarling cur, *Cerberus?* I have, in particular, an aversion to lap dogs. I wish I could cure it; because they are so often the fondlings of the ladies; and who would choose to be an enemy to any living thing, that is honoured with their affection? For such enmity, therefore, it is incumbent upon me publickly to account. I will cheerfully do it. In a certain war between France and Greatbritain, the latter sent to America my lord Loudon, as generalissimo of her army, to Quebeck. My lord had a lap dog, I do not remember its name; but I dare say it was at least as sweet as that of *Dulcinea.* It was a very great favourite of his lordship.—Whether or no he used to kiss it, I will not dispose: But he hugged it, and he stroked it, and he fed it in the morning with chocolate sweetened with loaf sugar. Either conceiving from his own fund of knowledge, or being so advised by the most eminent physicians, that the air of Newjersey would prove more salutary to the health of this charming tiny creature, than that of Newyork, the noble general sent it to Mr. West's, at Elizabethtown point, to be there boarded during the summer season. Full as solicitous about proper supplies and accommodations for this beautiful little play thing, as for those of his troops, he sent with it a careful assiduous nurse to attend it, with particular directions respecting its diet. Upon this I asked *myself* (for the lord, in the plenitude of his power, from his arbitrary disposition, was that kind of man, that I could not, without running the risque of being hanged, have asked the question of *another*) *will a general, who is so extremely attentive to a lap dog, ever conquer Canada?* My lord

---

*Livingston's original epigraph from Statius translates as "You, birds, having not eaten, fled the madness and violence of the dogs." From the Thebiad 1.625.

did not conquer Canada. What did he? Why, he made very free with the property of others, while very tenacious of his own. He protested, that the chancellor of Greatbritain had authorized him to hang any man in America without trial by jury; He played with his lap dog; and he accumulated an immense fortune, which might all have been saved by the British nation, had they but thought of appointing for the commander in chief of that army, that very same identical pretty little lap dog, instead of his lordship, which would have done just as much towards the reduction of Quebeck, without costing the crown any more than its board at Mr. West's. *My lord did not conquer Canada.* This glory was reserved for general Wolf, who never played with lap dogs. The little dog in question, or at least his lordship's unseasonable fondness for it, thus proving the fatal occasion of a most successless campaign, at a time, gentle reader, when you and I and all of us loved Greatbritain, though she did not love us, hath to this moment (asking the pardon of the ladies, and all the *lilies male* of the land) given me an aversion to all the canine breed, of that diminutive species.

As to *hounds,* it is a delicate point to say any thing to *their* prejudice. They are dogs of sport; and who would wish to spoil another man's sport? But twenty men, and twenty horses, and twenty dogs, in twenty hours chace, and trespassing on twenty times twenty of their neighbour's inclosures, for the important purpose of killing one fox! Peradventure, too, instead of a fox, as I have actually known it to happen, to dig out of a hole to which the *well scented* hounds had led the eager hunters, a miserable opossum. O the wonderful utility of hounds!

Respecting *puppies,* I will not say a word against them. They are very *numerous;* and no prudent man will unnecessarily create a multitude of enemies.

But to dogs in general I cannot be reconciled without drawing some publick benefit from them. They are great eaters. Some of them would distance at this exercise, the greatest epicure in a neighbouring state, along side of a haunch of venison or a green turtle. They often consume what were better bestowed upon the poor; and what would feed many hundreds. They are out of all humour with the moon, when in its brightest splendour, which argues their love of darkness, and probably for the works of it: They frequently tempt a horse to throw its rider: They frighten the ladies; and it is not long since that one of them ran away with, and finally feloniously murdered, the favourite parrot of Belinda, that had long been the entertainment of the whole family; and spoke as articulately, and generally more sensible, though not so vociferously, as our modern Demosthenes of Newjersey. They often bespatter the silk stockings of a wooer; and compel him to return home (painful interruption, considering his errand) for another pair: They continually break the peace amongst themselves; and we have no laws to punish their frays and riots: They bark at us in the day; and they disturb our repose by night; and whether from a guilty conscience or not; they frequently run mad; and for the bite of a mad dog, there are more recipes than cures.

From the supernumeraries of those, for the most part, very useless animals, a considerable revenue might be extracted, for the benefit of the state. A very small tax upon every dog above one in a family, and so in proportion for more than two, would amount to a great sum; and I cannot think the serious consideration of such an import, beneath the dignity of the legislature.

William Livingston, "Humorous: Thoughts on Dogs." *Massachusetts Magazine, or Monthly Museum* 5, no. 5 (May 1793): 293.

In Praise of Mops (1892)

The varieties to be found in the character of dogs have always appeared to us a most interesting study. What degrees of morality, intelligence, self-control do we not observe in their different families, from that narrow and uncertain-tempered specialist, the greyhound, to the universally popular and trusty fox-terrier whom you can "do anything with," as the saying is! This axiom means in particular that the habitual companion of so many Englishmen is, like that equally respectable creature the retriever, susceptible of discipline to no ordinary degree. Many a humane man has held up a terrier of the fox or bull type and beaten the animal as he loved it, and till his arm ached. Nor is it to be supposed that such a dog (whom we have seen struggle after an angry swan in mid-stream and triumphantly pull its tail feathers out) is exactly afraid to retaliate. The same may be said of the curly black brute (capable of carrying a good-sized child in its mouth) whom the keeper chastises to an accompaniment of "Ah! Ratt-*ell* you *breeute! Wood-jerrr!*" There are dogs of course, such as the wolf-hound that killed the unfortunate Frenchman the other day, that one would hesitate to chastise for the reason that Kingsley gives, in respect of the hero of his famous ballad:—

> The clerk that should beat that little Baltung,
> Would never sing mass again!

But as there are human natures, and those not always the worst, that do not take "punishment" kindly, so are there canine natures. The difference lies in a more refined sensibility both of soul and skin, and perhaps in a rarer, more feminine, if one may say so, and more spiritual nature.

Of such sort is the dog of whom we write. Mops is one of those long-haired terriers whom to know is to love. No one could ever venture to beat him; he would probably go wild with fright or passion; as it is, he has hardly ever had a rough word spoken to him. Mops is nevertheless in ordinary circumstances as good as gold. If his sensitive temper be ever hurt, that is generally the fault of some person who has approached him either without proper introduction, or in a manner unsuited to his dignity. It is his habit to mark these occasions by pretending not to know his dearest friends, as they pass while he lies on his particular mat in the hall; or (in very extreme cases) by retiring to the housekeeper's room, much to the elation of that elderly dignitary, and growling from the low and cushioned window-sill at all who venture into his presence with overtures of friendship. There are points in his character which, in such an animal, it is hopeless to attempt to alter; but these are not the low or mischievous tricks of common dogs. He would scorn to run after a chicken or a sheep. Once he caught a very little rabbit on the front lawn and brought it with tender fondlings, yet half alive, to bed with him in his basket by the drawing-room fire, whence the horrified housemaid removed its corpse during his absence at dinner-time. He has also been confronted with a live rat with which, though exasperated by its want of humor, he for long endeavored to play, till it bit him, when there was an abrupt end of the game, and of the rat. But Mops has decided instinctive notions about how certain things ought to be done, and equally decided aversions to certain people. To Mr. Buller, the local banker, who comes over to dine regularly once a fortnight, he will never be more than severely civil. Mops's olfactory nerves have doubtless informed him of this gentleman's secret preference for fox-terriers, of which an adorable specimen is, at home, cherished in his bosom; but there are possibly other reasons.

We have not mentioned yet that Mops is as beautiful as the day, though this is not a very appropriate simile for one whose first appearance suggests a chaotic heap, or dancing cloud, of dusky hair through which now and then you catch the sparkle of two gleaming dark-brown eyes. Such he appears (for his affections and enthusiasms are unbounded, and his conduct, when pleased, of the frantic order) bounding or rather rippling down the stairs to fly into the arms of some welcome arrival or (supreme joy!) to be taken out for a walk by the right person. At such a moment he will fling shrieking up and down the passage and over and under the furniture like an animated football; but when he stops dead short, or jumps upon your knees, shakes back his hair (which is really silver-grey, almost sky-blue in a strong light) with a prodigious effort, and grins ecstatically in your face, showing all his splendid teeth and preparing to inflict a vigorous kiss upon any unprotected feature, then indeed not the famed Peloton of Du Bellay,

Faisant ne sçay quelle feste
D'un gay braulement de teste,

was more bewitching. Having mentioned the subject of teeth, we must add that one of the greatest pleasures of Mops's life is to "play at rats" with some competent human friend. This pastime (which is only allowed on the old leather settle in the smoking-room) consists chiefly in your trying to bury him in cushions, which should not be of expensive material. Then, if you have an old velveteen coat, you may after a quarter of an hour come out of the game (which is deliriously exciting) with only a black and blue arm, for which you will be amply repaid by the sight of Mops erect, breathless, and in admired disorder, with his large eyes gleaming like coals of fire at you through their hairy curtain, simply dying to begin again.

It has been suggested that he is not what is vulgarly called a "sporting dog," and that is so. Though he has no idea of being all things to all men, like many an honest dog of our acquaintance, he can be anything he pleases (for his genius is rich and versatile) with the people he really loves. We often summon him to come partridge-shooting with us in the fields close round the house. If we find him not in the gun-room, we are used to give a low whistle. Instantly a responsive and piercing bark echoes through the back premises,—Mops's demand addressed to domestics in general to open some door in his way; then another, and louder, on the first landing to announce his approach; then the noise of a carpet being dragged swiftly down the front stairs,—and there is Mops. But when we carelessly pick up our breechloader (and this we always do in his presence) as though it were merely a stick, his excitement boils over, and his yells are but gradually allayed as we get outside the front door.

Among the turnips and potatoes he presents the strangest figure, his long hair draggled with the wet, and his pointed nose and broad head (for once visible in their natural shape) peering up every now and again to see how we are getting on. Though a little slow among cover which often hides him from sight, he will quarter his ground, work backwards and forwards at the wave of the hand, and set at his game in the most orthodox manner. Mops, we do verily believe, would scent a cock-chafer; and the only fault in his pointing (a thing beautiful to behold in its amateurish energy and self-consciousness) is that it almost as often indicates the presence of a thrush as of a partridge. As to passing by any living thing two inches high, he would never dream of it. Then will he return, his little legs plastered with mud and shrunk to half their size, and his splendid hair hanging down like a Cretan goat's, exhausted but supremely happy, and retire to the pantry to be brushed. For Mops is strong, very strong; a dog of this size need be strong to carry about pounds of soil and quarts of water in his coat all day. The coat, by the way, conceals the bull neck of his species, and the long and solid trunk is supported by substantial quarters and fine stout forearms, so that the animal is by no means only ornamental.

As to his use,—well, let this sketch be finished with the story of Mops's only real adventure.

Two years ago his owner was acting as land-agent in a much disturbed district of Ireland, and lived in a large and ugly mansion where, to tell the honest truth, someone else ought to have been living. But as an agent our friend, Major D., did his duty and was detested by the peasantry. At an earlier stage they had "carded" one of his herds, drowned and strangled his calves, and even fired at one of his daughters (a lovely girl of sixteen) as she sat in loose array at her window one summer night. The bullet is in the window-frame to this day. Her father, who was annoyed, replied with a shot-gun and two heavy sawdust cartridges from a lower story, it is believed, to some effect. This, however, is by the way. Once a week, at the time referred to, Major D. used to drive into the neighboring market-town, and on these occasions Mops (considerably to his relief) had never shown the slightest wish to accompany him further than the park gate. One Wednesday, however,—it was a day or two after some ill-looking fellows had been seen hanging about the park,—Mops suddenly changed his mind. He was determined to go. This was embarrassing to the major, who, apart from the trouble of looking after the dog, was afraid of risking so valuable an animal in a locality so distinguished for what is called in Ireland "agrarian feeling." What was to be done?

Mops was locked up in an empty room which the children used for carpentering. His lamentable howls gradually subsided, and the rest of the household went about their business. Meanwhile Mops, as afterwards appeared, was doing a little carpentering on his own account. The door was a good sound door, but the floor beneath it was rather worn. It is a pity that no one could have seen his muscular little form as it lay there curled up on one side, the shaggy head savagely shaking as at each *scrunch* of his gnawing teeth fresh splinters of the deal board came away, and were swept aside by his little paws. It must have been hard work, harder than scraping at any rabbit-hole, but probably more delightful!

Nearly four hours had passed when an astonished domestic noticed and duly reported the alteration just executed by Mops. At that moment a small dark form might just have been discerned in the dusk of the evening scudding across the fields. This was Mops going to meet the major,—and why in Heaven's name going at all?—and why going this way (the shortest cut as it happened) and not along the highroad? Who shall peer into the workings of that strange little mind,

or whatever we please to call it? It is certain that the point on the highroad aimed
at by Mops, consciously or unconsciously, was just about where an intelligent
being would have expected the major to be if he were walking home (as a rule
he drove) at his usual hour, and it is equally certain that the major was there. It
does not appear, moreover, that Mops had the slightest hesitation as to what he
meant to do, throughout the whole course of this, his one adventure. The major
was there, and nothing separated Mops from him but a high and rough stone
wall, such stone walls as are peculiar to Ireland, where they have witnessed, and
in their mute way assisted, many ugly deeds. One of these in fact was in process
when Mops arrived after a frantic struggle on the top of that wall.

Only twenty yards before reaching the point on the road the major, who for
reasons of his own had sent the carriage on and was walking home easily and
circumspectly with a cigar in his mouth and a double-barrelled shot-gun under
his arm, was suddenly confronted by a ragged and dirty masked ruffian who
seemed to have dropped from the skies, but who soon proved his infernal origin
by firing a heavy horse-pistol of antediluvian date right into the major's face.
As the heavy slugs whistled by the major's ear, the dirty ruffian turned and fled
down the deserted road into the gathering darkness.

Our friend, whose temper had been soured by the society of a disturbed
neighborhood, leant against the wall for a moment to steady himself and, allowing the proverbial forty yards' grace, deliberately let off two barrels into and
about the stern of his retreating enemy. The man howled fearfully, but continued his course. The major smiled, but the next moment cursed his folly with a
mighty oath, and turned to grapple with a second opponent who, having waited
his opportunity, sprang upon him while encumbered with his useless gun, and
in the surprise bore him almost to the ground. What this second monster, who
was also masked and unshaven, intended to do with the rude agricultural instrument, a sort of broken sickle, which he produced at this moment, must be left
to the imagination, for at this moment his attention was distracted.

With one of his curious little gurgling shrieks (like the bursting of a small
musical instrument) the breathless Mops jumped, or fell rather, on all fours from
the top of the wall. He did not spring at the man's calves, as dogs so often do;
he had no time to think of that,—and in fact alighted a little higher up. The
man wore moleskins, but what are moleskins to a little dog who makes a light
afternoon meal of a bedroom door? Before any one of the three knew very clearly
what had happened Mops had buried ten little teeth, each sharp as a new carv-
ing chisel, in the most fleshy part of the objectionable man's thigh. That was all,
and that was quite enough. The major, who had assisted (in the French sense)
at many an Irish row, and seen a good deal of service in Egypt, confesses that he

never heard a man swear as that ruffian did just before he was knocked down by the butt of the empty gun.

That night there was a good deal of coming and going of police. One of the individuals arrested will carry to the end of his life (which may be conterminous with the end of his imprisonment) such a "pretty pattern of No. 5" that the major has more than once expressed a wish "to send it to the makers," which, of course, is out of the question. The other carried away as lively a recollection of Mops as we shall any of us have, but for a different reason.

"In Praise of Mops." *Littell's Living Age* 192, no. 5 (January 1892): 251–53.

"Pillow Pattern, *Godey's Lady's Book*, 1861." *Godey's Lady's Book and Magazine* 62 (January 1861). Image courtesy of Special Collections and Archives, James B. Duke Library, Furman University.

Dogs (1829)

CATHARINE MARIA SEDGWICK

William Russel resides in one of our Massachusetts villages. He has recently been to New-York; and, on the evening after his return, while his brother and sisters were arranging their new toys, he began to describe, as well as he was able, the wonders he had seen in the great city. The toys were soon forsaken to listen to him; John's stag-hunt was but half set up; Anne's city looked as if an earthquake had tumbled down churches and houses in hopeless ruin; Mary's doll was permitted to remain half dressed; and even little Bess, the baby, caught the spirit of listening, ceased to jingle her silver bells, and, in sympathy with the rest, fixed her eager eye on William.

"Of all that I saw in the city of New-York," proceeded William, "that which pleased me most was the learned dog Apollo."

"That is exactly like you, William," exclaimed little Mary. "You always seem to care more about dogs than anything else."

"Not one half so much as I care about you, Mary," said the affectionate boy, kissing his sister's round, red cheek.

Mary's eyes sparkled; she threw her arm over her brother's shoulder. "Well, tell us all about Apollo, Will," she said.

William then went on to recount the wonderful performances of this most wonderful of all speechless animals. "Apollo," he said, "is a Greek by birth; like many other heroes, a native of the celebrated city of Athens; but he is owned and has been educated by an Englishman."

"Educated, William!" exclaimed John; "a dog educated! that is a good one!"

"Yes, educated, or taught, if you like that better, John; and, if you will please to listen instead of laughing, you will find that your education had been going on a long time before you knew as much as Apollo does. When he was exhibited, a circular piece of baize was spread on the floor, and twenty-six cards placed around its edge, with the alphabet printed on one side of them, and numbers, up to twenty-six, on the other. The spectators encircled the baize. They were requested by Apollo's master to ask him to spell any name that occurred to them. Several names were put to him, which he invariably spelt right."

"Could he speak?" asked Mary.

"Oh! no, no, Mary; I never heard of but one dog that could speak—a dog belonging to a peasant of Misnias; and he could pronounce but twenty-five words."

"A dog speak!" said Mary, shaking her head incredulously; "that I never will believe."

"Neither should I believe it, Mary, but papa read me the account, which is by Leibnitz, a great philosopher, who saw the dog; and I had rather believe a dog could speak, than that a great man would give a false report. But, though my dog Apollo cannot speak, he makes himself perfectly understood. For instance, I say, 'Apollo, spell Mary!' He walks slowly round the cards, stops before M A R Y, and puts his nose down to each; or, if you choose, he will bring them, and lay them at your feet."

"Ah, but Mary is a very, very short name; do you believe he could spell Alexander?" asked the little girl.

"Yes; I put that to him myself, and several other names; but he astonished me still more when he came to his arithmetic."

"Arithmetic!" exclaimed John; "well, if a dog can learn arithmetic, I hope I shall have a little more patience with it."

"Yes, arithmetic. He will multiply or subtract any number within twenty-five. For instance, you ask him, 'Apollo, how much is five times four?' and he will bring you the card on which twenty is printed. Or if you say, 'Apollo, add together three times five, and subtract six,' he will bring you the card on which nine is printed."

"Oh!" said John, "he could not know all that. It is a mere trick. I dare say his master makes him some private sign."

"Ah! John, as a gentleman said at the show, to get rid of one difficulty, you make a greater. Many of the spectators were watching the master, and they could not perceive the least communication between him and the dog; so the dog, to see these signs, which you suppose, must have had keener wits than any of us. He did many other things, but they did not appear so wonderful to me, because they were uniform answers to certain questions, which might have been often repeated to him. For instance, he would tell the capitals of all our states, and of the countries of Europe; where he was born; his age; the places he had visited, &c. He had even made acquaintance with the stars; could tell you the names of the planets; their distance from one another, and from the earth; the time they take to make their revolutions round the sun; and, in short," continued William, smiling, "he is quite a Newton among dogs."

After the children had exhausted their inquiries and expressions of admiration, William asked his mother if she did not think that, at some future time, there would be schools for dogs, as there were now for children. His mother thought not. "Men," she said, "teach one another. One race of boys educated, teaches the next; but God, in denying speech to dogs, has denied them the power of transmitting their knowledge. Apollo, learned as he is, cannot impart his knowledge to another dog; and it is not probable that man will ever make it his business to teach inferior animals, since such knowledge could be of no use after it ceased to be a curiosity. But, my children, we ought to be very glad to see the art of man employed on any other powers in dogs than the power of destruction. How much pains have been taken to train this interesting and useful animal to pursue and destroy other animals. In England, our mother country, dogs have been trained to fight and tear bulls for the amusement of the people. This disgusting sport was called bull-baiting. Even queens forgot the gentleness of their sex so far as to be present at these sports. Queen Mary entertained a French ambassador for two days successively with an exhibition of this kind, only fit for Hottentots; and was herself present."

"Perhaps, mamma," said William, "these horrid spectacles made her cruel; for that Mary was the queen who put to death so many of her own subjects that she was called 'Bloody Mary!'"

"Yes, William, such sports would certainly have a tendency to confirm a cruel disposition. You will find that most kind-hearted people are kind to animals. He who treats his horses and cows with care and tenderness, will not neglect his wife and children."

"You agree with the poet Cowper, mamma. Do you remember those lines you once pointed out to me?

'The heart is hard in nature, and unfit
For human fellowship, as being void
Of sympathy, and therefore dead alike
To love and friendship both, that is not pleased
With sight of animals enjoying life.'"

"Yes, my dear, and I thank you for remembering them. Cowper himself is a case in point. He was one of the most tender-hearted men that ever lived; and the history of his three little pet hares, Tiny, Puss, and Bet, which he has told so beautifully himself, and which you have all read, is a proof of his love of animals. But we were speaking of the cruelties taught to dogs. Do you know, William, that formerly bloodhounds were trained to pursue malefactors? This might be excused on the ground that murderers and robbers deserved no mercy; but no apology can be made for the French of St. Domingo, one of the West India Islands. Their slaves rebelled, and, determined to be free, carried on a war against their masters, by which they finally obtained their liberty. During this contest, the French trained bloodhounds to pursue and devour the negroes. I will read you the description of this mode of training the dogs, as it is given in the Encyclopedia." William's mother took down the book, and read the following extract:

"'In training the hounds to this inhuman pursuit, they are confined in a kennel, sparred like a cage, and sparingly supplied with the blood of other animals. The figure of a negro, in wicker-work, stuffed with blood and entrails, was occasionally exhibited in the upper part of the cage: the dogs struggled against their confinement, and, as their impatience increased, the effigy was brought nearer and nearer, while their usual subsistence was gradually diminished. At length the figure was resigned to them; and while voraciously tearing it up and devouring its contents, they were encouraged by the caresses of their keepers. Thus their hatred to black, and their love to white men, were at the same time excited. When their training was complete, they were sent out to the chase. The miserable negro had no means of escape; he was hunted down and torn to pieces, his wife and children, perhaps, sharing his misfortune. This, however, was not the full extent of the calamity. The dogs frequently broke loose, and infants were devoured in an instant from the public way; sometimes they proceeded to the neighbouring woods, and, surprising a harmless family of labourers at their simple meal, tore the babe from the breast of its mother, or devoured the whole party, and returned with their jaws drenched in gore.'"

The children were loud in their expressions of indignation at these base cruelties; and, turning from them to the more agreeable subject of Apollo, they again discussed his accomplishments.

"After all, mother," said Mary, "though I should like of all things to see Apollo, and I know I should admire him, yet I never could love him so much as I do poor Clara's little dog Foot."

"No, my dear; because, though talents in man, woman, child, or dog may excite our admiration, it is goodness that touches our hearts. Your eyes are wide open with wonder when you hear of Apollo; but the other day, when you witnessed the fidelity of Foot, they were moistened with tears of sympathy and tenderness."

"Tears! did we shed tears, mother?" asked Mary. "I am sure my feelings were pleasant."

"They were indeed, Mary; but some of our pleasantest feelings bring tears to our eyes."

That our young readers may understand what were the pleasant feelings that brought tears to the eyes of these good children, we must tell the story of Clara and her dog Foot.

Clara, or rather Clary (for I would give the accustomed sound to her name), is a poor girl in our village who has suffered from epileptic fits, which for the time suspend her faculties, and have gradually impaired them, till she has become, in country phrase, quite "underwitted." She leads, for the most part, an idle, vagrant life, straying about the field, gathering fruits, and collecting roots and wild flowers. She may be seen every day sauntering through our village street, in rain, snow, and driving wind, heedless of the weather, excepting in the bitterest cold of winter, when she steals to some kindly hearth, and putting to the fire her feet, which appear half frozen through her torn shoes, she looks up with a vacant smile, and says, like Shakespeare's fool, "Poor Clary's a-cold."

Her little terrier dog Foot is always by her side—the only living thing that seems to love her, the only one she loves. When she ploughs through the deep snows, he follows, jumping and frisking, and half buried at every plunge; and through the dismal rains, the poor fellow appears, still performing his forlorn duty, his head drooping, and his tail curled close to his legs. But in the fine, bright summer days, Foot has his pleasures too. When Clary is marching under the shade of the beautiful maples that line our streets, her torn frock trailing on the ground, her calico bonnet hanging back from her weather-beaten face, her alms-basket dangling on her arm, and her knitting (her constant occupation) in her hands, little Foot appears full of life and spirits. Every child in the street knows Foot; all respect his devoted friendship for Clary (for true friendship, even in dogs, is beautiful), and every little girl and boy gives him a kind word, or caress, or perchance a bit of gingerbread from the school-basket. Even the dogs—and there is an uncommon population of that race in our village—even the dogs bound towards little Foot with kind salutations, while he returns their greeting with a frolicksome play, and a short, joyous bark. But that which is most worthy of record about Foot, and that which excited the admiration of our young friends, yet remains to be told.

Poor Clary is sometimes seized with her fits by the roadside. During the paroxysms, and the long sleep which sometimes succeeds them, Foot never quits her side. I saw him on one of these occasions, his paws placed on her arm, looking intently in his poor mistress's face, and yelping most piteously. "What," thought I, "must be the tenderness of that Great Being, who has put such compassionate feelings into the breast of this little dog!"

Foot sometimes renders Clary essential service. Once, when she was returning from the field with a basket of fine strawberries, she sat down to rest herself, and was seized with a fit. A boy was passing with an empty basket. He espied Clary's beautiful strawberries; he saw she was unconscious, and he was tempted to steal them. He knew it was wicked to steal, and that this was cruel stealing; but the pleasure of gratifying his appetite with the delicious fruit was uppermost in his mind. He stole softly towards the strawberries, and was just emptying them into his own basket, when Foot sprang on him, grasped his coat between his teeth, and held him fast. The boy in vain tried to beat him off; he snarled and threatened to bite him, but did not quit his hold. The boy then thought of screaming for help; but then, whoever came to his relief would be a witness of his disgrace. He stood for a few moments pondering in silence, then stooped down, poured the pilfered strawberries again into Clary's basket, and placed it close to her side. When he had thus repaired his fault, Foot quietly released his prisoner and returned to his mistress's side. To the honour of the boy it should be told, that he afterward related the story himself; and said that no spoken reproof, no whipping, ever made him suffer so much as the shame he felt when he compared his dishonesty with the fidelity of this little brute.

I have often thought, when I looked on Clary and Foot, that there was no creature which walked the earth for whom God had not provided some pleasure. The possession of this little dumb friend seems in some measure to be a compensation to Clary for her misfortunes. I thought so last week, when I went to her mother's house on a sorrowful occasion. She has been the most afflicted woman in our village; and last week, her husband, an industrious, hard-working man, died after a few hours' sickness. When I entered their miserable dwelling, I found that some kind neighbours had already been there, and the poor man was decently laid out in an inner room. His son, a boy ten years old, who, a short time before, had his arm crushed in a mill, and afterward amputated, sat by him, weeping bitterly; the mother, a poor paralytic—one half of her body dead—was attempting to hush a famishing, crying baby; a little girl, the image of gentleness and patience, but pale and emaciated with disease, and deformed with dropsy, lay on a ragged coverlet in the middle of the floor. Clary sat on the doorstone, caressing Foot, in happy unconsciousness of the misery around her. Her eye rested on me for a moment while I sat feeding the baby, and she seemed to notice the tears I dropped on the helpless little thing, as if she half understood my emotion; but presently turning again to Foot, and renewing her play with him, she said, with one of her strange, vacant laughs, "But you and I have pleasant times, for all; don't we, Foot?"

I will not write out the moral of my story; for I well remember, when I was a child, how I hated those formal morals to Æsop's fables; how I thought them a dead weight, which almost crushed the life out of the pleasant story that went before them; and, besides, I do not doubt my readers have sagacity enough to perceive that little Mary preferred Foot on account of his affection and fidelity; and we hope that, like her, they will always set the qualities of the heart above the faculties of the mind; goodness above genius.

Catharine Maria Sedgwick, "Dogs." 1829. In *Stories for Young Persons*. New York: Harper and Brothers, 1855, 153–63.

The Fidelity of a Dog (1903)

CY WARMAN

The Baltynes came to Canada with plenty of money, but, as plenty is not enough for the average white man, Baltyne made more in the lumber-lands and more in the wheat-fields and flour-mills of Manitoba, and still more in the mines of the far Northwest. He was a big, wholesome, happy-natured man, but, as the years went by and his fortune grew with the growing country, there would come to him, in the logging-camp, in the wide wheat-fields, and in the miner's cabin, moments of utter loneliness.

Mrs. Baltyne had her moments of loneliness too. She longed and yearned for the sound of a baby's voice calling her mother. She was childless, and if she had married the commander of a submarine boat she would not have been much more alone, for so vast had her husband's fortune grown that they could scarcely see each other over the top of the heap.

At length, when she had sighed away six or seven summers, God blessed her and busied her with a beautiful baby boy. When the boy was two years old a friend of Baltyne's sent a pointer pup to play with him, and as no other heirs came to them the boy and the pup grew up together. Young Baltyne was a bright boy, and he taught the dog more tricks than most dogs ever learn. In summer they swam together, and in winter the dog, harnessed to a little red sled, gave the boy many a wild ride over the hard, snow-covered Canadian highways. Always they played together, and when the boy ate they ate together, for he would have nothing that he could not share with the dog, even to apples and oranges; and the dog, no matter how hungry he might be, if you gave him something blocks away, he would carry it and lay it at his master's feet.

When he was twelve years old the boy could say truthfully that there had not been a day in ten years that they had not seen each other sometime between the rising and setting of the sun. If the boy travelled by land or sea, the dog went by the same conveyance, and, if the boy could have his way, in the same carriage, car, or stateroom. The dog's whole life, from puphood to old age, had been spent in the boy's company, and never a cuff or a kick had he received. Is it any wonder, then, that the dog loved the lad?

One day—the first in all his life—he missed his little master. All day he hunted, searched, and waited for him, and all night those watching in the sick-room could hear him whining, which is only a dog's way of weeping, and when they passed out near the garden porch they could hear him walking, walking up and down, up and down, precisely as a human being would walk, and, I make no doubt, he suffered the same. Surely never was sorrow seen plainer in human eyes than in the anxious eyes of this devoted old dog.

The servants went tiptoe and conversed in stage whisperings. When they had outgrown the fear and dread of death that seemed to hover about "Brownwood," they spent long hours discussing the dog. They fed him regularly twice a day, and though no one of them had seen him eat, they believed he did eat, for all the solid food disappeared—all the bones were buried somewhere.

The pointer wasted day by day. The coachman said flippantly that the dog had spring fever. The gardener called it distemper, but old Auntie, the colored cook, said it was "totin' of his trouble" that made the old dog look "so po' an' mis'able like."

At the end of a fortnight he had lost all interest in his surroundings. If he lay in the shade of a shrub and the shadow shifted, he would not stir, but would lie for hours in the broiling sun rather than move. Sometimes, hearing a strange footstep, he would start up, look, listen, and then fall down again. Then he would take a long, deep breath, blow it out suddenly with a sigh, and lie perfectly still.

The robins rioted in the tulip-trees, the bluebirds built in the maples, and the woodpecker hammered away at the dead limb on the big sycamore down by the river, while the old dog lay under the lilac bush, listless, listening for his little master's footsteps. So the pointer passed the spring days, but of his nights and how he got through them no one knew. They knew he slept, if he slept at all, in his favorite corner in the garden porch, but they knew not how often through the long, lonely night, when tired of his bed he got up and walked, and when weary of walking lay down again.

One day Baltyne faced the Doctor in the hall. "Is he going?" he asked, almost demanded.

"Yes," was the answer, and it entered Baltyne's heart like a sword-thrust.

It was very still all about the big house that night, save for the smothered sobbing of a woman away off somewhere among the cushions where the lights burned low. But if any of the watchers passed out back, they heard the steady click,

click, click, click of the old dog's nails on the floor of the garden porch, like the measured ticking of the great clock in the hall, as he walked the hours away: up and down, up and down in the darkness, all alone.

At last the time was come. Hope had died with yesterday. The medicine bottles had been put aside. The nurse sat down, like the Doctor, to wait.

Often at intervals, during that day, the dying boy asked after his dog. Along in the afternoon he raised his head, and in his delirium called the dog, and instantly the pointer was at the window. For hours he had been walking, unobserved by the anxious watchers inside, up and down the narrow veranda that ran along the side of the boy's bedroom. At the sound of his master's voice he stood up and beat the window with his front feet. At the sight of him the boy seemed to forget his suffering and, smiling, begged them to let the dog in. Baltyne—big, brave Baltyne, with tears washing down his wind-browned face—looked at the door and the Doctor nodded. Then Baltyne opened the door that led to the little veranda and the dog glided in. His whole frame quivered as he entered the room, and as he caught sight of the boy he uttered a little, teetering whine that grew until he reached the bed. As the boy wound his arms around the dog's neck the whine swelled into a cry,—not a bark nor a growl, nor yet a melancholy howl that a dog will do away in the dark,—a sobbing cry, not unlike that which came from the other side of the bed where the boy's mother was kneeling. Almost immediately the boy became calm and sank into a sort of stupor that was like sleep. When he had closed his eyes, Baltyne lifted the old dog tenderly and put him outside the room. At the door the dog turned his head, looked back at the bed, and uttered a low, quivering cry,—that was all.

When the door was closed he resumed his walk, up and down, up and down along the narrow veranda.

That night the boy slept as he had not slept for weeks. The Doctor was surprised to find him fresher and stronger the next morning. He got out his bottles and began to help the boy, who continued to show some signs of improvement. He slept again in the afternoon, and on waking asked for the dog. The meeting between the little master and his mute friend was marked by the same mutual happiness, though neither was affected as on the previous day. The dog went out quietly this time. Like the boy, he had grown stronger.

The Doctor gave the family a little hope, and that night Mrs. Baltyne slept.

After a night's rest she rose somewhat refreshed and went out while the house was yet quiet. As she passed out under the great trees she saw the old dog dragging himself up the hill. When he saw her he picked up a nest that had been torn from a tulip-tree by the night-wind, brought it and put it down at her feet, and then fell down to rest. In the nest, rain-drenched, were two half-naked robins. "So like you, poor old dog," said his mistress, laying a hand lightly on the pointer's head.

From where she sat resting on a rustic seat she could see, away down by the swimming-pool, a little mound, where the wet leaves had been lately disturbed.

The next morning they missed the old dog, and Mrs. Baltyne, remembering her early morning experience of the day before, went down to the pool, and there she found the old dog hiding and hoarding like a miser to the last.

At the end of a month the boy was able to be wheeled down to the pool. The old dog romped out ahead, and when the nurse arrived with the invalid, followed by the parents, the old dog tore into the leaves, barking. "Here, Master," he was trying to say, "see, I have eaten nothing. Here, where we have feasted so often together, have I cached all my bones, waiting, waiting for you. It was hard—I was hungry sometimes, but I knew you'd come." And then, as if to set example, he began gnawing a fresh bone, for he *was* hungry.

Presently the Doctor joined them.

"What was it, Doctor," asked Mrs. Baltyne, "that came so near killing our boy?"

"The fever."

"And what was it that saved him to us when hope had gone?"

"The dog," said the honest old Doctor.

Cy Warman, "The Fidelity of a Dog." *Lippincott's Monthly Magazine* 71, no. 423 (March 1903): 361–63.

One Minute Longer (1919)

ALBERT PAYSON TERHUNE

Wolf was a collie, red-gold and white of coat, with a shape more like his long-ago wolf ancestors' than like a domesticated dog's. It was from this ancestral throwback that he was named Wolf.

He looked not at all like his great sire, Lad, nor like his dainty, thoroughbred mother, Lady. Nor was he like them in any other way, except that he inherited old Lad's stanchly gallant spirit and loyalty. No, in traits as well as in looks, he was more wolf than dog. He almost never barked, his snarl supplying all vocal needs.

The Mistress or the Master or the Boy—any of these three could romp with him, roll him over, tickle him, or subject him to all sorts of playful indignities.

And Wolf entered gleefully into the fun of the romp. But let any human besides these three, lay a hand on his slender body, and a snarling plunge for the offender's throat was Wolf's invariable reply to the caress.

It had been so since his puppyhood. He did not fly at accredited guests, nor, indeed, pay any heed to their presence, so long as they kept their hands off him. But to all of these the Boy was forced to say at the very outset of the visit:

"Pat Lad and Bruce all you want to, but leave Wolf alone. He doesn't care for people."

Then, to prove his own immunity, the Boy would proceed to tumble Wolf about, to the delight of them both.

In romping with humans whom they love, most dogs will bite more or less gently,—or pretend to bite,—as a part of the game. Wolf never did. In his wildest and roughest romps with the Boy or with the Boy's parents, Wolf did not so much as open his mighty jaws. Perhaps because he dared not trust himself to bite gently. Perhaps because he realized that a bite was not a joke, but an effort to kill.

There had been only one exception to Wolf's hatred for mauling at strangers' hands. A man came to The Place on a business call, bringing along a two-year-old daughter. The Master warned the baby that she must not go near Wolf, although she might pet any of the other collies. Then he became so much interested in the business talk that he and his guest forgot all about the child.

Ten minutes later, the Master chanced to shift his gaze to the far end of the room, and he broke off, with a gasp, in the very middle of a sentence.

The baby was seated astride Wolf's back, her tiny heels digging into the dog's sensitive ribs, and each of her chubby fists gripping one of his ears. Wolf was lying there, with an idiotically happy grin on his face and wagging his tail in ecstasy.

No one knew why he had submitted to the baby's tugging hands, except because she was a baby, and because the gallant heart of the dog had gone out to her helplessness.

Wolf was the official watch-dog of The Place, and his name carried dread to the loafers and tramps of the region. Also, he was the Boy's own special dog. He had been born on the Boy's tenth birthday, five years before this story of ours begins, and ever since then the two had been inseparable chums.

One sloppy afternoon in late winter, Wolf and the boy were sprawled, side by side, on the fur rug in front of the library fire. The Mistress and the Master had gone to town for the day. The house was lonely, and the two chums were left to entertain each other.

The boy was reading a magazine. The dog beside him was blinking in drowsy comfort at the fire. Presently, finishing the story he had been reading, the Boy looked across at the sleepy dog.

"Wolf," he said, "here's a story about a dog. I think he must have been something like you. Maybe he was your great-great-great-great-grandfather, because he lived an awfully long time ago—in Pompeii. Ever hear of Pompeii?"

Now, the Boy was fifteen years old, and he had too much sense to imagine that Wolf could possibly understand the story he was about to tell him; but long since he had fallen into a way of talking to his dog, sometimes, as if to another human. It was fun for him to note the almost pathetic eagerness wherewith Wolf listened and tried to grasp the meaning of what he was saying. Again and again, at sound of some familiar word or voice inflection, the collie would prick up his ears or wag his tail, as if in the joyous hope that he had at last found a clue to his owner's meaning.

"You see," went on the Boy, "this dog lived in Pompeii, as I told you. You've never been there, Wolf."

Wolf was looking up at the Boy in wistful excitement, seeking vainly to guess what was expected of him.

"And," continued the Boy, "the kid who owned him seems to have had a regular knack for getting into trouble all the time. And his dog was always on hand to get him out of it. It's a true story, the magazine says. The kid's father was so grateful to the dog that he bought him a solid silver collar. Solid silver! Get that, Wolfie?"

Wolf did not "get it." But he wagged his tail hopefully, his eyes alight with bewildered interest.

"And," said the Boy, "what do you suppose was engraved on the collar? Well. I'll tell you: *This dog has thrice saved his little master from death. Once by fire, once by flood, and once at the hands of robbers!* How's that for a record, Wolf? For one dog, too!"

At the words "Wolf" and "dog," the collie's tail smote the floor in glad comprehension. Then he edged closer to the Boy as the narrator's voice presently took on a sadder note.

"But at last," resumed the Boy, "there came a time when the dog couldn't save the kid. Mount Vesuvius erupted. All the sky was pitch-dark, as black as midnight, and Pompeii was buried under lava and ashes. The dog might have got away by himself.—dogs can see in the dark, can't they, Wolf?—but he couldn't get the kid away. And he wouldn't go without him. You wouldn't have gone without me, either, would you, Wolf? Pretty nearly two thousand years later, some people dug through the lava that covered Pompeii. What do you suppose they found? Of course they found a whole lot of things. One of them was that dog—silver collar and inscription and all. He was lying at the feet of a child. It must have been the child he couldn't save. He was one grand dog—hey, Wolf?"

The continued strain of trying to understand began to get on the collie's high-strung nerves. He rose to his feet, quivering, and sought to lick the Boy's face, thrusting one upraised white fore paw at him in appeal for a handshake. The Boy slammed shut the magazine.

"It's slow in the house, here, with nothing to do," he said to his chum. "I'm going up the lake with my gun to see if any wild ducks have landed in the marshes yet. It's almost time for them. Want to come along?"

The last sentence Wolf understood perfectly. On the instant, he was dancing with excitement at the prospect of a walk. Being a collie, he was of no earthly help in a hunting-trip; but on such tramps, as everywhere else, he was the Boy's inseparable companion.

Out over the slushy snow the two started, the boy with his light single-barreled shotgun slung over one shoulder, the dog trotting close at his heels. The March thaw was changing to a sharp freeze. The deep and soggy snow was crusted over, just thick enough to make walking a genuine difficulty for both dog and boy.

The Place was a promontory that ran out into the lake, on the opposite bank from the mile-distant village. Behind, across the high-road, lay the winter-choked forest. At the lake's northerly end, two miles beyond The Place, were the reedy marshes where a month hence wild duck would congregate. Thither, with Wolf, the Boy plowed his way through the biting cold.

The going was heavy and heavier. A quarter-mile below the marshes the Boy struck out across the upper corner of the lake. Here the ice was rotten at the top, where the thaw had nibbled at it, but beneath it was still a full eight inches thick, easily strong enough to bear the Boy's weight.

Along the gray ice-field the two plodded. The skim of water, which the thaw had spread an inch thick over the ice, had frozen in the day's cold spell. It crackled like broken glass as the chums walked over it. The Boy had on big hunting-boots, so, apart from the extra effort, the glass-like ice did not bother him. To Wolf it gave acute pain. The sharp particles were forever getting between the callous black pads of his feet, pricking and cutting him acutely.

Little smears of blood began to mark the dog's course; but it never occurred to Wolf to turn back, or to betray by any sign that he was suffering. It was all a part of the day's work—a cheap price to pay for the joy of tramping with his adored young master.

Then, forty yards or so on the hither side of the marshes, Wolf beheld a right amazing phenomenon. The Boy had been walking directly in front of him, gun over shoulder. With no warning at all, the youthful hunter fell, feet foremost, out of sight, through the ice.

The light shell of new-frozen water that covered the lake's thicker ice also masked an air-hole nearly three feet wide. Into this, as he strode carelessly along, the Boy had stepped. Straight down he had gone, with all the force of his hundred-and-ten pounds and with all the impetus of his forward stride.

Instinctively, he threw out his hands to restore his balance. The only effect of this was to send the gun flying ten feet away.

Down went the Boy through less than three feet of water (for the bottom of the lake at this point had started to slope upward toward the marshes) and through nearly two feet more of sticky marsh mud that underlay the lake-bed.

His outflung hands struck against the ice on the edges of the air-hole, and clung there. Sputtering and gurgling, the Boy brought his head above the surface and tried to raise himself, by his hands, high enough to wriggle out upon the surface of the ice. Ordinarily, this would have been simple enough for so strong a lad, but the glue-like mud had imprisoned his feet and the lower part of his legs and held them powerless.

Try as he would, the Boy could not wrench himself free of the slough. The water, as he stood upright, was on a level with his mouth. The air-hole was too wide for him, at such a depth, to get a good purchase on its edges and lift himself bodily to safety.

Gaining such a finger-hold as he could, he heaved with all his might, throwing every muscle of his body into the struggle. One leg was pulled almost free of the mud, but the other was driven deeper into it. And as the Boy's fingers slipped from the smoothly wet ice-edge the attempt to restore his balance drove the free leg back, knee-deep into the mire.

Ten minutes of this hopeless fighting left the Boy panting and tired out. The icy water was numbing his nerves and chilling his blood into torpidity. His hands were without sense of feeling as far up as the wrists. Even if he could have shaken free his legs from the mud, now he had not strength enough left to crawl out of the hole.

He ceased his uselessly frantic battle and stood dazed. Then he came sharply to himself. For, as he stood, the water crept upward from his lips to his nostrils. He knew why the water seemed to be rising. It was not rising. It was he who was sinking. As soon as he stopped moving the mud began very slowly, but very steadily, to suck him downward.

This was not a quicksand, but it was a deep mud-bed, and only by constant motion could he avoid sinking farther and farther down into it. He had less than two inches to spare at best before the water should fill his nostrils; less than two inches of life, even if he could keep the water down to the level of his lips.

There was a moment of utter panic. Then the Boy's brain cleared. His only hope was to keep on fighting—to rest when he must for a moment or so, and then to renew his numbed grip on the ice-edge and try to pull his feet a few inches higher out of the mud. He must do this as long as his chilled body could be scourged into obeying his will.

He struggled again, but with virtually no result in raising himself. A second struggle, however, brought him chin-high above the water. He remembered confusedly that some of these earlier struggles had scarce budged him, while others had gained him two or three inches. Vaguely, he wondered why. Then turning his head, he realized.

Wolf, as he turned, was just loosing his hold on the wide collar of the Boy's mackinaw. His cut forepaws were still braced against a flaw of ragged ice on the air-hole's edge, and all his tawny body was tense.

His body was dripping wet, too. The Boy noted that; and he realized that the repeated effort to draw his master to safety must have resulted, at least once, in pulling the dog down into the water with the floundering Boy.

"Once more, Wolfie! Once more!" chattered the Boy through teeth that clicked together like castanets.

The dog darted forward, caught his grip afresh on the edge of the Boy's collar, and tugged with all his fierce strength, growling and whining ferociously the while.

The Boy seconded the collie's tuggings by a supreme struggle that lifted him higher than before. He was able to get one arm and shoulder clear above the ice. His numb fingers closed about an upthrust tree-limb which had been washed down stream in the autumn freshets and had been frozen into the lake ice.

With this new purchase, and aided by the dog, the Boy tried to drag himself out of the hole. But the chill of the water had done its work. He had not the strength to move farther. The mud still sucked at his calves and ankles. The big hunting-boots were full of water that seemed to weigh a ton.

He lay there, gasping and chattering. Then, through the gathering twilight, his eyes fell on the gun, lying ten feet away.

"Wolf!" he ordered, nodding toward the weapon, "Get it! *Get* it!"

Not in vain had the Boy talked to Wolf for years as if the dog were human. At the words and the nod, the collie trotted over to the gun, lifted it by the stock, and hauled it awkwardly along over the bumpy ice to his master, where he laid it down at the edge of the air-hole.

The dog's eyes were cloudy with trouble, and he shivered and whined as with ague. The water on his thick coat was freezing to a mass of ice. But it was from anxiety that he shivered, and not from cold.

Still keeping his numb grasp on the tree-branch, the boy balanced himself as best he could, and thrust two fingers of his free hand into his mouth to warm them into sensation again.

When this was done, he reached out to where the gun lay, and pulled its trigger. The shot boomed deafeningly through the twilight winter silences. The recoil sent the weapon sliding sharply back along the ice, spraining the Boy's trigger finger and cutting it to the bone.

"That's all I can do," said the Boy to himself. "If any one hears it, well and good. I can't get at another cartridge. I couldn't put it into the breach if I had it. My hands are too numb."

For several endless minutes he clung there, listening. But this was a desolate part of the lake, far from any road, and the season was too early for other hunters to be abroad. The bitter cold, in any case, tended to make sane folk hug the fireside rather than to venture so far into the open. Nor was the single report of a gun uncommon enough to call for investigation in such weather.

All this the Boy told himself as the minutes dragged by. Then he looked again at Wolf. The dog, head on one side, still stood protectingly above him. The dog was cold and in pain, but, being only a dog, it did not occur to him to trot off home to the comfort of the library fire and leave his master to fend for himself.

Presently, with a little sigh, Wolf lay down on the ice, his nose across the Boy's arm. Even if he lacked strength to save his beloved master, he could stay and share the Boy's sufferings.

But the Boy himself thought otherwise. He was not at all minded to freeze to death, nor was he willing to let Wolf imitate the dog of Pompeii by dying helplessly at his master's side. Controlling for an instant the chattering of his teeth, he called:

"Wolf!"

The dog was on his feet again at the word, alert, eager.

"Wolf!" repeated the Boy. "*Go!* Hear me? *Go!*"

He pointed homeward.

Wolf stared at him, hesitant. Again the Boy called in vehement command, "*Go!*"

The collie lifted his head to the twilight sky in a wolf-howl, hideous in its grief and appeal—a howl as wild and discordant as that of any of his savage ancestors. Then, stooping first to lick the numb hand that clung to the branch, Wolf turned and fled.

Across the cruelly sharp film of ice he tore at top speed, head down, whirling through the deepening dusk like a flash of tawny light.

Wolf understood what was wanted of him. Wolf always understood. The pain in his feet was as nothing. The stiffness of his numbed body was forgotten in the urgency for speed.

The Boy looked drearily after the swift-vanishing figure which the dusk was swallowing. He knew the dog would try to bring help, as has many another and lesser dog in times of need. Whether or not that help could arrive in time, or at all, was a point on which the Boy would not let himself dwell. Into his benumbed brain crept the memory of an old Norse proverb he had read in school:

"Heroism consists in hanging on one minute longer."

Unconsciously he tightened his feeble hold on the tree-branch and braced himself.

From the marshes to The Place was a full two miles. Despite the deep and sticky snow, Wolf covered the distance in less than six minutes. He paused in front of the gate-lodge, at the highway entrance to the drive. But the gardener and his wife had gone to Paterson, shopping, that afternoon.

Down the drive to the house he dashed. The maids had taken advantage of their employers' day in New York to walk across the lake to the village to a motion-picture show.

Wise men claim that dogs have not the power to think or to reason things out in a logical way. So perhaps it was mere chance that next sent Wolf's flying feet across the lake to the village. Perhaps it was chance, and not the knowledge that where there is a village there are people.

Again and again, in the car, he had sat upon the front seat alongside the Mistress when she drove to the station to meet guests. There were always people at the station, and to the station Wolf now raced.

The usual group of platform idlers had been dispersed by the cold. A solitary baggageman was hauling a trunk and some boxes out of the express-coop on to the platform to be put aboard the five o'clock train from New York.

As the baggageman passed under the clump of station lights, he came to a sudden halt, for out of the darkness dashed a dog. Full tilt, the animal rushed up to him and seized him by the skirt of the overcoat.

The man cried out in scared surprise. He dropped the box he was carrying and struck at the dog to ward off the seemingly murderous attack. He recognized Wolf, and he knew the collie's repute.

But Wolf was not attacking. Holding tight to the coat-skirt, he backed away, trying to draw the man with him, and all the while whimpering aloud like a nervous puppy.

A kick from the man's heavy-shod boot broke the dog's hold on the coat-skirt, even as a second yell from the man brought four or five other people running out from the station waiting-room.

One of these, the telegraph operator, took in the scene at a single glance. With great presence of mind he bawled loudly:

"MAD DOG!"

This, as Wolf, reeling from the kick, sought to gain another grip on the coat-skirt. A second kick sent him rolling over and over on the tracks, while other voices took up the panic cry of "Mad dog!"

Now, a mad dog is supposed to be a dog afflicted by rabies. Once in ten thousand times, at the very most, a mad-dog hue-and-cry is justified. Certainly not oftener. A harmless and friendly dog loses his Master on the street. He runs about, confused and frightened, looking for the owner he has lost. A boy throws a stone at him. Other boys chase him. His tongue hangs out, and his eyes glaze with terror. Then some fool bellows:

"Mad dog!"

And the cruel chase is on—a chase that ends in the pitiful victim's death. Yet in every crowd there is a voice ready to raise that asinine and murderously cruel shout.

So it was with the men who witnessed Wolf's frenzied effort to take aid to the imperiled Boy.

Voice after voice repeated the cry. Men groped along the platform edge for stones to throw. The village policeman ran puffingly upon the scene, drawing his revolver.

Finding it useless to make a further attempt to drag the baggageman to the rescue, Wolf leaped back, facing the ever larger group. Back went his head again in that hideous wolf-howl. Then he galloped away a few yards, trotted back, howled once more, and again galloped lakeward.

All of which only confirmed the panicky crowd in the belief that they were threatened by a mad dog. A shower of stones hurtled about Wolf as he came back a third time to lure these dull humans into following him.

One pointed rock smote the collie's shoulder, glancing, cutting it to the bone. A shot from the policeman's revolver fanned the fur of his ruff as it whizzed past.

Knowing that he faced death, he nevertheless stood his ground, not troubling to dodge the fusillade of stones, but continuing to run lakeward and then trot back, whining with excitement.

A second pistol-shot flew wide. A third grazed the dog's hip. From all directions people were running toward the station. A man darted into a house next door, and emerged, carrying a shotgun. This he steadied on a veranda-rail not forty feet away from the leaping dog, and made ready to fire.

It was then the train from New York came in, and momentarily the sport of "mad-dog" killing was abandoned, while the crowd scattered to each side of the track.

From a front car of the train the Mistress and the Master emerged into a Bedlam of noise and confusion.

"Best hide in the station, Ma'am!" shouted the telegraph operator, at sight of the Mistress. "There is a mad dog loose out here! He's chasing folks around, and—"

"Mad dog!" repeated the Mistress in high contempt. "If you knew anything about dogs, you'd know mad ones never 'chase folks around' any more than typhoid patients do. Then—"

A flash of tawny light beneath the station lamp, a scurrying of frightened idlers, a final wasted shot from the policeman's pistol, as Wolf dived headlong through the frightened crowd toward the voice he heard and recognized.

Up to the Mistress and the Master galloped Wolf. He was bleeding, his eyes were bloodshot, his fur was rumpled. He seized the astounded Master's gloved hand lightly between his teeth and sought to pull him across the tracks and toward the lake.

The Master knew dogs, especially he knew Wolf, and without a word he suffered himself to be led. The Mistress and one or two inquisitive men followed.

Presently, Wolf loosed his hold on the Master's hand and ran on ahead, darting back every few moments to make certain he was followed.

"Heroism—consists—in—hanging—on—one—minute—longer," the Boy was whispering deliriously to himself for the hundredth time as Wolf pattered up to him in triumph across the ice, with the human rescuers a scant ten yards behind!

Albert Payson Terhune, "One Minute Longer." *St. Nicholas* 47, part 1, no. 2 (December 1919): 112–19.

The Education of Sam (1900)

CHARLES DUDLEY WARNER

Sam is comparatively a young dog, only eighteen months old, with the world before him. It is not his fault that he has not a romantic name; he did not choose it, nor did I. He came to our house simply as Sam. Although a puppy in months, he displayed an independence of character that accounted for the fact that he was not called "Sammy."

Sticklers about breeds declare that he is a pure mongrel. He has the head of a hound, with a large brain, a handsome face, and fine eyes, commonly sad in expression, but capable of sparkling with joy or beaming with affection, and of flashing with rage and excitement when he encounters an enemy or cannot have his own way. In color he is a glossy black-and-tan, with a round sinewy body, but with legs, alas! too short to carry out the idea of his face that he is a hound; but he is so immensely vigorous that he can go along almost as fast as a sparrow. The tail is not bushy, but if it had a knot of ribbon on the end it would resemble a Chinaman's queue, or the single braid of a school-girl. Many people say that he is not handsome, considered as a dog; and he is not, if a dachshund is a beauty or if a pug is considered presentable—a kind of dog cut off square at both ends, as if one of many sawed off from a scantling of dogwood to be sold by the dozen. Whatever is the meaning of the biblical dictum that "He taketh not pleasure in the legs of a man," those who know Sam best cease to criticize him in this respect.

If Sam were a child he would be described as a bad boy with an affectionate disposition; he has no more inclination to "mind" than a child, is quick to repent after a beating, and eager to do wrong again immediately, and to repent again and be forgiven. He has never been punished to the point of breaking his spirit, but he seems to know exactly when he has had enough, ceases his angry yelping, sits down and puts up his right paw in token that he yields, and is sweetness and affection itself to his instructor until some new idea comes into his head for another educational experiment. I have never known a dog exhibit so much affection for his master, and less disposition to obey him when there is a difference of opinion between them. He is often as winning as a child in his ways, but in intelligence and knowledge of the world no child of his age is to be compared with him. He not only knows more than any child of eighteen months, but he has more sense of responsibility. His development has been much more rapid. The point of interest is the study of his mind and its limitations.

With his great and early intelligence in many ways, it is incomprehensible that he should not go on beyond what is generally assumed to be the dog limit. It is from this point of view that I venture to consider his education. At the outset, however, it should be said that I am not trying to educate him in the common acceptation of that word, but am trying the new method of awakening his mind and letting him develop and educate himself like a dog and not like a man. The mistake is commonly made of training a dog to imitate people. I wish to teach him no tricks, nor to cram him for an examination or an exhibition. I should like to see him grow up a good, capable dog on dog lines.

It should be borne in mind that a dog has a much more difficult task in his development in this world than a child. The child has simply to be developed as a human being on well-defined lines. The dog is expected to develop as a dog, and at the same time to adjust himself to human life in our social state—to learn human ways and accommodate his nature to artificial conditions. He has, therefore, a double task.

In a state of savagery the dog is a savage—that is admitted,—and probably he would remain so without human companionship, though doubtless dogs differ in character when wild, and, if we knew, we should find among them noble dogs, generous and capable of leadership. The question is whether there is any possibility of the higher education of the dog as a dog, and not as a mere imitation of a man. His present education is generally through fear, or through hope of gratification. In the former case he becomes a cringing slave of his master, and in the latter a sort of hypocrite. I dislike a learned pig, and I have little pleasure in seeing the performance of a trained dog. It is, indeed, pathetic to watch the tricks of imitation, so un-doglike, induced by fear, or by hunger, or by an appeal to the appetite. But it is always agreeable to see a dog do anything for his master, or for another dog, out of affection.

How far Sam can educate himself, when his attention is called to the necessity, is, of course, a matter of experiment. It seems to be agreed that dogs are prone to take their character from their human environment. If brought up among vulgar and brutal people, they will be vulgar and brutal, whereas they will acquire a certain gentleness and even aristocratic fastidiousness with associations of a different sort. Without trying to educate Sam out of his nature, I have been trying to influence him to good and polite behavior by treating him with gentle firmness and uprightness. His great passion is for taking walks, preferably in the country rather than in the city streets, and while his companion walks a mile Sam will usually run five miles, following scents on the ground, and chasing birds and other objects, like cats, that excite his curiosity. In this way he works off his superfluous energy and gets into a good frame of mind. Since he has been indulged daily in these long and free rambles, especially in the fields and woods, he has grown much more amenable and inclined to listen to reasonable counsel, and the cook says he is a "changed dog."

Occasional chastisement has benefited him, but the chief hold on him is through his affection and his love of wandering with his master. He will do anything rather than be cut off from that privilege. No punishment equals that of being left home when one of the family goes for a stroll. As an illustration of this, I recall that one morning when we started out he was so full of uncontrollable spirits that he ran and barked violently at every carriage, automobile, or bicycle in the road. I remonstrated in vain; and after going a square or two, I took him home and shut him up. He understood perfectly what that meant, for when we went out again after lunch he behaved like a little gentleman, and only exercised his impetuous playfulness on sparrows and cats and small game. Did he remain good and obedient? No more than a boy. Line upon line is needed with a dog, and he continually does things he knows to be wrong, only gradually giving up his bad habits. It seems to be a struggle in his nature whether he shall please himself or please me, and he acts a good deal on lightning impulse, like a child.

Yet some lessons he can learn perfectly. One day, as we were quietly walking along, his attention was suddenly attracted to an electric-car sprinkler. It was a new thing, and he thought it would be fun to run alongside of it and bark. Instantly he was off like a flash, paying no attention to my call. It was going at high speed, and Sam went straight at it with all his might. Unfortunately, he had not noticed the sprinkling-boom that swept the street close to the ground. This instrument knocked him down, carried him along, rolled him over and over, and drenched him. The motor-man and his master thought the dog was killed; but he got up, stood a moment dazed by the attack before he comprehended the situation, and then came back to me with the most downcast and humiliated mien. A moment after, a sparrow on the walk attracted his attention, and he was off like a shot. This shows the thoughtlessness of youth. But the lesson was learned, and now when Sam sees a sprinkler he makes the most respectful circuit around it. Day by day he is learning, in a dozen ways, that it is not most comfortable for him to have his own way in everything.

In speaking of his education, I do not mean to say that he is likely to be amenable to any system or traditionary curriculum. Indeed, he seems to have the modern idea of taking only the electives. He is probably incapable of pursuing a regular course. At the best his education must be superficial, but it is all the more interesting to see what he will make of his opportunities. There is one thing, however, that he may escape: he will not be a victim of what may be called the electric education. It is well known that an electric automobile can only be charged to run a certain time or distance. After the charge is out it is a dead machine. In some of our schools this process is used with the pupils. They are charged, or filled up, or "crammed," as it is called, in order to pass an examination, or to go a certain "term," and after the term is up, or the examination is safely passed, they have nothing in them, and would need to be newly charged for another effort. Whatever learning Sam gets, I want him to absorb it, have it a part of his nature, so that he will not run down and come to a standstill when the artificial stimulus is wanting.

It would be worthwhile to study Sam's morals from an evolutionary point of view. In this respect he would be placed somewhere in the list of those described by the reporter who recently spoke of the fall of the rain, at a picnic, upon the just and the unjust and upon the middle class. He has one trait which is specially interesting to the scientist. He has always had it, but it has come into special prominence since he has learned to swim—which he did without learning—and to go into the water after a stick. He will get it, but he will not, for love or money, bring it to me or surrender it if he thinks I want it. He does not care for the stick, and he drops it and leaves it if let alone; but if I make any move to take it up, he promptly claims it. This disposition to keep all you can get hold of, mainly to keep it from other people, a common trait of individuals and of nations, was evidently in the dog in the remote evolutionary period before he diverged from the main stem. And the persistence of this trait in the human race, in its present development, shows how impossible it is that it can be educated or evolved out of the dog in any calculable period.

It is very difficult to gage Sam's mental capacity, or its limitations, and fairly to judge how much of it is chargeable to what we contemptuously call "instinct." The lack of a mutual medium of communication is in the way of this investigation. This is more my fault than his. He understands me better than I understand him. He is learning my language, while he cannot make me understand his language, which is mostly signs. He knows a great many words that I use, while I can little understand his bark, or interpret properly the wag of his tail or the wiggle of his body. He may be expressing joy or rage or dissatisfaction or the want of something, and I have no doubt he thinks I am very stupid not to comprehend him. I have seen him, at times, almost beside himself, in a frenzy of tearing about and barking, when he evidently wanted me to do something, or was trying to express some emotion, either of affection or dislike. He certainly has great capacity of attachment; or perhaps his affection for his master might be called adhesiveness; for he sticks to me, in all our waking hours, closer than an Italian flea.

It is clear that some of his senses are developed far beyond ours, and probably beyond that of savage man, certainly his senses of hearing and smell, though I doubt if his sight is as keen or as far-reaching as that of a trained woodsman or a prairie-dweller or of the natural man in freedom. But there is another respect in which he is superior, and that is the quickness with which he responds to a sensation, or a suggestion transmuted into an idea, conveyed by the motor nerves. For instance, a fly lights on the finger. The sensation caused by this is conveyed to the brain, and the brain orders a motor nerve to move the finger and get rid of the fly. An appreciable time is consumed in this operation, and the time differs in different people. There was, and perhaps is, a series of experiments carried on at Cambridge, with very delicate machinery, to test the muscular response in different individuals to sense impressions. In this school or laboratory—all our schools will probably be called laboratories before long—Sam would take a high rank among the subjects or pupils. His response to anything he hears, sees, or smells appears to be instantaneous. If anything attracts his attention, whatever he may be doing, he is after it like a ball from a catapult. The sensation, the making up the mind, and the muscular action appear to be simultaneous. This may show that he is a very highly organized being. He has the faculty of dropping asleep instantly whenever he chooses; but he must be a light sleeper, for any incident that interests him puts him instantly in motion, without wasting the time to "wake up" taken by people generally. Why should not this great alertness of body be evidence of great alertness of mind?

Some of Sam's limitations are discouraging to an educator. I doubt if he has any correct comprehension of numbers, or if he can compute the passing of time. His memory shows that he recalls the past, but there is no sign that he has any comprehension of a future, consequently none of any world except this. It seems a pity to bring up a dog a pagan in a Christian country. If he lived in Europe he would be in the way of going to church, and would not be driven out of a place of worship, like a Congregational dog. But he could not be a Roman Catholic, for even if he could get rid of his seven deadly sins,—one of which, as has been said, is barking at passing carriages, automobiles, bicycles, and people carrying packages,—he has no sense of repentance, only the common sorrow for wrong-doing that makes him suffer. He can, however, be taught conduct, but not by "absent treatment"; and though anything like a religious tendency is indiscernible, he might be made a better dog by the Society of Ethical Culture.

I cannot say that Sam is a fighting dog. If invited, he would probably join the Peace and Arbitration Society. This peacefulness of his would discredit him with most people, who like a fighting dog and eagerly see a dog-fight; that is, they like best in a dog that which is savage in him. This shows about how far the human race has got on in its evolution out of savagery. It likes to fight and kill, and the best part of the race boasts of love of fighting as an Anglo-Saxon trait. The bulldog quality is highly valued. The highest compliment that can be paid to a soldier is to call him a bulldog. Sam certainly is not a model of this sort of valor; and merely to fight in self-defense, like a Quaker pushed to the wall, gives at present no reputation for heroism. The subject has, of course, another side. Is a non-resistant dog fitted for this world? Would a dog so civilized as to fight only in self-defense be likely to fight even in a war of self-defense for his country? Would he volunteer? Is the fighting spirit still a necessary part of doghood as it is of manhood? I doubt if Sam would make even a good modern missionary, since it is necessary to send a Gatling gun before or behind every missionary. It is only when Sam loses his temper that he acts like a Jingo, and is no more amenable to reason than an Expansionist.

Bad as Sam is in many respects,—he seems to be aware that I am writing about him, as he lies by my chair,—I am confident that he must be educated through his affection, and that the discipline he gets must be so administered as not to make him cringing and mean-spirited. He really, at times, seems disposed to do what I wish, if he can understand what that is and it does not interfere with his own inclinations; and he likes being praised. Many of his imperfections are due to his youth, and I realize that the truth of the old saying that it is hard to teach a new dog old tricks. But I do not wish to teach him tricks, or to make him conceited, but to educate him to be a good companion, and not to pervert his dog nature.

When Sam, conscious of having done wrong, stands quite out of the reach of my stick, all affection tempered by humorous expression in his eyes, and all dodging alertness in his legs, I often say to him: "Sam, you rascal, if you only knew how I have yearned for you to be a good dog!"

Charles Dudley Warner, "The Education of Sam." *Century Illustrated Magazine* 61, no. 1 (November 1900): 56–59.

The Reform of Shaun (1903)

ALLEN FRENCH

I

Within the kennel yard were a dozen dogs—within, that is, all but their noses, which were thrust through the pickets. Without, Jim Weaver, the dog-fancier, talked with a patron. The gentleman's dog strained at his leash, and tried to rub against Brian, who sat at Jim's feet—old Brian Boru, the ancestor, in some degree, of every dog there. But Brian held aloof, and listened to the conversation.

The other dogs also listened, even the three-months' pups, who were just learning their English. And heedless Shaun, after his month in the world as eager to put on airs as a boy just from college, got no attention at all.

"You guaranteed him satisfactory, Jim," the gentleman was saying.

"Yes, Mr. Davis, so I did," returned the breeder. "Of course I'll take him back, or I'll exchange him for another."

"You have another?" asked Mr. Davis.

"Same litter. Well, I'm disappointed in Shaun. I took such pains with him."

"Utterly unmanageable, Jim. He ran with all the curs in the town, ate himself sick with the food he found in the street, and would stay for hours away from the house."

Jim reached down, detached the gentleman's leash from Shaun's collar, and snapped on one of his own. Shaun took the opportunity to rub closer to Brian, but Brian moved away and sat down on his haunches, still listening.

"Will you have the other dog now, sir?" asked Jim.

"No, in a few days my wife and I go away for a visit, and we can't have a dog with us that we're not used to. In two weeks I'll take him. Meanwhile, won't you have him with you in the house, and train him a little?"

"I will, sir."

Mr. Davis stooped and patted Shaun. "Good-by, old fellow," he said. Shaun paid no attention. His master pulled the dog to him, took his head in both his hands, and looked into his brown eyes. "Shaun," he said, "I did my best with you." But the dog began to tug and twitch to get away.

Mr. Davis rose. "You see, Jim, he pays no attention. He doesn't care."

"I see, sir. He's no dog for you."

Mr. Davis turned away, and Shaun, piqued at his small attention from the others, started to follow. The leash held him up. He uttered a yelp.

His master stopped and looked back. "No, Shaun," he said, sadly. "I gave you every chance." He disappeared out of the dog's sight.

II

Jim opened the gate to the kennel yard, but none of the dogs came running out, not even the puppies. They stood at the opening in a close-wedged mass, and looked at Shaun. None of the stumpy tails were wagging. None of the shining teeth were bared in welcome. Each stocky Irish terrier stood and glowered, and Shaun, for the first time in his boisterous life, felt ill at ease. He hung back as Jim pulled him toward the gate.

"You see," said Jim, "they understand you. Larry, come out."

Shaun's own twin trotted past him and took no notice of him. Jim thrust Shaun in among the others, took off the leash, and was about to close the gate. Then he paused. "Brian," he said to the old dog.

Master and dog looked at each other knowingly. Brian's stump-tail slowly moved. "Go in there for a few days," said Jim. "See if you can't teach him something." Brian walked in after Shaun, and the gate was shut behind him.

The other dogs crowded close beside Brian, following him to the back of the yard. Larry went with Jim into the house. Shaun, devoid of company, pressed up against the bars, and gazed at the corner around which his master had gone. Mr. Davis was in the bright and beautiful world; Shaun was in the dingy kennel once more. But his master did not return, and Shaun at last, with a toss of his head, turned to the other dogs.

An unnatural quiet was over them. None of the puppies were playing: they were sitting in a row. Some of the older dogs were curled up to sleep, but at his movement Shaun saw the wary eyes open, then slowly close again. Old Brian, his onetime tawny muzzle now nearly silver, sat calmly, and took no notice of his descendant. But Shaun wandered up to him. "Brian," he asked, beginning to feel a curious homelessness, "Brian, has my master left me?"

"Your master?" said Brian. "You don't deserve a master, or a home."

"Huh!" said Shaun, scornfully. Brian was his great-great-grandfather, the idol and model of the kennels, upon whose precepts Shaun had been instructed. But his respect for Brian, in fact, his respect for anything, was much lessened.

Brian made no answer. Shaun went to Nip, the next oldest dog. "Nip," he said, "how d'e do?"

But Nip was cross, always cross. "Get out!" he said, "you spendthrift swaggerer!"

Self-possession was Shaun's latest cultivation. "Oh," he said, jauntily, "glad to find you feeling so well, Nip." He passed on to another dog.

But this time he got no answer at all, and as he went still farther he was studiously neglected. The dogs were asleep, or appeared to be, curled up tight. But Shaun believed they were pretending.

It was irritating. More than that, it was depressing, for where was Mr. Davis? Was he really not coming back? And would none of the dogs speak pleasantly? Perhaps Mr. Davis had said something unkind, there at the gate. Shaun wished he had listened. He walked along the row of sleeping dogs; none moved, none made advance to him. Nip was awake still, but surly and bristling. Brian, after his oracular utterance, sat like a statue of ice. Again Shaun felt that curious homesickness.

He went back to the gate and sat down. Why did not Mr. Davis return? Homesickness increased. It began to press upon him. He could not help it—after awhile he whimpered. Shaun was not so very old. He looked around at the older dogs: none paid attention. He raised his muzzle and whimpered louder. Then the barriers broke, and he lifted his voice in a full-drawn howl. "Oh," cried poor Shaun, "nobody loves me!" His quivering nose pointed toward the unrelenting heaven.

III

After awhile Shaun became conscious that Brian had changed position—was, in fact, coming toward him. He kept on howling. Brian sat down at his side. Gradually Shaun became silent. He did not look at Brian, but he knew that Brian was looking at him.

"Tell me," said Brian, finally, "what have you done to earn any one's love?"

"Oh," cried Shaun, in despair, "I wish I were with Horton's Snap. He would treat me kindly."

"Well, then," asked Brian, patiently, "who is Horton's Snap?"

"Horton," said Shaun, "is the butcher in our town—Mr. Davis's town, I mean. Snap is his dog."

"What kind of a dog?"

"Why, a fox terrier with a bushy tail."

"A fox terrier with a bushy tail?" asked Brian, coldly. "What did he do?"

"Oh, just nothing," said Shaun, glad of a chance to talk of his world. "But he knew where there were such nice things to eat."

"With what other dogs did you associate?" pursued Brian, deliberately.

"Why," said Shaun, "there was Jack Rogers. He was half setter. And Mopsy Frost; he was a pug."

"Fond of eating?" asked Brian.

"Oh," cried Shaun, enthusiastically, "there was always such a fine pailful by his back door."

"Any other dogs?" inquired Brian.

"Well, I don't know;" and Shaun thought. "I don't count the Walton's Max. He was rather too fond of going with his master."

"A thing you seldom did, I suppose?"

"And what's the use?" said Shaun. "Why, in our town there's plenty to eat, and so a fellow helps himself. You can't expect anything else."

"I shouldn't think it very clean," remarked Brian, critically.

"Well, clean enough," said Shaun.

"And you don't seem in such good trim as when you left."

Shaun made no answer: he allowed his mind to wander. But the thought of his friends was presently too much for him, and he broke out again. "It's been such fun!" he said. "Do you ever bark at horses?"

"Not now."

"Well, of course you have to be pretty limber," went on Shaun. "Snap Horton showed me, but I can do it now as well as he. I almost made a horse run away once. And everybody gets mad."

"Your master, too?"

"He hated it," admitted Shaun, guilelessly. "He'd whip me and tie me up. But it's such fun!"

"Never struck you as being a little undignified?"

"Why," said Shaun, "no—I—That is, not exactly."

"And how were you treated in the house?" asked Brian.

"Why, pretty well, I must say. I had my own basket, and a cushion. My mistress was kind to me. Isn't it nice when a woman pats you? But she was particular, you know, just like Mr. Davis. She used to wash me once a week, and she would make me eat my food on a cloth. Why should people object to crumbs? And then they would never let me come in the dining-room. And she didn't like to have me bark at people that passed the house. You see, they kept me pretty close."

"Of course you barked just the same?"

"Of course," said Shaun.

"And didn't take pains about the crumbs?"

"Why—no."

"And slipped away whenever you could to join your aristocratic friends?"

"You talk," answered Shaun, impatiently, "like Caesar White."

"It's a pity you didn't listen more to him. But who was he?"

"Well," said Shaun, this time triumphantly, "you may sneer at the misfortune of Snap Horton's birth, but Caesar White is no better. He is mixed mastiff and bull."

Brian was not moved. "Very well," he said, "birth is not everything. I have seen some pretty poor specimens come out of the best kennels." (Shaun winced.) "You are young, Shaun, and have not yet learned that there is an aristocracy of merit. What did he do?"

Shaun was still argumentative. "You can't get me there," he cried, "either. He ran with a cart." His contempt was deep.

Brian's head drooped. "The pity of it!"

"There!" said Shaun.

"O Shaun," said Brian, "I thought you had learned these things. Tell me, is there any disgrace in minding your master's business? To run with a cart and guard it—for a horse cannot do that—is honorable."

Shaun's assurance vanished, and Brian waited for a moment for the reproof to take effect. Then he asked:

"And Mr. Davis, was he kind?"

"Well," said Shaun, "I thought he was at first. But after I made friends with Snap Horton, he used to whip me for the things I did; barking, you know, and eating, and coming home late. And Snap said, you know, he was a pretty hard master. He never let any of his dogs run loose."

"No," said Brian, "so your father said."

Shaun faltered. "Did my father know Mr. Davis?"

Brian looked at Shaun with a mild indignation.

"You don't remember much that was said to you, do you? Your father was Mr. Davis's own dog. Have you forgotten that Mr. Davis took you because he was so fond of your father? Why, I told you twenty times never to disgrace your family. In that town of all others, and with such a master!"

Shaun felt a sudden sinking. "I—I forgot," he said.

"Your father," went on Brian, "used to come here sometimes for a week in the summer, when his master and mistress went yachting. Your father," said Brian, "was a *dog*." It was as if he said, He was a *man*. "Jim has his picture in the house. He was the best dog that ever went out of Jim's hands. Better than me. There's not a pup in the yard that can't tell you all about him. And you forgot!"

Shaun held his head low.

"I remember," said Brian, "when the news came of his death. I was in the yard that day looking after your mother. Jim came to the fence and looked down on us all. The moment I saw him I knew that something was wrong, and when he said, 'Gillie's dead!' there wasn't one of us that didn't drop his tail. You were born next day.

"And you say," pursued Brian, grimly, "that Mr. Davis was a hard master. I know all about Mr. Davis. Your father said: 'A kinder master one couldn't have. It was a pleasure to obey him.' A hard master! Shaun, he came here one day, and sat down there in the house, and called me to him. 'Brian,' he said, 'Gillie's dead! Old dog, my heart is sore. Where shall I get such another?' And, Shaun, there were tears in his eyes. Don't you know we picked you out for him?"

Shaun shivered all up and down his spine, but his back was now turned, and he said nothing.

"One of Gillie's pups was to go to Mr. Davis," went on Brian. "We heard Jim saying so. We picked you out for him, your mother and I; we trained you up for him. Jim saw it, and so he took the mother's choice, as he always does. And now Larry's a good dog, but he's the last of the litter."

"What do you mean?" cried Shaun. "Isn't Mr. Davis coming back for me?"

"For Larry."

"And I?—and I?"

Brian answered, solemnly, "You'll stay here the rest of your life. Jim never lets a dog go out twice."

Shaun screamed with sudden fright.

IV

What human beings express by weeping and wailing and wringing of hands, Shaun manifested in his own way for many hours. He yelped, he barked, he howled, he ran up and down beside the pickets, he scratched at the gate. At midnight his distress had not abated. Old Jim got out of his bed and looked into the moonlight at the piteous form. "He takes it pretty hard," he said, and he patted Larry before he lay down again.

Near daylight Shaun, exhausted, slept. But his dreams were bad, and he twitched and whimpered in his sleep. The other dogs looked at him soberly as one by one they awoke; the puppies got many a lesson that morning. Jim came and fed the dogs, and at the noise Shaun woke. But he made no movement to join them, and Brian at last came and sat down by him.

"Well," he said, cheerfully, "I've some breakfast saved for you."

"I think," said Shaun, "I don't want any."

"Prefer something fresh from the swill-pail?"

"Brian!" cried Shaun, unhappily.

Brian couched, and lay thinking. "Your father—" he said, after a while. Shaun's ears dropped, and he turned his head away.

"Your father," said Brian, inexorably, "used to speak so fondly of his home. He used to thank me" (and the old dog's voice trembled a little) "for the training I gave him. He used to repeat to the puppies all the maxims: 'Obedience is a dog's virtue,' 'One dog can annoy a whole neighborhood,' 'A good home is more than everything,' and then again, 'Whatever comes of it, obey.' He used to say a good many things may not seem to pay—waiting at doors, not eating, not barking, coming when you're called. But they do pay just the same, when you find your master loves you. Mr. Davis, Shaun—"

"Don't!" cried Shaun.

"Mr. Davis cared. He said, when he left you yesterday, that he'd done his best with you. If you had noticed, you'd have seen how much he cared."

"Don't! Don't!" cried Shaun.

"And now," went on Brian, "you'll grow to be just like Nip here, fat and cross, and somewhat stupid. A gentleman tried him once, and couldn't keep him—"

"Don't!" cried Shaun. "Don't, oh, don't! It kills me. Oh, how could I forget?"

And Jim, again looking out of the window, said, "There's Shaun at it once more." He lifted Larry up to look.

V

It was the second morning. Shaun's second night had been quieter; he went to sleep before midnight. But again he refused his breakfast.

"You needn't talk to me any more about it all," he said to Brian, when the old dog came and sat by him again. "I think I understand now."

"Have I been unkind?" asked Brian.

"You had to be, I suppose. None of the other dogs have taken any notice of me since I came."

That was according to Brian's orders. And yet, thought the old dog, what was the use? Shaun's life was spoiled. He would have no chance to prove his repentance.

Suddenly Shaun jumped up. "Brian!"

"Well?"

"Jim has left the gate open!"

"Well," said Brian, calmly, "none of the pups will run away."

Shaun dilated, "*I* will run away."

"Why," said Brian. "Why—" He hesitated between duty to his master and affection for a favorite grandchild. But Shaun waited for no permission. He slipped out the gate. "I must go," he said. "Good-by!"

Once in the street he was like a chip upon the sea. Strange dogs ran at him, and growled. He avoided them only to meet others. This was no time to fight;

besides no dog has a right to fight except on his own territory. He was weak with thirty-six hours of strong emotion, and from lack of food. He glad he was when he saw a dog that ran with a cart!

"Please," he said, "oh, please, which way to Concord?"

The dog with the cart trotted on, minding his master's business. But he responded.

"Go on to the watering-trough," he said. "Then first left, and straight on for miles and miles."

Shaun obeyed. He found the long turnpike and followed it. First there were houses; they dwindled in number, and he ran between fields, then between tall trees. Then fields again, then more houses, then a town.

He passed through the town, then through the long vacant space where no one lived, then through another town, and another, and another. No Concord yet, but in every place he was followed by yelling mongrels. Another town, but not his own, and still the straight road led on. Then at last—surely that house was familiar, and that tree. Here was his own town—his own street—his own house, and Mr. and Mrs. Davis standing at the door. He crawled to them, pleading on his wretched little belly. "Shaun!" they cried, and stood speechless.

VI

"And so," said Brian, on the next day, "they've brought you back again."

Shaun's disappointment was too deep for expression. Brian could get nothing from him—nothing but moans, and tears from the brown eyes. It seemed as if Shaun were heartbroken. "He'll die of it," said Brian, and old Jim said the same. A day, two days passed, and Shaun was thin. Jim bathed him, combed him, brushed him. He brought him the best of food; Shaun would have none of it. "He'll die, surely," said Jim.

Brian came to him again and again. Shaun sighed, moaned, and could not respond. But at last, by long, perseverance, Brian made Shaun talk. "Oh," said the poor creature, "if they had only tried me! I should have been so good! Yet my mistress cried when I cried; sometimes I think of that, and it comforts me—a little. If I could only see her again!"

Brian was moved. "It must have cost her something to send you away, even the first time," he asserted.

Tears trickled down Shaun's nose. "I know it now," he said. "I remember now how she kissed me good-by, the first time. And this time, just as we were going away, and I was crying, 'Oh,' she said to Mr. Davis, 'don't let him come back again. I couldn't bear to part with him a third time!'"

"Then go again!" cried Brian.

"Jim will never let me out," said Shaun, sadly. "I heard him promise Mr. Davis."

"But I can get you out."

Shaun raised his head, then started up. "What—now?" he demanded.

"This night," said Brian. "Eat, Shaun—eat, and gather strength!"

That night's moon saw a strange sight. One after another the terriers relieved each other, digging a hole under the pickets. Shaun lay and waited, trembling with hope. Brian directed the work. When the hole was deep enough, Shaun squeezed through.

"Good-by, all," he said. "Good-by, Brian. You've been kinder to me than I deserve."

The two rubbed noses through the bars. "Good-by," said Brian. "Good-by," said all the others. "Good luck this time, Shaun!"

That was a long run in the pale moonlight. The road stretched onward like a silver ribbon, bordered by threatening shadows. Among the woods, the darkness seemed full of dangers; in the town, Shaun feared the persecuting curs. But no wild beast came from under the trees, and as he passed through the sleeping towns no one molested him.

As the day broke he reached his own town, and his own house. Thankful, humble, fearful of the future, he sat at the door and waited for the inmates to awake.

But while the town stirred into life, and carts began to pass and repass, no sound came from within the house. The milkman went by without stopping, and Shaun, wondering, became uneasy. Still, he did not dare to bark. He waited longer, till the sun stood high, and he could no more contain himself. Then he cried for admittance.

The neighbor's wife came to her door, and looked at him. "Why," she said, "there is Mr. Davis's dog come back again."

She came out and spoke to Shaun. "Doggie," she said, "they've gone. They've gone to stay a week."

"She doesn't understand," thought Shaun. "Perhaps they will come soon. I'll—I'll wait."

VII

The woman left him and he lay down. He was aroused by a voice, impudent and familiar. "Hullo, Shaun! Back again?"

There stood Snap Horton, grinning broadly, his bushy tail waving. "One on you, Shaun," he said. "They've gone on a vacation; everybody knows. But never mind, you sleep with me in our shed, and there's plenty of food about the town."

Every fiber of Shaun's body revolted at the sight of his old intimate—his tempter. He jumped up, growling. "Go away!" he cried.

Snap started back. "Shaun?"

"Go away!" repeated Shaun. "I hate you!" He took a step forward; his hair was bristling. "Shall I bite you?" Snap was a coward, and he fled.

The long day wore into the long evening. Shaun never left the steps. Toward night he saw a form coming down the street, and knew it for Jack Rogers on his evening rounds. In behind each house, reappearing slowly or quickly, as he found more or less to eat, occasionally emerging hurriedly, as if chased, came the second of Shaun's old cronies. Shaun watched him with growing shame. Once he had joyously accompanied Jack on these tours of gluttony; now it seemed a small and currish thing to do. Shaun turned his head away.

But he heard the fawning voice: "Why, Shaun, old boy! So glad to see you back. Folks away, aren't they? Well, come with me, and we'll get along together."

Shaun slowly rose to his feet, and if his legs trembled with weakness, they also trembled with rage. "See here, Jack Rogers—"

"Well, Shaun," said Jack, smoothly, "if you won't, you won't. Tomorrow, perhaps." He trotted on.

The neighbor's wife came to her door and called him. She had a dish in her hand, and Shaun looked away from the temptation. She came to him and put the dish down near him; a bowl also.

"A good bone," she said, "and some bread and milk. There, doggie, you look hungry. Now eat it all up." She patted his head, and waited to see him begin.

Shaun wagged his tail, but drew back.

"A good dog," he remembered, "lets only his master feed him." She pushed the food nearer, and the tempting smells came to his nostrils, but he still drew uncomfortably away. "It beats all," she said, at last. "But I'll leave them with him." She went back to her own house.

Night came. In the dark Shaun felt the desire to howl, but struggled with it and mastered it. "One dog can annoy a whole neighborhood." Mr. Davis had once called him a public nuisance; he would be one no longer. He paced up and down; at times he slept fitfully. At last the morning dawned—a dreary day.

Then came Mopsy Frost panting up the street. He seated himself on the steps.

"Snap told me he saw you yesterday," he said, in his husky voice. "A little out of sorts, weren't you? He said he expected an apology. Ha! ha!" He paused for comment, but found none. "I came to offer you a share of the contents of our bucket."

"Go!" cried Shaun.

"Shaun! When I've fed you so many times!"

"With your food," said Shaun, bitterly, "you betrayed me."

The dropsical beast got himself off the steps. "Well," he wheezed, "I see Snap was right. *I* sha'n't expect an apology." He went away.

The day dragged on. Shaun had much to think of, many resolves to make, and an enemy within him, hunger, to conquer. It was hard to resist with the food so close by. To forget it, he slept, and dozed away the hours—slept uneasily, with unpleasant dreams. Toward night he thought that someone was near him, and started up suddenly, crying, "Who's there?"

There was a rush of feet, and Snap Horton went flying away. But he bore in his mouth the bone for which he had sneaked up so quietly; and though the neighbor's wife, who had seen it all, came running out, it was too late. Shaun sat still, too proud to give chase, but his heart burned within him.

VIII

The night brought a late spring frost. Shaun could not sleep, he had to keep in constant motion. The early sun brought warmth, but no true comfort.

The neighbor's wife made it harder for him with fresh, more tempting food, and he carried his trembling little body away from her, across the street. But even when she was gone the food remained, and when he curled up on the steps to sleep the odors tantalized him. He repeated constantly, "I mustn't eat," and, warmed at last by the sun, he slept.

But sleep, which at first had been his comfort, now began to torture him as much as his waking. Hunger pursued him, he dreamed of beautiful dishes of food and woke in an agony, crying with fear lest he should taste them. Dozing again, he thought he was with Jack Rogers rooting in the garbage of the street, and woke with the strength of his hatred of himself. He was very thin; the gnawing at his stomach was unceasing. When he slept again the pain of his hunger waked him.

So passed a third day and night. People began to take notice of him, for the neighbors had told others. It irritated Shaun, in his weakness, to be stared at. It required all his strength to resist the temptations that were brought him. More than once he sank in a stupor that was not sleep; and when waking his head was not clear. And the fourth day revealed an evident difference in him: his bones were showing everywhere under his skin.

It was the middle of the afternoon. Shaun lay on the step, awake. His eyes were bright and strange, as if through them showed the fire of his energy, fitful just before its end. Snap Horton, Jack Rogers, Mopsy Frost, had not come near him again. But many others had spoken to him, new friends whom he remembered thankfully all the rest of his life. And the neighbor's wife was still with him, coaxing him to eat, and almost crying with pity. "If I knew where Mr. Davis was," she said to herself, "I'd write him."

A gentleman passed by, the postmaster, and she left Shaun hastily and called. Shaun recognized a friend of his master, and feebly wagged his tail. "Why, Shaun!" said the postmaster, and listened to the story of the woman. "Didn't he leave his address with you?" she asked at the end. "Cannot you write?"

The postmaster sat down on the steps and took Shaun's head on his knee. "Won't you eat, Shaun?" he asked. He took a piece of meat and held it to the dog's lips. "Here, try this." But Shaun would not allow his mouth to be opened.

The postmaster laid the dog gently down, then stood up hastily. "This isn't a case for writing," he said. "I'll telegraph. If I know Davis, he'll be here in the morning."

Shaun half understood, and through a blur of tears he saw them leave him. Still he lay without motion, scarcely responding to words or caresses.

Mercifully there was no more frost. All night long Shaun lay motionless, waiting for the day. Only the force of his will seemed to keep him alive. Through the dawn and the early daylight he lay battling his weakness, till all the town was astir.

At last a carriage came down the street, hurrying from the railroad station. Shaun heard it coming and opened his tired eyes. It stopped. He could not see, for his eyes were dim, yet familiar steps hastened to his side, and he heard voices which he knew.

"O Shaun," cried Mrs. Davis, "how thin you are! No, keep quiet, do not move." She put her arms around him.

Still he could not see, but he heard now the other voice, quiet and strong, for which he had listened so long. "Shaun," said Mr. Davis, "good dog! Here, boy, take this." He let his mouth be opened, and something flowed between his lips. It seemed to burn, but strengthened him.

What was this? Tears were falling on his head. "Oh," sobbed Mrs. Davis, "he shall never leave us now."

Shaun found her hand and kissed it.

Allen French, "The Reform of Shaun." *Everybody's Magazine* 9, no. 5 (November 1903): 664–72.

Where Is My Dog? or, Is Man Alone Immortal? (1892)

THE REVEREND CHARLES JOSIAH ADAMS

I

Which dog? I have had many—not because I am fickle in my attachments; I love all dogs. There is a look of faithfulness in a dog's eye that has always powerfully appealed to me. It is hard for me to pass a dog of any sort on the street without patting him on the head. Man's heart naturally yearns for a being upon whom he can rely under all circumstances. Are you successful? All men will stand by you. Do you fail? All men will desert you. Your purple or your black makes no difference to your dog. Your servant and your friend once, he is your friend and your servant always. Open the door of his cage, or slip the bridle from his head, and your bird or your horse will fly or gallop, with note or neigh of joy, to his own kind. Your dog is as naturally gregarious, but you can not even drive him away from you. He licks the hand that smites him, and rubs the whole length of his back upon the foot that kicks him. Your cat loves your house or your rug, not you. The love of place is a primary love with the cat. When you move into another street he will not follow you. The dog has the love of location as well. There is some particular spot in the house where he loves to sleep. The dog turns around before he lies down. Why? Because, we are told, his primitive ancestors had their home among the reeds of the Nile, and turned about to push those reeds away, that they *might* lie down. We can imagine the same reeds rising and bending each time any one of these early dogs arose from or lay down to his rest, because simply he had lain there before. You may form the modern dog's habit as to place, if he is *your* dog, by placing a garment which you have worn there. You may hear him settling upon it with a low sound of satisfaction, because it reminds him of you. The love of place is a secondary love with the dog. There are three upon whom man, in his virtue, may always depend—God, his mother, and his dog. This is the great trinity of love. There are two upon whom man may always depend so long as his iniquity is not proven—his mother and his dog. There is one upon whom man may always depend, no matter how miserably fallen—his dog. God must maintain the laws of His moral universe, the mother may be stabbed to death in her maternal pride, but the dog is absorbed in his master—lost in him as is a drop of water in the great deep.

Where is my dog? Which of them? I have been particularly unfortunate with my dogs. I come to write these sentences because a week ago my fox-terrier was stolen. The police force of a great city has been seeking a trace of her, but one has not been found, and now all hope is lost that one will ever be discovered. She did the best she could to wag her tail; that she did not wag it was not her fault. She had only about an inch and a half of a remnant of a tail; the rest had been cut off. Though, in the blindness of her puppydom, the operation may have cost her some pain, I hardly blame the operator. A fox-terrier with a tail to wag would be a monstrosity. How many things our taste demands, simply because we are accustomed to them! We had named her Clip. She had a market value. She came to us as a mark of esteem. She was a constant and very obtrusive activity in the house; she was "gritty;" she had the best of pedigrees. When conversation lagged, we could speak of the Duke of Devonshire, with whom she was directly and unquestionably connected. Then, what amusement we could give our guests by lifting her by the skin of her neck, by one ear, and by the little that remained of her tail, without her giving a whimper of dissent. She had the marks of her breed. We were proud of her. We are saddened by her loss, and grieved; but most of our pain is caused by the memories which that loss stirred. I can hardly say that I mean Clip, when I ask, Where is my dog? nor Dennis, though I had come to have a deep affection for *him.* He was a cur—half water-spaniel and half—no man knew what. This would be to his discredit with the managers of the bench-show, beyond question; but it was not so with me. Commend me to a cur with good brain-chambers. The blooded dog's mind goes out in some particular direction. The greyhound courses by sight; the blood-hound pursues royal game by scent; the fox-terrier has its specialty; the cur's mind may be directed. When I reached home late from my work, the family would be abed, asleep; but Dennis always met me with a lick of the hand and a wag of his rail-like tail—one of the ugliest, but also one of the most expressive tails that dog ever possessed; and often, especially in very rainy weather, when his long, coarse, curly black hair was dripping, and his great feet were muddy, he would leap upon me with a joy at meeting that ruined my clothes and threatened to overturn me. Master-like, I would—But I am ashamed of it now, poor Dennis having returned to the earth from which he came. Extremes meet. Dennis was so ugly that he was handsome. Everybody loved him. The boys made a companion of him, and I have seen two capitalists stop on the street, that one might introduce him to the other, saying with a great, broad, genial laugh, "This is Dennis." He went through one of those trials, which all clergymen have, with me. When those who disagreed with me in churchmanship turned their backs upon, and wagged their tongues at me,

Dennis always had a deep look of love in his eye and a wag of his tail—a wag that was ridiculously clumsy and pathetically hearty—for me, and a fondling lick of my hand. He made me friends. The reporters overwhelmed me. They were good fellows, and gentlemanly. I was always glad to see them. I would chat with them, talk about anything but church affairs. I remarked to one of them, one evening:

"My dog's name is Dennis, but he is not named after me."

The observation appeared in a morning paper. The city laughed. A gentleman afterward said that when he had read it he walked by my house and looked at the number, and felt a great anxiety to meet me and my dog. In due time he met us. He is my friend now, and was Dennis's friend until the dear fellow was buried. His end was sad. Those who murder others, thinking "they are doing God service," often stab them through their families. They poisoned me through my dog. A day or so after we missed him, we found him dead, swollen, in the cellar. In his death died all my respect for Pharisees. The man who will poison his enemy's dog—But leave him to that Justice which allows "not a sparrow to fall to the ground without His notice." Dennis was never a favorite with the mistress of the house. He was a great, sprawling, awkward brute, that made more noise and dirt than a whole pack of average dogs should have made. As a murderer of sleep he was worse than a critic or a tin bathtub, the faucet of which is defective, and which is constantly sucking into the escape-pipe what it appears to think the last gill of water. His snore was uniquely strident and discordant, and he never recovered from an omnivorous disposition to chew. He would chew whatever he could eat between his teeth. He has been with the majority some months now, but I seldom take from my pocket a handkerchief, or pull on a pair of socks, without first frowning and then smiling in remembrance of Dennis. Yesterday my handkerchief scratched my nose; I sought the cause. It was patched. That handkerchief should be preserved in a crystal case; it would always remind me of Dennis, and remain a monument to the painstaking economy of the president of my wardrobe. It was different in the case of Tip. The mistress of the house loved him as much as I or the boy did. When Dennis would get a rebuke, Tip would get a caress. Where Dennis would be stricken with the broom-stick, Tip would receive a gentle-voiced reprimand. Tip was even more widely known than Dennis. He was nearly as ugly. He was small—about two thirds as long, tail and all, as your arm—with eyes as deep and confiding as those of Dennis; they were brighter, more active, and seemed to be "the windows of a soul" that was anxious for the incoming of more light. He was very receptive; you had little trouble in conveying a simple idea, or even a plain thought, to him. When he understood what you said, or when he wanted you to do something for him, or when he had performed some one of the numerous tricks which we had taught him, his eyes fairly gleamed, and his beautiful tail (after the white spot on the very end of which he was named) waved and switched like a willow-wand in a storm. He would have been called a cur, I presume. He was pure in the cross between the Dandy Dinmont and the poodle. Excepting the spot on the tip of his tail to which I have referred, and a narrow white vest, he was as black as "the cloth." He had one bad habit, of which he could never be broken: he would bark. He never did nip anybody, but I have always believed that a trio of exquisite young gentlemen who boarded next door feared for their lavender pantaloons or the pink skin of their calves. At any rate, as I sat reading my paper one morning, I heard a cry from the wife in an adjoining room, and on looking up, saw through the folding-doors the poor little beggar roll over in a fit. I sprang to my feet and rushed for a physician. He sneeringly remarked that he did not treat dogs. I had only time to say, as I turned away, that I had, when a boy, owned a big bull-dog, Joe, that I would like to see treat him; but the remark did Tip no more good than a milder one would have done. When I reached home Tip was dead, and the wife, whom I had never before seen very demonstrative in grief, was sitting near where he lay on the floor, the tears running through the fingers of the hand which she held to her face, and convulsed with sobs. I went up to the boy's room—he not having risen yet—and told him what had happened. Shall I confess it? We cried together—the man as deeply moved as the boy, and as unable to control himself. Tip was gone from us, by the road by which Dennis went a couple of years later. He was poisoned. I was very anxious to know who did the miserable deed. Though—I might as well confess it, for it will crop out sooner or later—though a parson, I wanted revenge. Some one asked me, in a company of gentlemen, whether I would pray for the man who poisoned my dog, did I find him. I replied: "I would pound the daylights out of him," and added: "I might pray for him when I got so weak that he really needed it." And, on mature deliberation, I do not know that my remark was too strong. Fortunately, maybe for the parson, I never could certainly discover who brought Tip to his untimely end, though I always suspected the exquisite young men with the lavender breeches and the hypothetically pink calves. I am tempted to give such a detailed history of all the dogs that I have owned. Since I have had my own home, before Tip, I had exquisitely beautiful, long, silken-haired Curly—a poodle with a strain of Skye-terrier. I had not much more than received him as a present, when I was called away from home. But a few weeks had gone by, when I received a long letter, telling me of his death. After Tip, Dennis; after Dennis, Clip—named, not after her tail, or from a peculiarity of its point, as was Tip, but from its absence and the mode of its disappearance. In my early boyhood, Joe, or Old Joe, who could water and restall a stable of horses, and protect a bevy of children as well as "Old Uncle Dave," or any other man, black or white. A little later came Doctor and Prince—the former a terrier which could kill three rats in crossing a room sixteen foot wide; the latter a diminutive white rascal of a villainous temper, that I would carry in my overcoat pocket, into which I would have youngsters reach for apples and nuts, that they might be bitten—a diversion which I abandoned when I had unwarily reached into the wrong pocket myself half a dozen times with serious results, two or three of the scars of which I have to this day.

As I write, many pictures of those boyhood days come to my mind. One of them comes again and again. A beautiful valley, with great mountainous hills to the south, on which the thunder-clouds gather; somewhat lower ones to the east, over which the sun comes and on which the dew sparkles; still lower ones to the west, drowned in golden light at eventide; low, rolling undulations to the north—a beautiful valley, appropriately called Pleasant Valley—for in it at twilight the bells of going and returning cattle tinkle; at noon the meadows and the harvest-fields seem to breathe a great peace, or the half-plowed acres tell of the rests that come between labors. In this valley, quietly moving figures, one a bent man with hair long and white under a hat of broad brim and sober color; following in his steps a little boy, to whom the sheaves of wheat are obstacles to be circumvented, or the clods to be stumbled over; and, trotting between them, before them, behind them, two dogs—one, black, the other white. They are Doctor and Prince, sniffing at the scent of field-mice and other small denizens of the fields—small things, but whose lives are as important to them as Napoleon's was to him. What grown man is there in whose life the dog has not been a factor? Who pronounces the word "home" or "childhood" and sees not the dog in the pictures which rise before him? Is it any wonder that I raise the question: "Where is my dog?" Is he lost? Will I not spend money and time to find him? Not so much because he is worth anything, but because I love him. As a rule, the uglier the dog, the more his master loves him. Talk with the pound-keeper; he will tell you that all the tears are shed over curs. Is he dead? Where is he? Where are Dennis, and Tip, and Curly, and Doctor, and Prince? Where is Old Joe? Dead! Yes; but "does death end all" in the case of the dog any more than in the case of man? Man's life is so much more important. Are you sure? Who is to decide? Man, the dog, or God?

Charles Josiah Adams. *Where Is My Dog? or, Is Man Alone Immortal?* New York: Fowler and Wells, 1892, 9–16.

Gulliver the Great (1912)

WALTER A. DYER

It was a mild evening in early spring, and the magnolias were in bloom. We motored around the park, turned up a side street, and finally came to a throbbing standstill before the Churchwarden Club.

There was nothing about its exterior to indicate that it was a clubhouse at all, but within there was an indefinable atmosphere of early Victorian comfort. There was something about it that suggested Mr. Pickwick. Old prints of horses and ships and battles hung upon the walls, and the oak was dark and old. There seemed to be no decorative scheme or keynote, and yet the atmosphere was utterly distinctive. It was my first visit to the Churchwarden Club, of which my quaint, old-fashioned Uncle Ford had long been a member, and I was charmed.

We dined in the rathskeller, the walls of which were completely covered with long churchwarden pipes, arranged in the most intricate and marvelous patterns; and after our mutton-chop and ale and plum pudding, we filled with the choicest of tobaccos the pipes which the old major-domo brought us.

Then came Jacob R. Enderby to smoke with us.

Tall and spare he was, with long, straight, black hair, large, aquiline nose, and piercing eyes. I disgraced myself by staring at him. I didn't know that such a man existed in New York, and yet I couldn't decide whether his habitat should be Arizona or Cape Cod.

Enderby and Uncle Ford were deep in a discussion of the statesmanship of James G. Blaine, when a waiter summoned my uncle to the telephone.

I neglected to state that my uncle, in his prosaic hours, is a physician; and this was a call. I knew it the moment I saw the waiter approaching. I was disappointed and disgusted.

Uncle Ford saw this and laughed.

"Cheer up!" said he. "You needn't come with me to visit the sick. I'll be back in an hour, and meanwhile Mr. Enderby will take care of you; won't you, Jake?"

For answer Enderby arose, and refilling his pipe took me by the arm, while my uncle got into his overcoat. As he passed us on the way out he whispered in my ear:

"Talk about dogs."

I heard and nodded.

Enderby led me to the lounge or loafing-room, an oak-paneled apartment in the rear of the floor above, with huge leather chairs and a seat in the bay window. Save for a gray-haired old chap dozing over a copy of *Simplicissimus,* the room was deserted.

But no sooner had Enderby seated himself on the window-seat than there was a rush and a commotion, and a short, glad bark, and Nubbins, the steward's bull-terrier, bounded in and landed at Enderby's side with canine expressions of great joy.

I reached forward to pat him, but he paid absolutely no attention to me.

At last his wriggling subsided, and he settled down with his head on Enderby's knee, the picture of content. Then I recalled my uncle's parting injunction.

"Friend of yours?" I suggested.

Enderby smiled. "Yes," he said, "we're friends, I guess. And the funny part of it is that he doesn't pay any attention to anyone else except his master. They all act that way with me, dogs do." And he pulled Nubbins's stubby ears.

"Natural attraction, I suppose," said I.

"Yes, it is," he answered, with the modest frankness of a big man. "It's a thing hard to explain, though there's a sort of reason for it in my case."

I pushed toward him a little tobacco-laden teakwood stand hopefully. He refilled and lighted.

"It's an extraordinary thing, even so," he said, puffing. "Every dog nowadays seems to look upon me as his long-lost master, but it wasn't always so. I hated dogs and they hated me."

Not wishing to say "Really" or "Indeed" to this big, outdoor man, I simply grunted my surprise.

"Yes, we were born enemies. More than that, I was afraid of dogs. A little fuzzy toy dog, ambling up to me in a room full of company, with his tail wagging, gave me the shudders. I couldn't touch the beast. And as for big dogs outdoors, I feared them like the plague. I would go blocks out of my way to avoid one.

"I don't remember being particularly cowardly about other things, but I just couldn't help this. It was in my blood, for some reason or other. It was the bane of my existence. I couldn't see what the brutes were put into the world for, or how anyone could have anything to do with them.

"And the dogs reciprocated. They disliked and distrusted me. The most docile old Brunos would growl and show their teeth when I came near."

"Did the change come suddenly?" I asked.

"Quite. It was in 1901. I accepted a commission from an importing and trading company to go to the Philippines to do a little quiet exploring, and spent four months in the sickly place. Then I got the fever, and when I recovered I couldn't get out of there too soon.

"I reached Manila just in time to see the mail steamer disappearing around the point, and I was mad. There would be another in six days, but I couldn't wait. I was just crazy to get back home.

"I made inquiries and learned of an old tramp steamer, named the *Old Squaw*, making ready to leave for Honolulu on the following day with a cargo of hemp and stuff, and a bunch of Moros for some show in the States, and I booked passage on that.

"She was the worst old tub you ever saw. I didn't learn much about her, but I verily believe her to have been a condemned excursion boat. She wouldn't have been allowed to run to Coney Island.

"She was battered and unpainted, and she wallowed horribly. I don't believe she could have reached Honolulu much before the next regular boat, but I couldn't wait, and I took her.

"I made myself as comfortable as possible, bribed the cook to insure myself against starvation, and swung a hammock on the forward deck as far as possible from the worst of the vile smells.

But we hadn't lost sight of Manila Bay when I discovered that there was a dog aboard—and such a dog! I had never seen one that sent me into such a panic as this one, and he had free range of the ship. A Great Dane he was, named Gulliver, and he was the pride of the captain's rum-soaked heart.

"With all my fear, I realized he was a magnificent animal, but I looked on him as a gigantic devil. Without exception, he was the biggest dog I ever saw, and as muscular as a lion. He lacked some points that show judges set store by, but he had the size and the build.

"I have seen Void's Vulcan and the Wurtemburg breed, but they were fox-terriers compared with Gulliver. His tail was as big around as my arm, and the cook lived in terror of his getting into the galley and wagging it; and he had a mouth that looked to me like the crater of Mauna Loa, and a voice that shook the planking when he spoke.

"I first caught sight of him appearing from behind a huge coil of cordage in the stern. He stretched and yawned, and I nearly died of fright.

"I caught up a belaying-pin, though little good that would have done me. I think he saw me do it, and doubtless he set me down for an enemy then and there.

"We were well out of the harbor, and there was no turning back, but I would have given my right hand to be off that boat. I fully expected him to eat me up, and I slept with that belaying-pin sticking into my ribs in the hammock, and with my revolver loaded and handy.

"Fortunately, Gulliver's dislike for me took the form of sublime contempt. He knew I was afraid of him, and he despised me for it. He was a great pet with the captain and crew, and even the Moros treated him with admiring respect when they were allowed on deck. I couldn't understand it. I would as soon have made a pet of a hungry boa-constrictor.

"On the third day out the poor old boiler burst and the *Old Squaw* caught fire. She was dry and rotten inside and she burned like tinder. No attempt was made to extinguish the flames, which got into the hemp in the hold in short order.

"The smoke was stifling, and in a jiffy all hands were struggling with the boats. The Moros came tumbling up from below and added to the confusion with their terrified yells.

"The davits were old and rusty, and the men were soon fighting among themselves. One boat dropped stern foremost, filled, and sank immediately, and the *Old Squaw* herself was visibly settling.

"I saw there was no chance of getting away in the boats, and I recalled a life-raft on the deck forward near my hammock. It was a sort of catamaran—a double platform on a pair of hollow, water-tight, cylindrical buoys. It wasn't twenty feet long and about half as broad, but it would have to do. I fancy it was a forgotten relic of the old excursion-boat days.

"There was no time to lose, for the *Old Squaw* was bound to sink presently. Besides, I was aft with the rest, and the flames were licking up the deck and running-gear in the waist of the boat.

"The galley, which was amidships near the engine-room, had received the full force of the explosion, and the cook lay moaning in the lee scuppers with a small water-cask thumping against his chest. I couldn't stop to help the man, but I did kick the cask away.

"It seemed to be nearly full, and it occurred to me that I should need it. I glanced quickly around, and luckily found a tin of biscuits that had also been blown out of the galley. I picked this up, and rolling the cask of water ahead of me as rapidly as I could, I made my way through the hot, stifling smoke to the bow of the boat.

"I kicked at the life-raft; it seemed to be sound, and I lashed the biscuits and water to it. I also threw on a coil of rope and a piece of sail-cloth. I saw nothing else about that could possibly be of any value to me. I abandoned my trunk for fear it would only prove troublesome.

"Then I hacked the raft loose with my knife and shoved it over to the bulwark. Apparently no one had seen me, for there was no one else forward of the sheet of flame that now cut the boat in two.

"The raft was a mighty heavy affair, but I managed to raise one end to the rail. I don't believe I would ever have been able to heave it over under any circumstances, but I didn't have to.

"I felt a great upheaval, and the prow of the *Old Squaw* went up into the air. I grabbed the ropes that I had lashed the food on with and clung to the raft. The deck became almost perpendicular, and it was a miracle that the raft didn't slide down with me into the flames. Somehow it stuck where it was.

"Then the boat sank with a great roar, and for about a thousand years, it seemed to me, I was under water. I didn't do anything. I couldn't think.

"I was only conscious of a tremendous weight of water and a feeling that I would burst open. Instinct alone made me cling to the raft.

"When it finally brought me to the surface I was as nearly dead as I care to be. I lay there on the thing in a half-conscious condition for an endless time. If my life had depended on my doing something, I would have been lost.

"Then gradually I came to, and began to spit out salt water and gasp for breath. I gathered my wits together and sat up. My hands were absolutely numb, and I had to loosen the grip of my fingers with the help of my toes. Odd sensation.

"Then I looked about me. My biscuits and water and rope were safe, but the sail-cloth had vanished. I remember that this annoyed me hugely at the time, though I don't know what earthly good it would have been.

"The sea was fairly calm, and I could see all about. Not a human being was visible, only a few floating bits of wreckage. Every man on board must have gone down with the ship and drowned, except myself.

"Then I caught sight of something that made my heart stand still. The huge head of Gulliver was coming rapidly toward me through the water!

"The dog was swimming strongly, and must have leaped from the *Old Squaw* before she sank. My raft was the only thing afloat large enough to hold him, and he knew it.

"I drew my revolver, but it was soaking wet and useless. Then I sat down on the cracker tin and gritted my teeth and waited. I had been alarmed, I must admit, when the boiler blew up and the panic began, but that was nothing to the terror that seized me now.

"Here I was all alone on the top of the Pacific Ocean with a horrible demon making for me as fast as he could swim. My mind was benumbed, and I could think of nothing to do. I trembled and my teeth rattled. I prayed for a shark, but no shark came.

"Soon Gulliver reached the raft and placed one of his forepaws on it and then the other. The top of it stood six or eight inches above the water, and it took a great effort for the dog to raise himself. I wanted to kick him back, but I didn't dare to move.

"Gulliver struggled mightily. Again and again he reared his great shoulders above the sea, only to be cast back, scratching and kicking, at a lurch of the raft.

"Finally a wave favored him, and he caught the edge of the under platform with one of his hind feet. With a stupendous effort he heaved his huge bulk over the edge and lay sprawling at my feet, panting and trembling."

Enderby paused and gazed out of the window with a big sigh, as though the recital of his story had brought back some of the horror of his remarkable experience.

Nubbins looked up inquiringly, and then snuggled closer to his friend, while Enderby smoothed the white head.

"Well," he continued, "there we were. You can't possibly imagine how I felt unless you, too, have been afflicted with dog-fear. It was awful. And I hated the brute so. I could have torn him limb from limb if I had had the strength. But he was vastly more powerful than I. I could only fear him.

"By and by he got up and shook himself. I cowered on my cracker-tin, but he only looked at me contemptuously, went to the other end of the raft, and lay down to wait patiently for deliverance.

"We remained this way until nightfall. The sea was comparatively calm, and we seemed to be drifting but slowly. We were in the path of ships likely to be passing one way or the other, and I would have been hopeful of the outcome if it had not been for my feared and hated companion.

"I began to feel faint, and opened the cracker-tin. The biscuits were wet with salt water, but I ate a couple, and left the cover of the tin open to dry them. Gulliver looked around, and I shut the tin hastily. But the dog never moved. He was not disposed to ask any favors. By kicking the sides of the cask and prying with my knife, I managed to get the bung out and took a drink. Then I settled myself on the raft with my back against the cask, and longed for a smoke.

"The gentle motion of the raft produced a lulling effect on my exhausted nerves, and I began to nod, only to awake with a start, with fear gripping at my heart. I dared not sleep. I don't know what I thought Gulliver would do to me, for I did not understand dogs, but I felt that I must watch him constantly. In the starlight I could see that his eyes were open. Gulliver was watchful too.

"All night long I kept up a running fight with drowsiness. I dozed at intervals, but never for long at a time. It was a horrible night, and I cannot tell you how I longed for day and welcomed it when it came.

"I must have slept toward dawn, for I suddenly became conscious of broad daylight. I roused myself, stood up, and swung my arms and legs to stir up circulation, for the night had been chilly. Gulliver arose, too, and stood silently watching me until I ceased for fear. When he had settled down again I got my breakfast out of the cracker-tin. Gulliver was restless, and was evidently interested.

"'He must be hungry,' I thought, and then a new fear caught me. I had only to wait until he became very hungry and then he would surely attack me. I concluded that it would be wiser to feed him, and I tossed him a biscuit.

"I expected to see him grab it ravenously, and wondered as soon as I had thrown it if the taste of food would only serve to make him more ferocious. But at first he would not touch it. He only lay there with his great head on his paws and glowered at me. Distrust was plainly visible in his face. I had never realized before that a dog's face could express the subtler emotions.

"His gaze fascinated me, and I could not take my eyes from his. The bulk of him was tremendous as he lay there, and I noticed the big, swelling muscles of his jaw. At last he arose, sniffed suspiciously at the biscuit, and looked up at me again.

"'It's all right; eat it!' I cried.

"The sound of my own voice frightened me. I had not intended to speak to him. But in spite of my strained tone he seemed somewhat reassured.

"He took a little nibble, and then swallowed the biscuit after one or two crunches, and looked up expectantly. I threw him another and he ate that.

"'That's all,' said I. 'We must be sparing of them.'

"I was amazed to discover how perfectly he understood. He lay down again and licked his chops.

"Late in the forenoon I saw a line of smoke on the horizon, and soon a steamer hove into view. I stood up and waved my coat frantically, but to no purpose. Gulliver stood up and looked from me to the steamer, apparently much interested.

"'Too far off,' I said to Gulliver. 'I hope the next one will come nearer.'

"At midday I dined, and fed Gulliver. This time he took the two biscuits quite without reserve and whacked his great tail against the raft. It seemed to me that his attitude was less hostile, and I wondered at it.

"When I took my drink from the cask, Gulliver showed signs of interest.

"'I suppose dogs get thirsty, too,' I said aloud.

"Gulliver rapped with his tail. I looked about for some sort of receptacle, and finally pulled off my shoe, filled it with water, and shoved it toward him with my foot. He drank gratefully.

"During the afternoon I sighted another ship, but it was too distant to notice me. However, the sea remained calm and I did not despair.

"After we had had supper, I settled back against my cask, resolved to keep awake, for still I did not trust Gulliver. The sun set suddenly and the stars came out, and I found myself strangely lonesome. It seemed as though I had been alone out there on the Pacific for weeks. The miles and miles of heaving waters, almost on a level with my eye, were beginning to get on my nerves. I longed for someone to talk to, and wished I had dragged the half-breed cook along with me for company. I sighed loudly, and Gulliver raised his head.

"'Lonesome out here, isn't it?' I said, simply to hear the sound of my own voice.

"Then for the first time Gulliver spoke. He made a deep sound in his throat, but it wasn't a growl, and with all my ignorance of dog language I knew it.

"Then I began to talk; I talked about everything—the people back home and all that—and Gulliver listened. I know more about dogs now, and I know that the best way to make friends with a dog is to talk to him. He can't talk back, but he can understand a heap more than you think he can.

"Finally Gulliver, who had kept his distance all this time, arose and came toward me. My words died in my throat. What was he going to do? To my immense relief he did nothing but sink down at my feet with a grunt and curl his huge body into a semicircle. He had dignity, Gulliver had. He wanted to be friendly, but he would not presume. However, I had lost interest in conversation, and sat watching him and wondering.

"In spite of my firm resolution, I feel asleep at length from sheer exhaustion, and never woke until daybreak. The sky was clouded and our craft was pitching. Gulliver was standing in the middle of the raft, looking at me in evident alarm. I glanced over my shoulder, and the blackness of the horizon told me that a storm was coming, and coming soon.

"I made fast our slender provender, tied the end of a line about my own waist for safety, and waited.

"In a short time the storm struck us in all its tropical fury. The raft pitched and tossed, now high up at one end, and now at the other, and sometimes almost engulfed in the waves.

"Gulliver was having a desperate time to keep aboard. His blunt claws slipped on the wet deck of the raft, and he fell and slid about dangerously. The thought flashed across my mind that the storm might prove to be a blessing in disguise, and that I might soon be rid of the brute.

"As I clung there to the lashings, I saw him slip down to the further end of the raft, his hind quarters actually over the edge. A wave swept over him, but still he clung, panting madly. Then the raft righted itself for a moment, and as he hung there he gave me a look I shall never forget—a look of fear, of pleading, of reproach, and yet of silent courage. And with all my stupidity I read that look. Somehow it told me that I was the master, after all, and he the dog. I could not resist it. Cautiously I raised myself and loosened the spare rope I had saved. As the raft tipped the other way Gulliver regained his footing and came sliding toward me.

"Quickly I passed the rope around his body, and as the raft dived again I hung on to the rope with one hand, retaining my own hold with the other. Gulliver's great weight nearly pulled my arm from its socket, but he helped mightily, and during the next moment of equilibrium I took another turn about his body and made the end of the rope fast.

"The storm passed as swiftly as it had come, and though it left us drenched and exhausted, we were both safe.

"That evening Gulliver crept close to me as I talked, and I let him. Loneliness will make a man do strange things.

"On the fifth day, when our provisions were nearly gone, and I had begun to feel the sinking dullness of despair, I sighted a steamer apparently coming directly toward us. Instantly I felt new life in my limbs and around my heart, and while the boat was yet miles away I began to shout and to wave my coat.

"'I believe she's coming, old man!' I cried to Gulliver; 'I believe she's coming!'

"I soon wearied of this foolishness and sat down to wait. Gulliver came close and sat beside me, and for the first time I put my hand on him. He looked up at me and rapped furiously with his tail. I patted his head—a little gingerly, I must confess.

"It was a big, smooth head, and it felt solid and strong. I passed my hand down his neck, his back, his flanks. He seemed to quiver with joy. He leaned his huge body against me. Then he bowed his head and licked my shoe.

"A feeling of intense shame and unworthiness came over me, with the realization of how completely I had misunderstood him. Why should this great, powerful creature lick my shoe? It was incredible.

"Then, somehow, everything changed. Fear and distrust left me, and a feeling of comradeship and understanding took their place. We two had been through so much together. A dog was no longer a frightful beast to me; he was a dog! I cannot think of a nobler word. And Gulliver had licked my shoe! Doubtless it was only the fineness of his perception that had prevented him from licking my hand. I might have resented that. I put my arms suddenly around Gulliver's neck and hugged him. I loved that dog!

"Slowly, slowly, the steamer crawled along, but still she kept to her course. When she was about a mile away, however, I saw that she would not pass as near to us as I had hoped; so I began once more my waving and yelling. She came nearer, nearer, but still showed no sign of observing us.

"She was abreast of us, and passing. I was in a frenzy!

"She was so near that I could make out the figure of the captain on the bridge, and other figures on the deck below. It seemed as though they must see us, though I realized how low in the water we stood, and how pitifully weak and hoarse my voice was. I had been a fool to waste it. Then an idea struck me.

"'Speak!' I cried to Gulliver, who stood watching beside me. 'Speak, old man!'

Gulliver needed no second bidding. A roar like that of all the bulls of Bashan rolled out over the blue Pacific. Again and again Gulliver gave voice, deep, full, powerful. His great sides heaved with the mighty effort, his red, cavernous mouth open, and his head raised high.

"'Good, old man!' I cried. 'Good!' And again that magnificent voice boomed forth.

"Then something happened on board the steamer. The figures came to the side. I waved my coat and danced. Then they saw us.

"I was pretty well done up when they took us aboard, and I slept for twenty-four hours straight. When I awoke there sat Gulliver by my bunk, and when I turned to look at him he lifted a great paw and put it on my arm."

Enderby ceased, and there was silence in the room save for the light snoring of Nubbins.

"You took him home with you, I suppose?" I asked.

Enderby nodded.

"And you have him still?" I certainly wanted to have a look at that dog.

But he did not answer. I saw an expression of great sadness come into his eyes as he gazed out of the window, and I knew that Jacob Enderby had finished his story.

Walter A. Dyer, "Gulliver the Great." 1912. In *Gulliver the Great and Other Stories*. New York: Century, 1916, 3–28.

"Barking at the moon." Thomas W. Knox. *Dog Stories and Dog Lore.* New York: Cassell and Company, 1887. Image courtesy of Special Collections and Archives, James B. Duke Library, Furman University.

Coda

All the Good Dogs (1954)

GEORGE AND HELEN PAPASHVILY

What purpose did they serve, all the good dogs that once ran through the world and wait now in the shadowy quiet of the past?

They lightened our burdens and drove away our enemies and stayed when others left us. They gave aid and comfort, protection and security. They held a mirror wherein we might see ourselves as we long to be. They gave us a glimpse of the world beyond the narrow confines of our own species.

Although we make dull students, slowly they help us learn how to command and to protect with wisdom and justice and imagination.

They taught and still teach us the joy of giving generosity and kindness and love—without thought of gainful return.

And now—all the fleet hounds, the staunch mastiffs, the loyal shepherds, the dancing toys, the fumbling puppies, pets on silk pillows, workers plodding at their tasks, the special ones you loved best, those of ours we still miss—all the good dogs, goodbye, until on some brighter day, in some fairer place you run out again to greet us.

George and Helen Papashvily, "All the Good Dogs." In *Dogs and People*. Philadelphia: J. B. Lippincott, 1954.

INDEX